HOMER ECONOMICUS

HOMER ECONOMICUS
The Simpsons and Economics

Edited by
JOSHUA HALL

STANFORD ECONOMICS AND FINANCE

An imprint of Stanford University Press

Stanford, California

Stanford University Press
Stanford, California

Special discounts for bulk quantities of titles in the Stanford Economics and Finance imprint are available to corporations, professional associations, and other organizations. For details and discount information, contact the special sales department of Stanford University Press.
Tel: (650) 736-1782, Fax: (650) 736-1784

Printed in the United States of America on acid-free, archival-quality paper

Library of Congress Cataloging-in-Publication Data

Homer economicus : The Simpsons and economics / edited by Joshua C. Hall.
    pages cm
  Includes bibliographical references and index.
  ISBN 978-0-8047-9097-0 (cloth : alk. paper) —
  ISBN 978-0-8047-9171-7 (pbk. : alk. paper)
1. Microeconomics. 2. Economics. 3. Simpsons (Television program) I. Hall, Joshua C., editor of compilation.
  HB172.H66 2014
  330—dc23
                    2013047797

ISBN 978-0-8047-9182-3 (electronic)

Typeset by Bruce Lundquist in 10/14 Minion

CONTENTS

PART III: APPLIED MICROECONOMICS

PREFACE

Joshua Hall

I was living in a suburb of Columbus, Ohio, when I got my first taste of teaching economics. I was asked at the last second to fill in on a principles of economics section at a small university near my home called Capital University. Though I had been a teaching assistant for many classes while earning a masters degree in economics, I had never had complete control over the classroom. It seemed to me that there were two main questions I needed to answer: What did I want my students to learn? and Did I want to be a "guide on the side" or a "sage on the stage?"

Answering the first question was easy (and not just because I knew the name of the course!). Since my graduate school days, I had been concerned that we were going about teaching principles all wrong. Most people who take an economics course are never going to take another one in their lives. Knowing that, principles courses should not be focused on preparing students for advanced study of economics but instead giving them tools and insight that will help them at work, at home, and at the ballot box. My job as a teacher was to show them how economics explained the world around them, not just some lines on a chalkboard. The bigger question was how to do it.

While the first couple of days convinced me that I preferred to lecture, I also realized that a two-hour lecture was just too long if you didn't break it up every thirty minutes or so. How could I break things up and show students that economics was everywhere? At first I would just stop the lecture and illustrate a topic with an example from that day's newspaper or by discussing how a scene from a classic movie or television show illustrated a concept. I soon realized that most of my examples were coming from *The Simpsons*, and as luck would have it, the first couple of seasons of that program were just starting to come out on DVD. So I began to show brief snippets of episodes in class when appropriate. I quickly found that students loved to talk about *The Simpsons* and to learn by using examples from the show. Students began to come up to me and say things like, "Did you see in last night's episode Homer's fear about donating a kidney to his dad illustrated the trade-offs organ donors face?" In my mind, that was a clear sign that using *The Simpsons* was getting them to engage with the course material.

Nearly a decade later, I have taught thousands of students using *The Simpsons*, authored one article[1] and coauthored another[2] on how to use *The Simpsons* in the classroom, and edited the book you hold in your hands. The origins of this volume began with a conversation I had over dinner with two economists, Deirdre McCloskey and Bob Lawson. I told them I was writing an article on using *The Simpsons* in the economics classroom, and I planned on calling it "Homer Economicus," a play on the Latin phrase *homo economicus*, which is often translated as "economic man."[3] McCloskey's response was roughly, "A title like that deserves a book."

So while I did originally ignore McCloskey's advice, after running into dozens of economists over the years that were using *The Simpsons* in the classroom, I realized that she was right. A title like that did deserve a book, and the only question was how to get it done. After all, I could write it, but what fun would that be? Instead, I contacted dozens of excellent economics teachers and scholars who were also *Simpsons* fans and asked them if they would be willing to contribute to a volume explaining how the show illustrates *homer economicus* in action. The response was tremendous, as my inbox was flooded by essays using *The Simpsons* to illustrate concepts in economics from general ones such as money or unintended consequences to very specific areas of inquiry such as health economics or the economics of prohibition. Luckily for me everyone clearly understood that the book is about how *The Simpsons* reflects concepts or ideas from economics, not about how much money Matt Groening has made from the show!

The book is organized into three sections. Because *The Simpsons* is primarily about the Simpsons family and the other residents of Springfield, the book focuses primarily on microeconomics. Microeconomics is the study of human behavior in small units, such as individuals, families, or firms. The first three chapters constitute Part I, and they deal with "the economic way of think-ing" and primarily focus on understanding individual behavior and decision making. I tell my students that studying economics is like putting on a pair of glasses that let you see the world in a different way. The basic economic lessons about individual behavior, the market process, and tracing out the effects of policies are all laid out in these three chapters.

Part II of the book comprises six chapters on "money, markets, and gov-ernment," and these essays primarily cover issues beyond isolated individual decision making and behavior. For example, in Chapter 4, West Virginia Uni-versity's Andrew Young details how money serves to facilitate exchange and then asks the important question of whether Milhouse can be said to be money. Other important topics covered in this section include how best to un-derstand Homer's serial entrepreneurship (Chapter 6) and the role of profits and losses (for Homer, mostly losses) in a market economy. Chapters 7 and 8 discuss situations when free markets might not lead to desirable outcomes, such as monopolies and externalities (think Springfield Nuclear Power Plant). The economic analysis of politics concludes this section, as John Considine ex-plains how a television clown such as Sideshow Bob can become mayor. (Really, is it so different than Al Franken becoming senator?)

The third and final section of the book discusses topics in applied microeco-nomics. Basically, these are the tools of economics that were discussed in the first two parts applied to particular policy areas and topics. So we have explanations of the economics of immigration (Chapter 10), labor markets (Chapter 11), and health care (Chapter 12) as seen in *The Simpsons*. Mark Thornton, the author of *The Economics of Prohibition*, tells us in Chapter 13 how Springfield's experience with prohibition in the episode "Homer vs. the Eighteenth Amendment" is sim-ilar to the United States' experience in the 1920s and 1930s. The social costs of Marge's gambling problem and other issues related to gambling are dealt with in Chapter 14. An overview of the relatively new field of behavioral economics is given in Chapter 15, and the book concludes with a thought-provoking chapter by Steven Horwitz and Stewart Dompe on how changes in the lifestyle of the Simpsons illustrate how the economic progress that has occurred over the past two decades is contrary to some economic statistics.

While this book is in not meant to be a comprehensive introduction to eco-nomics (after all, most economics textbooks run several hundred pages long), it does encompass the basic concepts covered in any principles textbook as well as provide a look at how economists think about topics such as health care and politics. While many popular economics books eschew foot- or endnotes, I encouraged my authors to provide notes to accessible articles and texts that curious readers can follow to learn more about a topic. Most important, however, I hope you find that this book lets you revisit your favorite *Simpsons* episodes while at the same time giving you a new perspective on them.

ACKNOWLEDGMENTS

I would like to thank the Social Philosophy and Policy Center at Bowling Green State University for the support of its Visiting Scholar program during the summer of 2009. The uninterrupted research time provided by Jeff Paul and Fred Miller was invaluable in getting this project started. I would like to thank Bob Lawson for encouraging me to write my first paper on *The Simpsons* when I was just a lecturer. In addition, let me thank my editor, Margo Fleming, for her patience and guidance in helping to bring this book to market. Last, I would like to dedicate this book to my wife and two boys. I can think of no one else with whom I would rather experience each new *Simpsons* episode.

PART I
THE ECONOMIC WAY OF THINKING

SCARCITY, SPECIALIZATION, AND SQUISHEES

The Simpsons as *Homo Economicus*

Anthony M. Carilli

THROUGHOUT THE PAST TWENTY-ODD YEARS we have turned to *The Simpsons* for irreverent humor, mindful distraction, inside jokes, and, it turns out, lessons in basic economics. *The Simpsons* is a perfect vehicle for illustrating basic economic concepts. Economics is the study of choice and its consequences, both intended and unintended. Of course, dealing with human beings unraveling the complexity of these consequences can be daunting. While there is *never* any doubt about Homer's intentions, *ever* ("Mmm . . . beer" or "Mmm . . . donuts" or "Mmm . . . porkchops"), somehow, Homer can't ever seem to anticipate or predict the longer-term consequences of his choices. In fact, no matter how many times he's been burned, Homer doesn't even consider that there might be unintended consequences to his choices, yet there always are. It wouldn't surprise us, as viewers, to see Homer sit down at Moe's one night to enjoy a Duff Beer, somehow resulting in Maggie not going to college. As the nineteenth-century French political economist, statesman, and author Frederic Bastiat taught us, economics is about the seen and the unseen; good economics traces out not just the seen but also the unseen consequences of any choice.[1]

Bastiat demonstrates the lesson of the seen and the unseen by using the famous example of the broken window.[2] Suppose Bart dares Milhouse to throw a brick through the window of the Kwik-E-Mart. Imagine that as Apu rushes out to catch the boys, a crowd gathers. As the crowd laments the terrible act of vandalism, Mayor Quimby instead extols the boys' virtue. Far from being hooligans, Milhouse and Bart are, in fact, heroes because they have created a series of jobs for Springfield. Mayor Quimby assures the townspeople by reasoning that the broken window will create economic benefits for the community, because a glazier must be hired to fix the window and will earn an income from the repair of the window, which he will in turn use to buy a new pair of shoes from the cobbler, thereby creating work for the cobbler. The cobbler will receive an income and perhaps buy a new suit, thereby generating income for the tailor. The tailor will use the income to . . . and so on and so on. . . .[3] However, Apu had intended to purchase a new Squishee machine, not a new window, and as he listens to this dramatic reversal of his fortunes, he knows that he will not be able to purchase both. The Squishee machine salesman has lost his commission, which he had planned to celebrate with a Duff Beer at Moe's; Moe loses the income he would have earned from selling the beer, Duff produces less beer and therefore hires fewer employees.[4] In the end, what really happens is that Apu has just a window instead of a window *and* a new Squishee machine.

The lesson is that a good economist looks at not only the short-run consequences but also the long-run consequences of actions; at not only the visible effects of actions but the subtle invisible effects of actions. "In the economic sphere an act, a habit, an institution, a law produces not only one effect, but a series of effects. Of these effects, the first alone is immediate; it appears simultaneously with its cause; *it is seen*. The other effects emerge only subsequently; *they are not seen*; we are fortunate if we *foresee* them. There is only one difference between a bad economist and a good one: the bad economist confines himself to the *visible* effect; the good economist takes into account both the effect that can be seen and those effects that must be *foreseen*."[5] *The Simpsons* does that, exactly. Every episode shows us what Homer sees and what he doesn't see. *The Simpsons* offers a humorous look at the choices its characters make and the consequences that follow wherever they may lead. Economics, like *The Simpsons*, is about everyday life.

The intended consequences are, of course, less interesting in many ways than the unintended. When Homer chooses a Duff Beer at Moe's we know his intentions: "Mmm . . . beer!" Mr. Burns intends to produce nuclear power. The intended consequences are interesting because it is the intended action of the individuals that leads to the more interesting and nuanced unintended consequences. Homer doesn't intend to forget Marge's birthday when he is drinking Duff Beer, nor does he intend to provide Moe with a living. Mr. Burns doesn't intend to make it easier for Apu to make a living by providing cheap reliable electricity to the Squishee machine, but he does. *The Simpsons* is an exercise in exploring the consequences of the decisions made every day by the people of Springfield; *The Simpsons* is about economics because economics is about, well—everything. The purpose of this chapter is develop some simple economic concepts with the help of Homer, Marge, Mr. Burns, Apu, Lisa, Lenny, and, of course, Bart.

Economics is based on the simple premise that individuals choose or act; that is, they apply means (resources) to ends (goals) according to ideas. When Homer wants dinner, he knows (has the idea) that pork chops (his means) will alleviate his hunger (his end). The limits to Homer's ends seldom reveal themselves, but his ability to use means to satisfy his goals is limited by the scarcity of the means and by Homer's ideas about how the means can be connected to the ends. Homer's ends are rarely in doubt, but his choice of means often doesn't prove an effective or efficient way of bringing about his ends. Frequently, Homer finds his access to means limited by his budget, whether it be monetary means or physical ability or mental ability (nah . . .) or lack of foresight or whatever. At its most basic level, every episode of *The Simpsons* is about economics; the consequences of choice within some sort of constraints. The foibles of Homer and Bart are basically about choice and its consequences within the confines of a budget constraint, which is just fancy economist talk for whatever people have to spend.[6] Homer makes decisions in reaction to the trade-offs he perceives within the context of the constraints he faces. The brilliance of *The Simpsons* is in the tracing out of the consequence of their choices, both intended and unintended. Unlike some other animated shows, they rarely let the fact that they are not "real" prevent them from being "realistic."

Ten Basic Concepts

The Simpsons is a great device for demonstrating the basic introductory ideas in economics. While economics really is a way of thinking as opposed to a list of concepts to be memorized, there nonetheless are some basic concepts that make up the core of the economic way of thinking, and *The Simpsons* provides many examples to demonstrate all of these concepts.[7] I will list ten basic concepts that all students of introductory economics should appreciate, briefly explain each one, and provide examples from *The Simpsons* for each concept. The basic concepts are

- Scarcity necessitates choice.
- The opportunity cost of an action is the value of the next-best alternative that must be sacrificed to take the action.
- Efficiency is best understood as a relationship between ends and means.

- To economize means to allocate available resources in a way that yields the most value to the economizer.
- Pursuing comparative advantage means sacrificing that which is less valuable for the sake of something more valuable.
- Specialization is another word for
  - pursuing one's comparative advantage.
  - the division of labor.
  - producing at a comparably lower opportunity cost.
- The "law of demand" in economic theory asserts that people will purchase less of a good when its price rises, and vice versa.
- A market is a process of competing bids and offers.
- In an informed and uncoerced exchange, both parties receive more in value than they give up.
- Economic growth entails an increase in the rate of production of wealth, and wealth is what we value.

Nearly all introductory or principles of economics texts have similar lists. For example, Mankiw includes, among others, people face trade-offs, the cost of something is what you give up to get it, rational people think at the margin, people respond to incentives, trade can make everyone better off, markets are usually a good way to organize economic activity, and so on.[8] Gwartney and colleagues have "Eight Guideposts to Economic Thinking," which are trade-offs must be made, individuals choose purposefully, incentives matter, individuals make decisions at the margin, information is costly, beware of secondary effects, value is subjective, and the test of a theory is its ability to predict.[9] Frank and Bernanke call their first chapter "Thinking Like an Economist" and include the scarcity principle and the cost-benefit principle as two of the basic building blocks of economics.[10] Again, economics is the science of choice and its consequences, both intended and unintended. While each author has his unique approach, they all focus on the choices made by individuals in the face of scarcity.

Scarcity Necessitates Choice

Homer's wants are limitless, but his means to attain them are not, so he cannot have everything he wants and he must choose which ends to satisfy. Life is full of trade-offs—that is, forsaking one thing to choose another—and Homer runs into this brute reality over and over again. In "The Tell Tale Head," Homer talks to Maggie about a bowling ball from the *Bowl Earth Catalog* being the best use of his $50 of gambling winnings. In "There's No Disgrace Like Home," Homer decides the family needs to go to counseling and, after looking at all the counselor commercials on television, decides Dr. Marvin Monroe is the best (and at only $250!). The scene is an economic lesson on trade-offs (and how value is subjective), since Marge is concerned about the cost of therapy while Homer is willing to give up the kids' college fund. Then after realizing the college fund only had $88.50 in it, Homer is willing to make the ultimate sacrifice and pawn the family TV. Unwilling to give up the TV, Marge offers her engagement ring, only to be reminded by Homer that they need to pawn something worth at least $250.

Opportunity Cost

Trade-offs imply opportunity cost. The act of choosing is, at the same time, the act of setting aside. Homer can't have his donuts and eat them too. The cost of choosing is the value of what has been set aside or not chosen. That is, the value of what has been traded off by choosing one thing over another is the opportunity cost. Closely related to opportunity is the concept of sunk cost; a sunk cost is a cost that cannot be affected by the individual's choice and should therefore be ignored. While the concepts of opportunity cost and its evil twin sunk cost may appear to be straightforward, together they are most often the most difficult concepts in economics to apply consistently.[11] The difficulty in applying opportunity cost theory is that it lies squarely in Bastiat's realm of the unseen; the opportunity cost of any action or choice is the value of what is not chosen and therefore not experienced or seen. Opportunity cost represents a hurdle to choice, but once the choice is made the "loss" cannot be experienced.[12] The misapplication most often manifests itself as the denial of the most basic tenant of scarcity: "There ain't no such thing as a free lunch."

Since cost is related to action and choice, if there is no action or choice there is no cost. Or, more succinctly, "no verb, no cost." Different actions toward the same object have different costs; in other words, "different verb, different cost." So the cost of holding something is different from the cost of obtaining it and is different from the cost of using it. Since only one action or choice can be made at the same time, the opportunity cost of action is the value of the action not taken.

Typically, the confusion lies in misunderstanding the relevant choices. Imagine Marge gives Homer a ticket to the Springfield Isotopes versus Shelbyville Shelbyvillians game for his birthday; does it cost him nothing to go the game? The answer, of course, is no, Homer does in fact have to bear a cost to attend the game. Suppose the game was for the coveted Lemon Tree Trophy, and when Homer shows up to the game, Fat Tony, who is scalping tickets, offers Homer $1,000 for the ticket. If Homer goes to the game, he just paid $1,000 for the ticket; as he mulled over his decision, Homer had one hand on the $1,000 and one hand on the ticket—he had to let go of one of them. The cost of attending (verb) the game was $1,000 (plus the value he places on not disappointing Marge because the $1,000 would have helped pay for Lisa's braces). It doesn't matter what he paid to obtain the ticket because that is not the relevant decision now, the relevant choice is attend or not attend the game.

The opportunity cost of the therapy with Dr. Marvin Monroe is the value of receiving the education that will be foregone because Homer has raided the college fund. The concept of time preference is also present in this decision. Homer, like everyone else, has a positive rate of time preference; he would, other things equal, prefer to have things now rather than later. A significant part of the charm of Homer is his very high (childlike) rate of time preference. Homer regularly discounts the future very heavily, meaning he places very little value on it and therefore places a high value on the present.

Homer's motto is *carpe diem*. In "The Way We Was," when Homer joins the debate team he is faced with the resolution, "The national speed limit should be lowered to fifty-five miles per hour." Homer's response recognizes immediately the opportunity cost of such a proposal when he notes that while there will be fewer deaths, millions of people will be late. In "Tree House of Horror," while Homer is trying to convince Marge that the haunted house is worth the purchase by telling her it's a fixer-upper and therefore worth the low price, Marge counters that the savings are not worth living in a house of evil. The exchange recognizes that value is subjective. To Homer, trading a little evil is worth the money; to Marge, the opportunity cost is too high.[13] Opportunity costs are the constant obstacles to Homer's choices that not even he can ignore.

Efficiency

Efficiency is best understood as a relationship between ends and means. The idea of efficiency means nothing absent a goal, which is to say that *things* cannot be more or less efficient. Choices can be more or less efficient. Given a set of means, efficiency is choosing the most valuable ends, or, given an end, efficiency is choosing the cheapest means to bring about that end. Even physicists recognize that efficiency is inherently an evaluative term when they define it as work out divided by work in; that is, how much of the energy put in comes back out as *useful* energy. Since *useful* means the extent to which the end is accomplished, efficiency is an evaluative term. A choice is efficient if the benefit from the decision is greater than the cost in prospect. To put it another way, a decision is more efficient if, given a cost, that choice yields a greater benefit than the original or if, given a benefit, the cost is lower than the original choice.

Homer's choices are ripe with implications about efficiency. Someone who has a rate of time preference as high as Homer's frequently makes choices that don't appear to be efficient. This is especially the case after he experiences *ex post* regret; that is, he discovers that he was wrong in his estimation about the future cost or benefit. In the opening scene of "One Fish, Two Fish, Blowfish, Bluefish," Homer's incredibly high rate of time preference is on display when Marge tells him his meatloaf will be ready in eight seconds and he wonders if there is any way it can be cooked faster. It is further displayed when, disappointed that it is meatloaf night again, Lisa tells Homer that he is always trying to get them to be adventurous and live richer lives, to which he responds that she doesn't know what she's talking about as no one in the family is trying to teach that lesson. Homer can't be troubled to think far enough ahead, that is, to lower his time preference enough, to think about his daughter's future.

Marge urges Homer to try something new for her sake and Lisa's sake. The Simpsons decide to try sushi, which of course Homer is against because he perceives a low benefit for a high cost—giving up Friday night pork chop night. For Homer, pork chops are more efficient than sushi. Reluctantly, Homer agrees, and the family goes to the Happy Sumo restaurant for sushi. Homer discovers that he loves sushi and orders everything on the menu except fugu (blowfish). Homer then decides that he must have the fugu, even when told that it will kill him if prepared improperly, which naturally the apprentice chef does.[14] When Homer is informed that he is poisoned and now has twenty-four hours to live (in other words, his means are now severely limited), he tries to use those twenty-four hours as efficiently as possible (that is, apply those means to the most valuable ends he can imagine). He makes a list of fourteen things to do with his final day that include making the list, eating a hearty breakfast, and being intamit [sic] with Marge.

As he attempts to move through the list, he discovers that his means are more limited than he thought (and he oversleeps on his last day on earth so he misses the sunrise), so he has to cut down on the ends he is capable of attaining. While making peace with his father he discovers that he has underestimated the cost of making that peace, so he has to give up a few more things on his list (opportunity cost). Homer crosses out beer with the boys, plant a

tree, and go hang gliding. He is anxious to get to being "intamit" with Marge, so
the cost of spending time with his father has risen above the benefit, such that
it is now inefficient to spend time with his father. Later, as he moves further
down the list, a low-cost opportunity to tell off his boss presents itself. While
driving home with Barney, Homer spots Mr. Burns and Smithers sitting in the
park ogling women's ankles. He has Barney slow down so he can tell Mr. Burns
to eat his shorts. Homer recognized that serendipity made another item on his
list become efficient to do, and thus clearly even Homer recognizes that some
decisions are more efficient than others.

Economizing

To economize means to allocate available resources in a way that yields the most
value to the economizer or chooser. That is, all choice is aimed at maximizing
profit, properly understood. Profit is merely the excess benefit over cost, so all
choice is made with the goal of maximizing profit in mind. In "Homer vs. Lisa
and the 8th Commandment," both Bart and Homer make attempts at economizing (maximizing profit). Homer can't afford to pay for cable TV, so he takes a
$50 offer to hook up cable for free. When Marge asks him about how they could
afford it, Homer tells her they can swing nothing a month. Later, Bart discovers
some of the other channels available on cable, such as Top Hat Entertainment
adult programming. This is an entrepreneurial discovery for Bart, as he now has
access to something valuable. He then uses the resources he has at his disposal
to yield something very valuable to him—fifty cents per ticket. Bart invites his
schoolmates to watch the most beautiful women in the world for just fifty cents.

In the "Simpsons Roasting on an Open Fire," Marge economizes after she
discovers that Bart has a tattoo of a heart with "Moth" written in the middle.
She doesn't want Bart to have a tattoo, so she takes the Christmas money and
applies it to a more highly valued end—removing Bart's tattoo. It is important
to understand that economizing does not mean to "be cheap," but only to use
available resources in the most valuable way or to attain an end in the least costly
way while understanding that the cost is the value of the foregone alternative.

Comparative Advantage

Pursuing comparative advantage means sacrificing that which is less valuable
for the sake of something more valuable. Comparative advantage is not just
for countries; it applies to individuals as well. That's why the husky kid catches
and the skinny kid plays centerfield even if the skinny kid is a better catcher. An

individual has a comparative advantage when he can do something relatively more cheaply than someone else. An individual who has the lowest cost of pursuing any activity has a comparative advantage in that activity. No one can have a comparative advantage at all activities, and everyone has a comparative advantage at something. Which is a lucky thing for Homer.

An individual discovers her comparative advantage in her everyday interactions within the market; she learns through repeated interaction about what she is relatively best at. Every time Homer ventures away from the Springfield Nuclear Power Plant (SNPP), he finds his way back because that is where his comparative advantage is. In "Homer's Odyssey," Homer is fired for an accident at the plant, which leads him to look for another job with some help from Lisa. When Lisa finds him a job at the fireworks factory, Homer isn't interested because the folks at the fireworks factory are perfectionists. We know (and Homer knows) he does not have a comparative advantage at being perfect. With no success in his job hunting, Homer decides to kill himself by throwing himself off a bridge. However, on his way to do so he is nearly killed at a busy intersection. After his family catches up with him he informs them that the intersection is dangerous and needs a sign. With that, Homer thinks he has discovered his comparative advantage, making Springfield safe from all manner of dangers.[15] As only Homer can, he lets his success go to his head and takes on the SNPP. In doing so, he ends up getting his old job back.

In "Simpson and Delilah," Homer attempts to pursue an occupation in which he doesn't have a comparative advantage. Mr. Burns confuses Homer with a young go-getter and promotes him to an executive position after Homer has managed to scam himself some Dimoxinil—a miracle cure for baldness—and grow some hair. While Mr. Burns is convinced that Homer is a management genius because of his full head of hair, Homer understands that his comparative advantage is built on sand. Throughout the episode we can feel Homer's discomfort because he knows his stint as an executive is doomed because he is out of his league.

In the end, Homer always sacrifices that which is less valuable to him for that which is more valuable; in other words, he follows his comparative advantage. Marge reminds Homer that his safety inspector job has always brought food to the table. It's when Homer strays from his comparative advantage of safety inspector at the SNPP that he fails to put food on the table, whether it is to be an executive, a safety crusader, a tow truck operator, an astronaut, a monorail conductor, a sanitation commissioner, a singer (in the Be Sharps), a Krusty Impersonator, a sideshow freak, a snowplow driver, a beer baron, or an inventor. In what seems likes hundreds of jobs Homer has had, it always turns out that he is relatively better at being a nuclear safety inspector. His many failed attempts at other jobs show us that while Homer is bad at all jobs he is the least bad at being a nuclear safety inspector relative to the others, so that gives him a comparative advantage. Homer can't be worse than everybody at everything, therefore he must have a comparative advantage at something, whether Frank Grimes likes it or not!

Specialization and the Division of Labor

Specialization and the division of labor follow directly from the pursuit of comparative advantage.[16] To specialize means to concentrate one's efforts in certain aspects of production.[17] Division of labor is the act of splitting up a task to allow for specialization. The division of labor is on constant display in Springfield, where everyone specializes right down to the town drunk and the schoolyard bully. We can't imagine many of the characters in any other occupations than those they are in because they just "seem" to have a comparative advantage. Try imagining Otto as anything other than a bus driver, or Chief Wiggum as other than the police chief, or Moe as other than a bartender, or the Reverend Lovejoy as manager of the Kwik-E-Mart, or Apu as the reverend. The reason we can't is because these individuals are pursuing their comparative advantages. The cast of characters themselves are a kind of division of labor. Each character specializes in *something*. For example, Ned Flanders specializes in being the goody two shoes, Mrs. Krabappel *is* an elementary school teacher, and Willie *is* a groundskeeper. It's through this specialization and division of labor that Springfield functions and prospers. As the founder of economics, Adam Smith, puts it, "It is the great multiplication of the productions of all the different arts, in consequence of the division of labour, which occasions, in a well-governed society, that universal opulence which extends itself to the low-est ranks of the people."[18]

The Law of Demand

Economics is about choice, and the concept of demand relates choice and cost. Economists use the concept of demand to represent how much of something someone would choose to acquire as the amount that he must sacrifice to ac-quire that thing changes. Demand represents the plans of buyers. If Bart and Milhouse are headed to the Kwik-E-Mart to buy a Squishee, each has some idea of the price (sacrifice) of the Squishee and therefore each has an idea (plan) about how many Squishees he will buy. If that sacrifice changes, each will change his plans.

A second way in which plans can change is that resources available for the sacrifice change. In "Three Men and a Comic Book," Bart finds the original issue of *Radioactive Man* for sale and plans to not buy it because he can't afford it, that is, he doesn't have enough resources. He convinces Martin and Milhouse to combine their money with his to buy the comic book. Clearly when he accumulated more resources his plans changed. A third way plans may change is if the sacrifice for a related good changes. If the price of Krusty-O's changes, then the plans to obtain Krusty-O's changes, and that in turn will change Bart's plans to buy Squishees.[19]

The "law of demand" in economic theory asserts that people will purchase less of a good when its price rises, and vice versa. Individuals will do more of something the smaller the sacrifice and less of something the greater the sacrifice, other things equal. We already saw this earlier in "One Fish, Two Fish, Blowfish, Blue Fish," when the "price" of telling Mr. Burns to eat his shorts fell; because Barney was driving Homer by Mr. Burns in the park, Homer chose more harassing of Mr. Burns. In "Simpson and Delilah," after Homer sees a commercial for Dimoxinil, a hair restoration product, he learns the price of it is $1,000 by visiting the store selling it. Homer breaks down in tears and leaves because the price is too high. Later, back at the power plant, Lenny and Carl suggest that with some creative paperwork Homer can have insurance pay for the Dimoxinil. With the new price of zero, Homer purchases the Dimoxinil. As the price falls, the law of demand even works for Homer!

The law of demand applies to all choosing beings, including aliens. In "Treehouse of Horror," the aliens are showing the Simpsons their entertainment center, noting that they get over one million channels from around the galaxy. In response to a question from Bart, however, they note that they do not get HBO because that would be extra. That is, as the price rises the quantity demanded is lower; even aliens react to incentives.

The law of demand derives from the law of diminishing marginal value; the more of something we have the less we value having one more of it. This principle is on display in "New Kid on the Block" when Homer discovers The Frying Dutchman all-you-can-eat restaurant. Homer eagerly orders the all-you-can-eat dinner, and even before the waiter can give him his plate, Homer is at the buffet car, carting away an entire tray of shrimp. Once Homer has decided to pay for the buffet, the price of additional food is zero, so Homer tries to eat until the marginal benefit (value) is equal to zero.

Together, demand and the law of demand can be represented by a demand curve as in Figure 1.1. The curve itself represents the plans (the willingness and ability) of the buyers to purchase different quantities at different prices. The downward slope of the curve represents the law of demand; as the price of the good falls, the quantity demanded increases. So at the lower price, p′, more q′ will be purchased than at the higher price p.

A Market Is a Process

A market is not a physical place; it is the negotiation of suppliers and demanders. In the episode "Homer and Apu," Apu handles the customers in his customary fashion at the Kwik-E-Mart. When they want a 29-cent stamp, he quotes them $1.85. When they pump $2 of gas, he charges them $4.20. In the real world, of course, such hikes would not be tolerated if there were rival suppliers.

It is in this process that the plans of the buyers and the plans of the sellers are coordinated. The market can be the Kwik-E-Mart or Moe's Tavern, or it can be the negotiation between Bart and Martin ("Bart Gets an F"). The market process as one of plan coordination is important to the functioning of Springfield, or anywhere for that matter; without plan coordination, Moe's doesn't get beer; Apu doesn't make Squishees; and Mr. Burns does not provide electricity to Moe, Apu, or the city of Springfield.

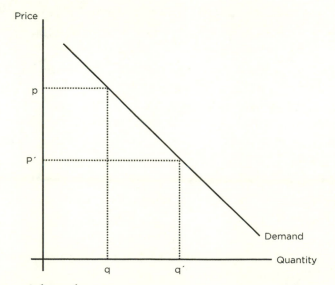

FIGURE 1.1. A demand curve

Exchange Is Mutually Beneficial

In an informed and uncoerced exchange, both parties receive more in value than they give up. Each person in an exchange values what the other has more than what he himself has. If this were not the case, the trade would not take place. Nearly every time Apu makes an appearance on the show, we are reminded that exchange is mutually beneficial. Apu prefers the money to the Squishee, and Homer prefers the Squishee to the money. The same is true at Moe's Tavern and for the Springfield Nuclear Power Plant. Each earns profit by providing individuals with something they value more than what they give up.[20]

Voluntary exchange takes place between someone who has something someone else wants and wants what someone else has; a Squishee-loving Duff owner needs a Duff-loving Squishee owner. So in every exchange a supplier meets a demander. Supply represents the plans of the owners (possessors) of a good to sell (exchange) that good at different prices (or for other goods).[21] Supply is analogous to demand in the sense that the more of something one has the less he will value it at the margin, and the less of something he has the more he will value it at the margin. Supply can be represented as an upward sloping curve for the same reason that demand is represented as a downward sloping curve. An example is given in Figure 1.2.

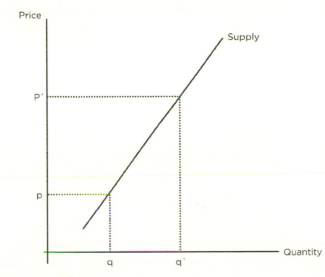

FIGURE 1.2. A supply curve

At low prices owners are willing to sell less (demand more) in hope of making a sale later to someone who values it more (is willing to give up more in exchange); that is, the opportunity cost of not selling at lower prices is relatively small, so less will be offered for sale. At high prices the opportunity cost of not selling is higher, so the more likely it is that the seller will plan to offer more. Therefore, other things equal, as the price of a good rises, sellers plan to sell more, and as the price of a good falls, sellers plan to sell less.

Market prices are determined by the interactions of sellers and buyers. Sellers meet buyers in markets and make offers, while buyers meet sellers in markets and make bids; it is through the process of bids and offers that the plans of the buyers and the plans of the sellers are coordinated through market prices. If sellers plan to sell more at a price than buyers plan to buy, the plans of the sellers will change to alleviate the surplus. Some sellers will offer to accept lower prices, and as they do, some buyers will agree to buy more as the opportunity cost falls, while still other sellers will offer less as the opportunity cost of selling falls. As lower prices are offered, the plans of both buyers and sellers will change until a price is reached at which the plans of the buyers and the plans of the sellers are coordinated. As seen in Figure 1.3, at a price of p the plans of the buyers, q_d, are not compatible with the plans of the sellers, q_s. The price will

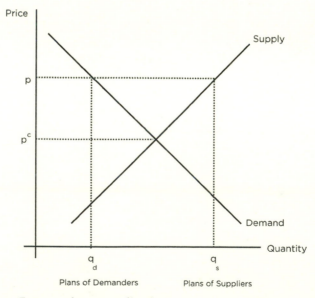

FIGURE 1.3. From surplus to coordination

fall toward p^c, at which point the plans of the sellers and the plans of the buyers will be coordinated and the market will clear.

In the case in which demanders plan to buy more at a price than sellers plan to sell at that price, plans are not coordinated and will therefore change. Demanders will bid up prices in an effort to get sellers to change their plans, and as the opportunity cost of not selling rises, sellers will offer more to buyers. While some sellers will plan to increase sales, some buyers will find that the price is "too rich for their blood" and plan to buy less. As the price rises through the process of bidding and offering, plans will change until they are coordinated. As seen in Figure 1.4, at a price of p the plans of the buyers, q$_d$, are incompatible with the plans of the sellers, q$_s$. The price will rise toward p^c, at which point the plans of the buyers and plans of the sellers will be coordinated and the market will clear.

The process of bids and offers brings about plan coordination, as buyers compete with buyers for the attention of sellers and sellers compete with sellers for the attention of buyers. This competition allows for the cooperation of buyers and sellers to reach mutually beneficial exchanges in which both the buyers and sellers are better off.

In "Bart Gets an F," Bart's choice not to read his book for his book report on *Treasure Island* earned him an F. Despite his best intentions, the benefits of

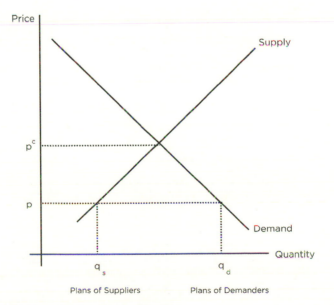

FIGURE 1.4. From shortage to coordination

watching TV outweigh the cost of studying, and Bart is unprepared for his history test. With another failure, Homer, Marge, and Bart meet with Dr. J. Loren Pryor, who suggests that Bart be held back in the fourth grade. Bart vows to pass the fourth grade. Later, while he is daydreaming in the schoolyard about being in the fourth grade well into his forties, Bart is hit on the head with a baseball. The ball rolls over near Martin, who awkwardly throws the ball back to the other kids and thus gets ridiculed. This gives Bart an idea. He offers Martin a trade—if Martin helps Bart pass the fourth grade, he will help Martin become less of a social outcast. Both boys end up being better off (wealthier) than before because of a mutually beneficial exchange.

Wealth Is What We Value

Economic growth entails an increase in the rate of production of wealth, and wealth is what we value. The production of material things is not necessarily wealth enhancing. Consider what occurred when Homer attempted to build Marge a spice rack in "Itchy and Scratchy and Marge." Despite having the means and the recipe from the *Complete Handyman's Bookshelf, Volume 1: Spice Racks* to bring about an end, Homer's labor, his garage of tools, and some wood produced a clump of wood that barely resembles a spice rack. So much for the labor theory of value![22] Despite his best intentions and hard work, Homer managed to reduce the value of his means, leaving the family worse off.

Homer discovers he has a long-lost brother, Herbert ("Oh Brother, Where Art Thou?"), who is the millionaire owner of Powell Motors. Herbert offers Homer any car he wants, but when none of them are to Homer's liking, Herbert hires Homer to design a car. Homer's design becomes progressively more garish and tacky as he adds features such as bubble domes and shag carpeting. The result of all of these extras is an $82,000 car. While it used lots of labor, material, and energy to produce, no one was willing to exchange resources worth anywhere close to its costs of production, and thus Powell Motors went out of business. Homer (and definitely Uncle Herb) learned the lesson that just because it is material and produced does not make it wealth.

Conclusion

One definition of economics is that economics is the study of the allocation of scarce resources amongst competing means. When economics is viewed as such, economics is about as enticing as watching *The Simpsons* in an episode on the proper disposal of oil after an oil change or watching a nuclear power documentary. Luckily for us, *The Simpsons* and economics is about people, the choices they make, and the consequences of those choices. Economics, like *The Simpsons*, is something we can look forward to watching and studying.

The intended consequences are, of course, less interesting in many ways than the unintended consequences. When Homer chooses a Duff Beer at Moe's, we know his intentions. With the help of Homer, Marge, Mr. Burns, Apu, Lisa, Lenny, and of course Bart, we learned that economics is about choice and its unintended consequences and the effects both seen and unseen. Economics, like *The Simpsons*, is about everything.

2

WHERE THE INVISIBLE HAND HAS ONLY FOUR FINGERS

Supply, Demand, and the Market Process in Springfield

Douglas Rogers and Peter J. Boettke

THE TOWN OF SPRINGFIELD can be a chaotic place. Aside from the occasional meltdown at the nuclear plant, however, the world of *The Simpsons*, much like our own, is characterized by a good deal of social order. A good way to understand this order is through the theoretical lens of economics.

Consider the scene from "Round Springfield" in which the hot dog vendor follows Homer everywhere, including to a cemetery. Homer's gluttonous desire for hot dogs is satiated despite the fact that he is in a graveyard, far from his beloved Kwik-E-Mart. Although seemingly inconsequential, this event helps shed light on the main puzzle underlying economics, the puzzle of social cooperation under the division of labor. It is one thing to explain how Homer would satisfy his desire for hot dogs if we find him at home with a supply of hot dogs already in his possession and a grill or stove at his disposal. It is quite another to explain how Homer's demand for hot dogs is satisfied in the market through specialization and exchange. Both economizing and exchanging are critical aspects of human behavior.

The fact that social cooperation is as ubiquitous as it is should be surprising. Millions of people, all with various ambitions, interact in a complex web of associations to produce the multitude of goods and services that we all enjoy. There is no central authority that plans all of these interactions; the market economy is a spontaneous order. The force behind spontaneous order, introduced by Adam Smith in his 1776 book *An Inquiry into the Nature and Causes of the Wealth of Nations*, is known in economics as the "invisible hand."

To understand just what Smith means by an invisible hand, it is important to emphasize a fundamental proposition of the economic way of thinking: "All social phenomena emerge from the actions and interactions of individuals who are choosing in response to expected additional benefits and costs to themselves."[1]

The invisible hand, as well as the four-fingered invisible "yellow" hands of the Simpsons, applies to more than what people usually consider to be the narrow scope of economic activity. Economics helps us understand not only social cooperation at the Kwik-E-Mart and Monstromart but also the behavior we see portrayed at Mayor Quimby's office and Springfield Elementary.

Scarcity, Trade-Offs, and the Market Process

To understand why social cooperation is so important and also why economic problems exist in the first place, it is necessary to introduce the concept of scarcity. The wants or desires of individuals are limitless. Homer Simpson is a wonderful illustration of this fact. After selling his soul to the devil, portrayed of course by Ned Flanders, Homer spends the day in hell, where his ironic punishment is to be continually stuffed with donuts ("Treehouse of Horror IV"). In accord with his super-human gluttony, Homer happily continues eating all the donuts hell can muster. Although the wants of individuals are limitless, the means that individuals have to satisfy these wants, with the apparent exception of heaven or hell, are quite limited, that is, scarce.

Life is not like the fantasy version of Germany that Homer Simpson dreams about, where everything, even the rain, is made out of chocolate ("Burns Verkaufen der Kraftwerk"). As is stressed in every basic economics course worth taking, utopia is not an option. The ever-present problem of scarcity forces individuals to make trade-offs. For an individual to consume something, whether that is a donut, a ride on the monorail, or an hour playing the saxophone, she must forgo something else that those resources or time could have been used for. Something is scarce if someone has to sacrifice something to get it, whether that is time, money, or both. The activities that one sacrifices, the alternative desires that could have been fulfilled, are called opportunity costs. Consider the episode "Bart the Fink," in which Bart wants a hundred tacos for $100 and Lisa wants to contribute $100 to the Corporation for Public Broadcasting. Marge recognizes the opportunity cost of their spending and, after stating that she won't let them waste their money, makes them put their $100 in the bank.

Individuals respond to scarcity by using their limited means to fulfill as many of their desires, what economists refer to as utility, as possible. One thing that the episode just described illustrates is that utility is in the eye of the beholder. Only individuals know what they want and how best to use their scarce resources to attain their goals. They weigh their prospective marginal benefits (MB) against the expected marginal costs (MC) of any activity and pursue that activity until MB = MC. Individuals are driven by this desire to get the most utility possible out of what they have available.

To see how competitive pressures work to coordinate human behavior, consider the checkout line at the Monstromart ("Homer and Apu"). Marge and Apu find themselves stuck in line as attention-starved Grandpa Abe Simpson rambles to the cashier about nickels. Apu suggests they go to the longest line because it is filled with sad single men buying only a few things with cash. By switching lines, Marge and Apu get through the checkout faster. They are both engaging in the sort of optimizing behavior at the individual level that produces complex and desirable social cooperation.

In this case, customers leave the slow-moving line for the faster-moving line, but it could just as easily be producers leaving an industry in which they incur losses for an industry in which they can make profits. In regard to the lines at the Monstromart, the slow line is now not as crowded, and thus not as slow as it was before. The tendency in either case is for the optimal behavior at the individual level to lead to socially desirable results. This case illustrates the same logic that is behind the law of one price in a standard economic presentation of the competitive market process. A profit opportunity known to all is realized by none, and $20 bills do not persistently lay there on the sidewalk unexploited, unless they cost $21 to pick them up. There is more to say on this issue later in the chapter.[2]

Economics Is About Exchange and the Institutions Within Which Exchange Takes Place

What is good for the individual is not always good for society as a whole. The criminal Snake Jailbird, for instance, makes a career out of stealing everything he can get his hands on. Whether or not individually optimal behavior produces socially desirable results thus depends on what economists refer to as institutions, or simply the "rules of the game."

Consider the Springfield Isotopes, the town's AA minor league baseball team. The Isotopes are expected to follow certain well-defined rules in the course of a game. Three strikes and the batter is out, three outs in an inning, and so on. If the rules were to arbitrarily change, chaos would ensue. A good example of this chaos is when Homer acts as referee for Lisa's soccer games ("Marge Gamer"). Lisa uses this opportunity to her own advantage by acting as if other players are fouling her. Homer the impartial ref goes as far as to rule that not only does Lisa get a penalty kick for being fouled, all the other players in the game have to pay her $1. The other players, as well as spectators, are out-raged and conflict ensues. When the rules of the game are not well-defined or impartially enforced, the game begins to break down.

The rules of the game are especially important in economic activity. The most important of these rules are property rights. Property rights assign ownership and specify who may, or may not, use or sell certain things. Property rights provide an incentive for individuals to put their property toward its highest-valued use and are necessary if the invisible hand is to function properly. Consider the multitude of exchanges that occur every day in Spring-field. By pursuing their own self-interest, property owners such as Apu and Montgomery C. Burns provide valuable goods and services to the residents of Springfield. This is because property owners can trade or exchange their prop-erty for something that they value more. Thus, as long as property rights are well-defined and enforceable, individually optimal behavior produces complex and desirable social interaction.[3]

The act of trade, exchanging property rights over one thing for property rights over something else, is fundamental to market processes and a critical element of economic growth. To understand trade, it is first necessary to in-troduce some additional concepts. For economic goods, more is preferred to less. Homer's proclivity for donuts and Duff Beer indicates that these are goods to him, and the more of these that he has, the happier he is. Moreover, these are scarce goods. Homer is willing to sacrifice money in order to obtain them. An economic bad, on the other hand, is anything for which less is preferred to more. For Homer, much like most people, work is an economic bad. This does not mean that these things are "bad" in the normative sense, just that, all things considered, Homer would prefer to do the least amount of work possible. At one point he goes as far as placing a mechanical drinking bird at his work key-board to constantly hit the "y" key to respond "yes" to safety related questions so that he can go to the movies ("King-Size Homer"). This helps to explain why people pay for economic goods, such as beer, and must be paid in order to ac-cept economic bads, such as work.

Something that should be clear is that whether something is a good or a bad depends on the preferences of the individual. Just as work is a bad to Homer, it is actually a good for Frank Grimes, the self-made man and opposite of Homer who prides himself in being a workaholic. Not even Duff Beer can always be considered a good, at least not to do-gooders such as Ned Flanders. What is important to keep in mind is that economic goods are whatever people value. Wealth, the end product of a well-functioning market economy, is just the possession of those things that people value.

One way that markets produce wealth is through trade. Consider the infamous Bart-Milhouse soul exchange ("Bart Sells His Soul"). Bart thinks that souls do not exist and thus have no value, whereas Milhouse thinks they are extremely valuable. Bart thus agrees to sell his soul to Milhouse for the price of $5. Bart summarizes his preferences later to Lisa by noting that everything he has is for sale, including his conscience and sense of decency.

It is important to note that no new production has taken place. Prior to the exchange there were two souls and after the exchange there are still only two souls. The lesson here is that both parties are made better off simply through the act of trade: Milhouse exchanges $5 for something he considers to be very valuable, whereas Bart exchanges something he considers to be worthless for $5. Simply by exchanging property rights, wealth has been created. Once again, the worth, or value, of something is dependent upon the preferences of the individual.

One way for individuals to get even more out of trade is by focusing their production on those goods that they are "best" at producing, what economists refer to as specialization. Specialization is simply when people focus on producing those goods for which they have a comparative advantage. Returning to the concept of opportunity costs, one has a comparative advantage in production if he or she has the lowest opportunity costs for producing something. Consider Doctor Hibbert and Groundskeeper Willy. Both produce economic goods for a living: Dr. Hibbert provides medical care, whereas Willy keeps Springfield Elementary clean. Let us assume for the moment that Dr. Hibbert, being a smart fellow, is better at both jobs, that is, he has an *absolute advantage* in production. Since like all economists we love assumptions, let us also assume that Willy has transferred to Springfield Hospital, just to make the example clear. Dr. Hibbert can choose *either* to perform five surgeries *or* to clean ten hallways in a day's worth of work. Willy, on the other hand, can *either* perform one rather shoddy Dr. Nick-like surgery *or* clean nine hallways in a day's work. These facts are summarized in Table 2.1.

TABLE 2.1. Comparative advantage and specialization

	Surgeries	Hallways	Opportunity Cost of One Surgery	Opportunity Cost of One Hallway
Dr. Hibbert	5	10	2 hallways	1/2 of a surgery
Groundskeeper Willy	1	9	9 hallways	1/9 of a surgery

It may seem as though there are no grounds for trade. Why not have Dr. Hibbert do both tasks and fire poor old Willy? Even though Dr. Hibbert is better at both activities, both parties can still be made better off by trade. To understand why trade is still mutually beneficial, consider the opportunity costs. Remember that opportunity costs are the alternative activities that one sacrifices by doing something else. If either man were to clean a hallway, the opportunity cost is however many surgeries they could have performed in that time, and vice versa for each surgery performed. Dr. Hibbert has the lowest opportunity cost for producing surgeries, and Willy has the lowest opportunity cost for cleaning hallways. Thus, even though Dr. Hibbert is better at both jobs, he should specialize in performing surgeries.[4]

Consider the possibility of trade. If Dr. Hibbert were to specialize in surgeries and Willy were to specialize in cleaning hallways, the total amount of work that they could get done in a day would be five surgeries and nine hallways cleaned. If the hospital were to fire Willy and have Dr. Hibbert perform both tasks, the total amount of work he could do if he split his time between both activities would be two-and-a-half surgeries and five hallways cleaned.[5] Thus, if the two were to trade, let's say that Dr. Hibbert hires Willy to clean hallways and pays him one third of the price of each surgery he performs, both can be made better off.[6] Dr. Hibbert can trade two surgeries for six hallways cleaned. Thus he ends up after hiring Willy with three surgeries and six hallways cleaned. This is more of both surgeries and hallways than Dr. Hibbert had before trading with Willy!

Specialization is important because it increases the overall productive capabilities of everyone involved. The more specialization and subsequent trade that takes place, the more wealth that is produced. How does one know what to specialize in? This important question leads us to the role that prices play in a market economy.

Let us return to the demand, or consumer, side of things. Remember that individuals try to get the most they can out of the scarce resources that they have. This leads us to the *law of demand*. This law states, *holding all other factors constant, if the price of a good increases, the quantity demanded will decrease; if the price of a good decreases, the quantity demanded will increase.*

Consider Stampy the elephant ("Bart Gets an Elephant"). After Bart wins the elephant as a gag on a radio contest, Homer quickly comes up with the idea of charging neighborhood kids $1 to see Stampy and $2 for a ride. At that price, many people are willing to part with their scarce dollars to see and ride Stampy. Homer thinks he has made $58 in profit the first day, until Marge points out that Stampy eats $300 in food a day. Realizing that something must be done, Homer changes his prices to $100 to look at the elephant and $500 to ride.

The quite predictable result is that no one wants to either see or ride Stampy anymore. The price has been increased more than tenfold, and as a result, the quantity demanded has fallen in accord with the law of demand. What is important to note here is that prices send signals that help consumers get the most out of their scarce resources. When prices are sufficiently low, they signal to consumers that the opportunity costs of consumption are low, in other words, they will not have to sacrifice a lot of consumption in alternative areas. When prices are high, they signal to consumers that the opportunity costs of consumption are high and that they should consider consuming something else. Once again, prices, like property rights, help to coordinate individual behavior to produce complex and desirable social cooperation. This produces desirable social cooperation because it incentivizes individuals to cut back their consumption of very valuable goods, so that only those who value them the most, that is, those that are willing to pay the most, actually get them.

Prices are most often measured in terms of money. Indeed it is much simpler and easier to trade using money than in abstract units such as hallways or units of Milhouse ("Trilogy of Error"). We will not get into the specifics here, but as Homer's internal voice mentions in "Boy-Scoutz 'n the Hood," money can be exchanged for goods and services. One critical function of measuring prices in terms of money is that it allows for accurate economic calculation. At the individual level, this means that individuals are able to get the most utility out of their scarce resources, that is, the most bang for their buck. At the level of society, or social cooperation, this means that resources flow to their highest-valued use.[7]

We already saw this in action with the law of demand. Prices help individuals respond rationally by leading them to consume less when goods are especially scarce and highly demanded (high opportunity cost) and vice versa when the opportunity cost is low. This calculation is critical, not only so the individual can get the most utility out of his or her scarce resources, but also at the larger level of social cooperation. Absent the economic calculation facilitated by market prices, we would quickly run out of relatively scarce, valuable goods. Unless prices are allowed to reflect relative scarcities, resources will not flow to their highest-valued use.

The Profit Signal: Even Hippies Follow It

At this point, it is important to remember the fundamental proposition mentioned at the beginning of the chapter. Individuals make choices, that is calculate, in response to expected additional costs and benefits. This leads us to an important result regarding supply and demand: *individuals will continue to consume until the marginal benefits of consumption equal the marginal costs. Individuals will continue to produce until the marginal benefits of production equal the marginal costs.* To explain another way, if the additional benefits of doing something outweigh the additional costs, you should do more of it because it will increase your overall level of utility. If the additional costs outweigh the additional benefits, you should do less of it. Thus the tendency is for individuals to stop doing more or less of something once they have balanced the costs and the benefits. At first glance, this might seem obvious to the point of irrelevancy. Understanding this basic principle, however, is critical to understanding economics.

Consider Homer's participation in a six-pound-steak-eating contest ("Maximum Homerdrive"). We can expect Homer to continue eating until the marginal costs of eating equal the marginal benefits. Since the marginal costs are zero, that is, Homer pays nothing for each additional bite of food, we can expect him to continue eating until the marginal benefits are also zero.

The tendency for individuals to equate marginal costs and marginal benefits goes a long way toward explaining market processes and social cooperation. Consider the concept of profits. The technical definition of profit is total revenue, the total money brought in from sales, minus opportunity costs. To say that profits are positive is just another way of saying that the marginal benefits of production are greater than the marginal costs of production.

The existence of profits thus elicits entry into the market. If profits are positive, that is a signal that society values the production of a good more the opportunity costs of producing it. Profit-seeking businessmen will thus have ample incentive to give people more of what they want. Once again, profits show in the context of the marketplace how the optimal behavior at the level of the individual produces complex and beneficial social cooperation.

The role of loss—that is, negative profits—is just as important. To say that profits are negative is to say that the marginal benefits of production are less than the marginal costs. When a producer incurs losses it means that the resources put into producing that particular good or service are not being put to their highest-valued use. Thus it is essential to a well-functioning market economy that producers that continue to incur losses go out of business so that resources can be reallocated to more valuable uses. Even the hippies in "D'oh-in in the Wind" recognize that profits are necessary to keep an organization in business.

Profits, like prices, are signals that coordinate behavior in a market economy. The spontaneous order of the market that we have been discussing throughout this chapter is only possible because of the function that these signals play. Absent private property, market prices, and the profit and loss signal, the spontaneous order of the market no longer functions to produce wealth.

Conclusion

The most basic lessons of economics are that incentives matter, information about the value of scarce resources is necessary, and accurate feedback is required for individuals to make prudent decisions within a market economy. Property rights produce incentives, prices provide information, and profit and loss accounting gives feedback to decision makers. The competitive price system steers economic activity via the structure of incentives and the flow of information so that dispersed individuals within a society will coordinate their plans—the production plans of some will dovetail with the consumption demands of others, and they will do so in such a way that eventually all the gains from exchange will be exhausted and all least-cost methods of production are utilized. Working through this argument from individual choice through institutional specification to equilibrium properties is a thing of intellectual beauty to the teacher of economics, and the explanation of the interconnectedness of activity throughout the world and the coordination of the vast division of labor to produce even the most mundane products is a source of wonderment to the student of economics.

3

A PILE OF KRUSTY BURGERS EMBIGGENS THE FATTEST MAN

Obesity, Incentives, and Unintended Consequences in "King-Size Homer"

Art Carden

A SMALL HANDFUL OF IDEAS IN ECONOMICS do most of the heavy lifting.[1] They're usually listed in the first chapter of introductory economics textbooks. They're also on display in "King-Size Homer," a *Simpsons* episode from season 7 in which Homer tried to balloon up to three hundred pounds in order to be classified as "disabled" under the Americans with Disabilities Act. Since "hyper-obesity" is a disability in the episode, a three-hundred-pound Homer would be allowed to work from home at his employer's expense. The episode illustrates a number of important economic principles. People act. People respond to incentives. People are generally rational. People make decisions at the margin. There are no free lunches. They compare costs and benefits. Finally, actions and policies have consequences that are sometimes difficult (or impossible) to foresee.

Before looking at how these principles are illustrated in the episode, a quick synopsis is in order. The episode is set against a backdrop of company-sponsored calisthenics at the Springfield Nuclear Power Plant. Some of Mr. Burns' heavies find Homer in a bathroom, where we learn that he is trying to avoid the morning calisthenics. Homer is dragged kicking and screaming to the area where Mr. Burns is leading his employees through some simple exercises. We observe several employees following as Mr. Burns leads them in jumping jacks while an exhausted Homer is sweating profusely and trying unsuccessfully to keep up.

Homer is extremely unhappy after the exercise session, and he expresses his frustrations to his friends and co-workers, Carl and Lenny. He learns of another co-worker who was able to go on disability following a workplace injury.

Homer decides that he is going to find a way to disable himself so that he too can go on disability, and walks around trying to hurt himself. He deliberately places himself in harm's way by going into a hard hat area and waiting for something to fall on him.

While reading a pamphlet titled "Are You Disabled?" and learning that he does not suffer from protected conditions such as "lumber lung" and "achy-breaky pelvis," Homer happens on "hyper-obesity," which would allow someone who weighs over three hundred pounds to work from home on his or her employer's expense. He decides that this is the way to go, and Lisa upbraids him for abusing a law that was *intended* to help the less fortunate. *Intended* is in italics because it's an important idea that will play a role later in the discussion.

First, Homer tries to consult Dr. Julius Hibbert for advice on how to get up to three hundred pounds. The Simpsons' family physician responds that doing so is negligent and that he cannot help in good conscience. He does, however, recommend Homer to Dr. Nick Riviera, a graduate of Hollywood Upstairs Medical College who gives Homer an alternative food pyramid, which includes "the whipped group" and the "chocotastic." He is advised to chew bacon instead of gum and use Pop Tarts instead of bread. With determined effort, Homer grows to three hundred pounds, and a remote workstation is installed at the Simpson home that will allow Homer to do his job as a safety inspector at the nuclear power plant remotely.

Suffice it to say that Homer's weight gain puts a strain on his marriage and his family life even though he (apparently) enjoys the newfound freedom that comes with working from home. Marge isn't sure how to get through to him on this, and when they are compiling a "pro" and "con" list about his new weight (an exercise in the analysis of costs and benefits), she reveals that she finds him less attractive than she did previously.

One day, Homer decides to take off and go to the movies. He has a small drinking bird toy set up to press the "y" key on his remote terminal because apparently "yes" is the correct answer to every question he is asked (like "vent gas"). He is denied admission to see the movie "Honk If You're Horny" because he is apparently too large to fit in the seats. He resolves to go home and show the world that fat people aren't lazy, undisciplined, and irresponsible, but he discovers that the toy drinking bird he had set up to press the Y key has fallen over. An explosion at the power plant is imminent unless he can shut things off manually. His fingers are too fat for him to use the phone and call the plant, the tires on the car explode when he tries to get in, Bart's skateboard breaks when he tries to get on it, and no one picks him up when he tries to hitchhike. He ends up hijacking an ice cream truck, driving it to the plant, and saving the day.

Human Action

What is known as the "Austrian School" of economics emphasizes the importance of individual action in the explanation of social phenomena.[2] One of the leading exponents of this approach was Ludwig von Mises, who was honored as a fellow of the American Economic Association for his contributions to the discipline. He titled his magnum opus *Human Action* because he wanted to develop an entire set of theory based on a very simple insight: man *acts* (or in a gender-neutral setting, people act), which is to say that people employ means to attain consciously chosen ends. Action is purposive, which means that it aims at the accomplishment of some kind of goal.

Goals range from the mundane and pedestrian to the enormous and ambitious. In this case, Homer's goal is pretty mundane: he seeks to gain the 35 pounds that will take him from his current 265 pounds to the 300 pounds that will make him officially obese and able to work from home. To do this, Homer employs some simple means: his time, his mental energy, and all the food he can find. Indeed, when he is weighing himself for his possible last day of work, he discovers that he needs another half-pound to get to 300 pounds. However, he has eaten everything in the house, including tarragon and soy sauce. Maggie comes to the rescue by making Homer a donut out of modeling clay. Homer eats it and the scale tips to 300 pounds.

The message is relatively simple. Homer chooses ends, simple though they may be, and then uses means to get there. From the very simple insight that people act, we can get the entire body of economic theory and show how Homer's quest to become hyper-obese (and others' reaction to his efforts) illustrates basic economic principles.

Rationality

Economists often assume that people basically are rational. This is controversial because people make a lot of mistakes and do a lot of things that seem to be irrational. Indeed, obesity is seen as evidence that undermines the rationality postulate. The argument is that people would like to be thin, long-lived, and happy, but they make irrational (or short-run focused) decisions that reduce their welfare.[3]

Economists often mean something much weaker than this when we say that people are rational. We don't mean that they make the right decision all the time or even that they learn quickly. We mean that they will tend to do things that give them outcomes they like, they tend not to do things that give them outcomes they don't like, and their mistakes tend to be revealed eventually.

In this episode, we see several examples of rationality, even though some of them are questionable at first glance. Homer tries to choose the appropriate means that will help him gain weight (a pile of Krusty Burgers, for example, and a banana split sans the banana). Later in the episode, Homer decides that he has chosen unwisely and that he needs to undertake different means to make amends with his family. The important point is that when Homer's perceptions of the costs and benefits of hyper-obesity change, he changes his behavior accordingly.

Incentives

This brings us to the importance of incentives. One of the most important insights that inform economic analysis is the idea that people respond to incentives. Indeed, economist and textbook author Steven Landsburg once said that economics could be boiled down to "people respond to incentives," with everything else merely being commentary.[4] People act in response to the costs and benefits of different courses of action, and they will tend to do more of things that get cheaper or more remunerative. They will do less of things that get more expensive or less remunerative. In Homer's case, the benefits embedded in the Americans with Disabilities Act increase the benefits of weighing over three hundred pounds. This provides him with an incentive to gain weight. It's an incentive to which Homer responds with verve, and the results are, of course, hilarious.

The results haven't been so funny for people who have actually been harmed by the Americans with Disabilities Act. Lisa's protestation to the contrary, the evidence suggests that the Americans with Disabilities Act reduced employment opportunities for some disabled workers. For example, the economists Daron Acemoglu and Joshua Angrist find that disabled men of all ages and women under forty exhibited a sharp decline in employment after the passage of the Americans with Disabilities Act.[5] Similar results can be found in DeLeire.[6]

Costs, Benefits, and Trade-Offs

The episode begins with a company-sponsored calisthenics program. But why would the company want to offer such a thing? Why would they want people exercising, and on company time, no less? There are a few possible reasons. First, if the firm is responsible for paying the employees' medical costs, it will have a vested interest in healthier employees. Second, healthier employees might be happier and more productive employees. Third, group calisthenics might serve the same purpose as a company softball team. The exercises might build an *esprit du corps* that increases worker morale and, therefore, productivity.

Regardless of the motivation, the fundamental fact about a company exercise program like this is that the people who initiated the program expected the benefits (morale, health, whatever) to be greater than the cost (morale, time, whatever). Outside observers—intellectuals, cable talking heads, magazine writers, economists—spend a lot of time and energy debating whether this venture or that venture was good for a particular company. Fortunately, in a market economy, profits and losses tell us whether our decisions have or have not created value. An increase in company profitability as a result of the calisthenics program would tell Mr. Burns that he has chosen wisely. A reduction in profitability as a result of the calisthenics program would tell Mr. Burns that he has chosen poorly. While it is entirely possible that Burns might misidentify the effect of the exercise program, he has a much greater incentive than anyone else to try to identify the program's true merits.

When Homer decides that he is going to try to find his way onto the disability rolls, he ventures into a hard hat area and waits for something to fall on him. Something falls. Homer moves to where the object hit. Another object falls somewhere else. Homer moves again. A wheelbarrow filled with bricks falls and squashes another gentleman. On reflection, Homer realizes that it is good that he didn't get hit. This reflects cost-benefit reasoning on Homer's part. He is willing to take on added risks in order to go on disability, but his willingness to do so has limits. Homer would like to retain most (if not all) of the benefits of his conscious existence. The thought of going through life as a paraplegic or as a vegetable is unappealing.

At the end of the episode, Mr. Burns asks what he can do to repay Homer for saving the power plant from a nuclear meltdown. Homer looks at his family and asks if Mr. Burns can make him thin again. We then see king-size Homer in his underwear trying to do a sit-up as an increasingly exasperated Mr. Burns tries to count to one through a megaphone. Finally, Mr. Burns gives up and just pays for liposuction.

As Homer is struggling to do sit-ups, Mr. Burns is revising his expectations about Homer's capabilities. He finally decides that the expected cost of helping Homer lose weight through diet and exercise is greater than the expected cost of liposuction. He decides that the liposuction is the least-costly way to obtain the benefit he has promised—a thin Homer.

Decisions Are Made at the Margin

People make a common error when analyzing policies when they say, "Well, the average person isn't going to try to gain weight just to go on disability" or "Most people aren't going to gain weight just because they could go on disability." This confuses the average with the margin: when we increase the benefits of something, we can be pretty sure that somebody somewhere will do more of it. This is what happens in "King-Size Homer." After reading a pamphlet about disability, Homer discovers that the benefits of hyper-obesity are higher than he had first thought. Most people wouldn't increase their weight just because it could help them go on disability, but Homer Simpson isn't most people. In response to changes in the marginal benefits of additional weight, Homer put on lots of additional weight.

There's No Free Lunch

Economists are fond of saying that there is no such thing as a free lunch, which is a saying whose origin is unknown but was popularized by the science fiction writer Robert Heinlein in his 1966 book *The Moon Is a Harsh Mistress*. In other words, everything has a cost. Homer's decision to gain weight is no different. In one scene, Homer and Marge list the pros and cons of Homer's decision to gain so much weight. Homer lists the pros—he is able to work from home, for example—while Marge's cons include the facts that they are constantly running the air conditioner and that Marge no longer finds him sexually attractive. These examples show that the additional lunches Homer has consumed in order to gain weight most certainly were not free and have in fact come at a steep price.

Homer's hyper-obesity also limits him in other ways. He isn't able to get into a movie theater because their facilities cannot accommodate him, and he can't dial his phone because his fingers are too fat. His tires explode when he tries to drive to work. His wife no longer finds him attractive. He has to wear a muumuu (although to him this seems to be a benefit). And so on. Homer achieves his goal of becoming hyper-obese, but he does so at a cost.

Unintended Consequences

One lesson that emerges in this episode is the importance of the law of unintended consequences. While Homer is considering gaining enough weight to qualify for disability, Lisa upbraids him for taking advantage of a program that is intended to help the truly unfortunate. The problem with policies and programs, though, is that they change incentives and give people reasons to alter their behavior. These changes in incentives cannot be ignored when people are evaluating whether policies are wise or not. Increasing the benefits or reducing the costs of becoming hyper-obese give people incentives to become obese.

A lot of policies intended to help the poor or the disadvantaged make them worse off. Rent control creates housing shortages. Minimum wages increase unemployment. The Americans with Disabilities Act made it more expensive to hire people with disabilities and, therefore, reduced their employment opportunities. No matter how good their intentions, public policies that interfere with the market process tend to have undesirable and unforeseen consequences that, in some eyes, necessitate further government intervention. The problem is that these interventions often have further negative consequences. The only solution is not to start, because the unintended consequences of the policies that are supposed to fix particular problems are often worse than the problems themselves.

The law of unintended consequences also appears when Homer is denied admission to "Honk If You're Horny" at the local movie theater. When Homer tries to buy a ticket, the cashier is unsure of what to do and consults a manager. The manager tries to be as diplomatic as possible and tells Homer that their facility is not prepared for a man of his needs. Of course, Homer does not understand such indirect language, causing the manager to become more direct and point out that he can't fit into their seats. Homer is obviously willing to work with him and offers to sit in the aisle. The theater manager responds that he can't allow it because it would violate the fire code. There is no room to bargain as it has been cut off by regulation. A transaction that might have created wealth—Homer watches "Honk If You're Horny" while sitting in the aisle and the movie theater earns revenue—is rendered illegal by regulation.

At first glance, the regulation appears sensible. Fire codes that prohibit people from sitting in the aisles are there (presumably) to prevent people from dying in a fire because of obstructed exits. After all, it has been argued that the right to speak freely does not extend to the right to shout "fire!" in a crowded theater, so why should the right to trade extend to the right to sit in such a way as to block the exits to a crowded theater?

This is, unfortunately, a rather short-sighted and heavy-handed way of dealing with one kind of risk.[7] There are markets, or potential markets, for all kinds of risks. The risk associated with the probability of injury from Homer sitting in the aisle could be capitalized into the ticket price, or Homer, the theater manager, and the other patrons could arrange a side bargain. The theater manager offers Homer a garbage bag filled with popcorn if he will leave quietly; presumably, he should be able to offer a similar benefit to patrons who might be threatened by the risk an obese Homer in the aisle might pose. The assumption that there is One Right Way for theater patrons to be organized—and that One Right Way means no one sitting in the aisles—reduces gains from trade and limits innovation.

Homer's offer also reveals that he is willing to accept a degree of risk in order to see "Honk If You're Horny." Since he is not allowed to exercise this preference for risk at the theater, he might exercise it in another activity that is riskier but less heavily regulated. The unintended consequence could be that the fire code, while it reduces the harm from fires in crowded theaters, increases the harm from other risky activities. The net effect is ambiguous, but it is entirely possible that the net effect of the regulation is to increase harm.

The early nineteenth-century French economist Frederic Bastiat identified an important principle in his classic essay "What Is Seen and What Is Not Seen," and Henry Hazlitt expanded on this in his book *Economics in One Lesson*; they argued that actions and policies have hidden costs and consequences that are difficult to see but that are no less real than the visible benefits and consequences.[8] The classic example is the fallacy of the broken window, first identified by Bastiat. If a window is accidentally broken, it might appear to everyone that this is actually economically beneficial. After all, the window's original owner has to buy a new one, which creates income for the glazier. The glazier uses his new income to employ workers and to buy things he likes. And so on. The fatal flaw, however, is that the money that went to pay the glazier was taken away from some other, unseen line of employment.

This principle helps to explain why some policies that waste resources and that hurt the people they are intended to help nonetheless remain very popular. Restrictions on international trade are among economists' favorite examples. Competition is a process of creative destruction, to use a term popularized by Joseph Schumpeter, and it is often a process wherein the benefits are dispersed across a large population and very difficult to see while the costs are concentrated on a small but very visible segment of the population.

Suppose restrictions on international trade were relaxed and Springfielders were allowed to import more beer. If they switch almost completely from domestic beer to imported beer, this would reduce earnings and profits for domestic producers such as Duff Beer. If the Duff brewery were to close, the costs would be very visible: a shuttered brewery, temporarily unemployed workers, and ripple effects for firms that served Duff, and its employees would likely make headlines in the *Springfield Shopper* and, perhaps, lead to calls for restrictions on imported beer. The benefits—a few extra dollars in consumers' pockets, more savings, more investment, and more innovation—will be much more difficult to see and difficult if not impossible to trace directly to the liberalization of the beer trade.

This is also illustrated in a later episode, "Coming to Homerica," which illustrates the cultural and economic benefits of free immigration as the newly unemployed people of Ogdenville move to Springfield. The benefits—cheaper, better services and newer cultural goods—are difficult to see while the costs in terms of fewer unskilled jobs for native Springfielders are very visible.

Fire codes that prevent Homer from watching "Honk If You're Horny" from the aisles in the movie theater produce similar visible benefits and opaque costs. If there were an emergency requiring evacuation, it would be easy to point at the regulation and claim that it helped those who might have been injured in the emergency. It would be more difficult to see the harm that might result. The regulation increases the price of movie tickets. Therefore, people substitute away from trips to the movies and toward movies watched at home. This reduces opportunities in the movie theater industry and increases opportunities in DVD player manufacturing, which might be more dangerous than movie theater operation. Fewer people are injured in theater accidents, to be sure, but more people will be injured through contact with industrial chemicals and compounds in electronics factories. The degree to which this will result in additional injury is an empirical matter, but theory predicts that we will pay for fewer theater injuries with other kinds of injuries.

Conclusion

Some of the most important principles of economics are illustrated in the episode "King-Size Homer." Homer's decision to gain weight in order to qualify for disability and work from home shows how people respond to incentives, how they make decisions at the margin, and how policies often have negative unintended consequences. Over the long run, we would expect to see firms such as the Springfield Nuclear Power Plant hire fewer people—like hyperobese Homer—who are now more expensive to hire as a result of the Americans with Disabilities Act.

Beyond the simple principles and the facts of unintended consequences, "King-Size Homer" illustrates the importance and usefulness of economics as a way of thinking about the world. People act. They employ means to achieve ends. By changing incentives, policymakers sometimes encourage people to pursue destructive ends. We all have a tendency to truck, barter, and exchange, to borrow from Adam Smith. When policymakers make policy without recognizing these tendencies, they create disasters.

PART II
MONEY, MARKETS,
AND GOVERNMENT

4

TWENTY DOLLARS
CAN BUY MANY PEANUTS!

Money and *The Simpsons*

Andrew T. Young

IN "BOY-SCOUTZ 'N THE HOOD," Homer Simpson is on the couch finishing off a jar of peanuts. To his dismay, he tosses the last peanut wide of his mouth and it goes behind the couch. Searching desperately for this peanut while covered in the leftovers from the rest of the jar, Homer instead retrieves a $20 bill from under the sofa. Initially he is disappointed because it is not a peanut. However, his brain reminds him that $20 can be exchanged for goods, including a lot of peanuts, which causes him to cheer up.

Homer—or, rather, his inner (smarter) voice—has successfully articulated a defining characteristic of money. But why *can* you exchange money for goods and services? Homer's $20 bill is composed of at most a few cents worth of paper and ink. What makes that particular type of paper into money? Moreover, what exactly *is* money?[1]

In the United States, money is much more than simply the sum of dollar bills and coins. The large majority of money is created by private banks rather than directly by the government. The Federal Reserve (the U.S. central banking system) reports that, in June of 2010, the most commonly used measure of the money supply, M2, was about $8.6 trillion. At the same time, bills and coins (*currency*) totaled only $883 billion. The remainder of M2 was primarily bank deposits (about $5.5 trillion).[2]

Not just any private institution—or any government, for that matter—can create money. Homer finds this out the hard way when he buys "Itchy and Scratchy money" at an amusement park ("Itchy and Scratchy Land"). When Homer asks what it is, the park attendant assures him that it works just like U.S.

currency but is "fun." Homer is sold and takes $1,100 worth. Unfortunately, Homer quickly finds out that the money only works *in the amusement park*.[3] But why? Why are people not likely to accept a piece of paper issued by a large, household-name amusement park? Why are they more likely to accept a piece of paper (a check) written on a small bank halfway across the country that they've never heard of?

In this chapter we'll explore (with the help of the residents of Springfield, including its most famous family) what makes something *generally* accepted as a means of payment for goods and services. *What makes something money?* We'll discuss the functions that genuine monies must serve as well as the properties that allow something to fulfill these monetary functions. We'll also briefly discuss our modern U.S. money supply and how, historically, we came to value little green pieces of paper.

The Functions of Money

In the "Trilogy of Error," caught with illegal fireworks by Chief Wiggum, Milhouse exclaims, "I can't go to juvey! They use guys like me as currency!" Could Milhouse actually become money in the juvenile hall? To answer this question we first have to know what functions Milhouse would have to serve to legitimately be called money. Second, we have to know what properties (or characteristics) Milhouse would have to possess to serve those functions.

Let's start with functions. For something—call it an *asset*—to be considered money, it typically must function as three things:

- A medium of exchange
- A unit of account
- A store of value

These functions are not mutually exclusive. The extent to which an asset serves one function largely determines to what extent it serves the other two functions.

Medium of Exchange

A *medium of exchange* is something that can be widely used as payment for goods and services. When Bart wins a radio contest and chooses an elephant as a prize rather than $10,000, Homer asks him to reconsider by noting that with $10,000 they'd be millionaires and could buy anything they want, including love ("Bart Gets an Elephant"). Actually, $10,000 doesn't make you a *million*aire, and it can't (necessarily) buy you love, but Homer got one thing right: money can be used toward the purchase of almost any good or service. When Homer's inner voice declares that $20 can be used to buy more peanuts, it could just as well speak of buying more coffee, donuts, or Duff Beer.

Going back to poor Milhouse, if he were to truly end up as juvey money then he would have to function as a medium of exchange. In the penitentiary economy, other inmates would be able to exchange Milhouse for other goods and services available "on the inside." Even inmates who didn't find Milhouse particularly valuable as a physical commodity would still recognize his *exchange value*. They would value Milhouse for the fact that other inmates would give goods and services in exchange for him.

Unit of Account

Besides being a medium of exchange a monetary asset also functions as a *unit of account*—something that is used as a measure of value. Without having some common unit that the value of goods and services are stated in terms of, essential tools of commerce such as double-entry bookkeeping and the reporting of profits can be prohibitively costly.[4]

In the United States, the dollar is the unit of account. It is used to reckon the values of different goods and services relative to one another. Even if one is exchanging goods or services directly for other goods or services (in other words, *barter*), the relative values are still reckoned in terms of the monetary asset. In a world where consumers and businesses have to make decisions about how much to buy and sell across innumerable goods and services, a unit of account to facilitate comparison is crucial.

If Milhouse became the juvey unit of account, people would reckon the values of other juvey goods and services in terms of him. A carton of cigarettes might be quoted at a price of 0.05 Milhouses. A prison tattoo might be quoted at a price of 0.65 Milhouses. If you wanted to bribe a guard to let you escape, the going rate might be 7 full Milhouses for such a risky task. Of course, there's only one Milhouse, and he's not—well—quite the same if you carve him up. So he couldn't possibly be used as the medium of exchange in all of these transactions. However, if he functioned as the unit of account, the values of the goods and services transacted for would still be quoted in terms of him.

Store of Value

Last, if you want an asset to be a stable medium of exchange or unit for reckoning value, then you will want it to hold its value over time. For example, tobacco served Virginians well in the 1700s as a monetary asset in part because it stored for long periods of time and retained its value as a commodity. In other words, tobacco was an effective *store of value*. It held its purchasing power over time, exchangeable for goods and services not only today, but tomorrow, and the next month, and the next year. Furthermore, that purchasing power remained fairly stable over time.[5]

In the episode "Old Money," Abe Simpson inherits $106,000 and asks Springfield's residents to offer worthy causes for the money. To Abe's disgust, Mr. Burns shows up to beg for the money because he is fearful of the day when that much money is worth too little to beg for. Someone as old as Montgomery Burns has lived through decades of persistent (though typically mild) *inflation*: the general rise in prices. Mr. Burns realizes that, given enough time, $100,000 won't buy enough to bother groveling for (just like 10 cents can't buy a loaf of bread, a gallon of milk, and a pint of beer the way it did in the 1930s).

When inflation is low on average, and prices rise only slowly year after year, money retains its effectiveness as a store of value. However, if the rate of inflation gets too high—in the extreme, when it becomes a *hyperinflation* such as in post–World War I Germany—the ability of money to purchase goods and services falls dramatically. Once an asset loses its ability to function as a store of value, it risks losing its role as money. In the episode "The Old Man and the 'C' Student," *The Simpsons* references the 1998 Russian currency crisis when the annual inflation rate reached 84 percent! The Russian representative at an International Olympic Committee meeting suggests holding the games in Moscow because the American dollar buys seven rubles. Before the conversation is up, however, his beeping pager alerts him to the fact that one American dollar buys a thousand rubles. Such a crisis can ruin the effectiveness of an economy's money as a store of value.

Would Milhouse be a good store of value? Well, there's little risk of inflation. Inflation typically occurs when the supply of money grows faster than the number of goods and services available.[6] (Imagine that all currency and bank account balances were suddenly increased by a factor of ten—that is, every $1 bill suddenly became a $10 bill. No new workers in the economy, no new factories, and no new technologies; just more units of money. Predictably, prices would simply end up higher by a factor of ten.) Milhouse can only grow so much, and there's not about to be an increase in the number of Milhouses. However, there are other properties that an asset must possess in order to serve as a store of value. We now turn to those properties, as well as the properties necessary for an asset to function as a medium of exchange and a unit of account.

The Properties of Money

When an asset functions as a medium of exchange, a unit of account, and a store of value, it becomes a monetary asset and is highly *liquid*. Liquidity refers to the *ease with which an asset can be converted into the means of payment for goods and services generally.*

Homer is often making financial blunders because he does not distinguish between liquid and illiquid assets. His mishap with "Itchy and Scratchy money" is one example. Another is when Bart and Homer enter Santa's Little Helper in the "Ugliest Dog in Springfield" contest ("Judge Me Tender") and Homer points out that if they win they get a gift certificate. While Bart is curious what the gift certificate is for, Homer doesn't care what the gift certificate is for. But it matters! A gift certificate can be easily converted into only a relatively small number of goods and services. It cannot be converted into goods and service generally. (Treating a gift certificate like it is money is unwise, especially when you don't know what it's a gift certificate *for*.)

What properties make an asset highly liquid, enough so that it becomes a good candidate for money? Economists most often speak of four: *widely valued, portable, divisible*, and *durable*. Historically, the first monies arose from commodities that greatly embodied most or all of these properties. It is little wonder that precious metals—most often gold—became the most popular forms of money historically. Gold has long been widely valued for its beauty as ornamentation. Minted into coins it is relative easy to transport from place to place (portable). It can be divided into pieces of any size without changing the substance fundamentally (divisible). (From smaller pieces it can also be melted down and combined back into larger pieces.) Finally, gold is a very durable material. It does not corrode or tarnish.

Widely Valued

When an asset is widely valued, it can come to be perceived as having not only *use value* but also *exchange value*. Even if you are someone who doesn't have a use for a widely valued commodity, you probably know many people who do have a use for it *and* possess other goods and services that you *do* want. So you may still desire to obtain that widely valued commodity for the sake of exchanging it for other goods and services.

A hallmark of money is that its exchange value is greater than its use value, at least for most people. Consider the pirates that Bart imagines while he and Lisa search for backyard treasure using Grandpa Simpson's metal detector in "Natural Born Kissers." A pirate captain and his crew are on a desert island contemplating their chest of booty (largely consisting of gold coins). The captain wants to bury the treasure, when one of the crew asks if this time they can use it to buy stuff they want. In Bart's fantasy this pirate is promptly shot by his captain for insubordination. The remaining pirates immediately begin digging a hole in the hope of avoiding the same fate. However, they most likely agree with their fallen mate.

Even more so than gold, our modern currency (paper dollars and coins) exemplifies a situation in which exchange value is far greater than use value. This is why, in the Simpson's "Behind the Laughter" mockumentary episode, we find it funny when Marge states that the family was using $50 bills as toilet paper. Yes, there's scatological humor here (which is always funny). However, there is also the absurdity of having such a large number of green pieces of legal tender that one would turn to using it as a simple commodity rather than money. This absurdity is also the source of standard gags such as Homer lighting a cigar with a dollar bill ("Homer vs. Patty and Selma") and Krusty lighting a cigarette with a $100 bill ("Homie the Clown").

Portable

While a commodity has to be widely valued to develop exchange value, it also has to be convenient for use in actual exchanges. This requires some desirable physical properties. First, you want to be able to carry it to different places to buy different goods and services. Homer finds this out when he tries to pay his $900 gas bill using only a water cooler jug filled with pennies ("Homer's Phobia"). Homer only manages to carry the jug three steps out the front door before dropping it *through* the yard. Pennies are indeed money, but if they were the *only* form of currency they would soon be discarded in favor of some other medium that was more portable.

Interestingly, pennies now have use value *greater* than their exchange value; the commodity value of the metal used to manufacture a penny is *greater* than one cent![7] Since you can "buy" a penny for one cent by law, a good strategy for profit would be to collect pennies and melt them down for sale of the metal. A few people in the United States have done this. It is not a widespread phenomenon probably only because destroying U.S. legal tender currency is against the law.

Divisible

One reason that pennies are still actively used as money is because we rarely buy things using only pennies. Rather, pennies (combined with nickels, dimes, quarters, and paper bills of various denominations) contribute to a U.S. currency that is highly divisible. We can quote prices in terms of the dollar (our unit of account) down to the hundredth. On the other hand, many widely valued goods are indivisible. For example, almost every U.S. household has at least one television. Consider the conundrum that Principle Skinner finds himself facing in the episode "In Marge We Trust." He complains to Reverend Lovejoy that his mother put cardboard over her half of the television. The value of one half a TV is less than one half the value of a TV. Televisions would make a poor medium of exchange and a nonsensical unit of account!

Durable

Last, a good candidate for money must be durable. For money to be a good store of value, not only must it hold its exchange value (as will be true when inflation is low and stable), the physical units must also be sturdy. For example, Homer might believe that donuts are one of the most widely valued commodities in the world. Even if this were true, they would make lousy money because they go stale in a matter of days. On the other hand, while dollar bills sometimes do get damaged or eventually wear out (as Homer discovers when a vending machine won't take his mutilated dollar in "Brother, Can You Spare Two Dimes"), anyone who's mistakenly run their pants through the wash with cash in the pockets knows that our green pieces of paper can take a good deal of abuse.

Milhouse Money?

We are now in a position to ask whether Milhouse would likely become currency in juvenile hall. Would he be widely valued? To say for sure, we require knowledge of the tastes and preferences of the other prisoners based on field research, which I, for one, am loath to pursue. On the other hand, is Milhouse portable? Yes. Though awkward to carry, Milhouse can walk from place to place like the cattle that were used as money in ancient Europe.[8] Given the many misadventures that Bart includes his hapless friend in, we can also surmise that Milhouse is quite durable. *But* Milhouse would probably be a poor candidate for money because he is not divisible. There is only one Milhouse, and the sum of his parts is undoubtedly less than the whole in terms of value.

Milhouse can be contrasted to a commodity that reportedly *has* historically served as money in prison: cigarettes.[9] In the episode "Dumbbell Indemnity," *The Simpsons* references this true-life phenomenon. Homer is arrested stealing Moe's car as part of an insurance scam and ends up in jail. Bart visits with a gift of cigarettes for Homer to use to buy stuff while in prison. Homer promptly tries to trade the cigarettes back to Bart for a candy bar.

Prison is a stressful place! One can easily imagine that cigarettes are widely valued. They are portable, lightweight, and easy to carry and conceal. Cartons are divisible into packs and packs are divisible into individual cigarettes. Last, especially if you don't open the packs, cigarettes take a good while to go stale (in other words, they are durable).

Money in the United States

Even Homer can realize that in the United States we use green pieces of paper for money and green paper isn't widely valued! So how is it money? If the green pieces of paper in your wallet didn't have all the appropriate markings, stating that they are "legal tender for all debts public and private," then their value would fall dramatically. In fact, those green pieces of paper would be basically worthless to the vast majority of Americans. Bart recognizes this fact when Homer hands him three green pieces of paper printed by the Montana Militia for fetching the mail ("Kill the Alligator and Run").

Present-day U.S. money is certainly portable, divisible, and durable, but *it is not widely valued as an actual physical commodity*. Money in our country is widely valued only as—well, *money*. Our money only has significant exchange value. Its use value is basically nil.

However, U.S. money *did* evolve from a widely valued commodity—namely, *gold*! From its beginning through 1933, our nation's monetary asset was gold.[10] This is what people refer to as the *gold standard*. (There were also a couple of experiments with silver as an additional monetary asset, but they were less than successful.) People used gold coins to carry out market transactions, or they used paper currencies that were redeemable in gold by the government or an issuing bank. (In the latter case these pieces of paper were called "banknotes.") Our unit of account—the "dollar"—represented a definite quantity of gold: 1/20th of an ounce. Gold was valuable both as money and as a physical commodity.

World War I, the Great Depression, and World War II represented crises during which periodically—and then permanently—the U.S. government suspended its promise to redeem paper currency in gold. However, people had grown accustomed to using portable pieces of paper to exchange for goods and services. This fact, combined with people's confidence in their government, allowed the monetary supply to be effective without redemption for gold. The U.S. government, in principle, continued to promise redemption in gold to foreign governments until 1971. In that year Richard Nixon declared that the United States would no longer honor its promise to redeem dollars in gold to anyone, anywhere. (In "Treehouse of Horror IV," we find that Nixon, as a result, is currently serving in hell on the "Jury of the Damned." You probably thought he was there for Watergate. Nope. He's there for pulling the life support on the gold standard.)[11]

Today the Federal Reserve prints paper currency that only has exchange value because people are willing to use it and the government declares it legal tender (in other words, it is a pure *fiat currency*). When it comes to money that only has exchange value, people's willingness to use the money is at least as important as the government fiat. There are innumerable real-world examples of governments declaring some asset to be money and finding that its citizens are simply unwilling to use it in exchange.[12] Even in the United States this sometimes happens.

Consider Marge's revision of Lewis and Clark's exploration of the Louisiana Purchase ("Margical History Tour"). Arriving at the Pacific Northwest, Lewis and Clark (Lenny and Carl) promise their Native American guide, Sacagawea, a great honor for her efforts. According to Marge, the promise is today fulfilled in a coin made of copper and brass. Bart and Milhouse, respectively, initially mistake the coin for a quarter or a Chuck E. Cheese token. Marge corrects them and notes that it can be taken to the bank and exchanged for a real dollar! In reality, the coin was introduced with much fanfare to the American public in 2000. Despite being legal tender by government fiat, they just didn't catch on and were not minted for general circulation after 2001.

As stated at the beginning of this chapter, paper currency and coins are only part of the U.S. money supply. Deposits at private banks (that is, checking and savings accounts) are also money. They are very liquid; it is very quick and easy to use those funds to purchase goods and services by writing checks, using debit cards, or making withdrawals at ATMs or bank branches. In fact, most purchases in the United States do not involve physical currency.

Perhaps Homer should become a bank. Not only are bank deposits money, banks actually *create* new money. Deposits are backed by fiat currency but only partially. Let's say that you go into your bank and deposit a $100 bill into your checking account. You can write a check for $100, withdraw $100, or make a $100 dollar purchase with your debit card at any time. You most definitely have $100 of money. However, a typical bank will proceed to loan out at least $90 of that new deposit. Whoever borrows the money (for example, someone taking out a car loan) will be able to immediately spend that $90. *They most definitely have $90 of money.* All of a sudden, where there was only $100 before you made the deposit, *there is now $190!* The bank has created $90 worth of brand new money.

In fact, when you hear about the Federal Reserve (or "Fed," as it is called for short) increasing or decreasing the nation's money supply you may think of it printing more or less green pieces of paper. However, in reality the Fed's control over the money supply comes more from its ability to entice banks to create more or less money. It does this by purchasing or selling financial assets from or to people in the economy. The Fed then counts on people depositing the proceeds (in the case of purchases) into their bank accounts or withdrawing from their deposits (in the case of sales) in order to pay the Fed for the assets. When this happens, if banks find themselves with new deposits they create additional new money by loaning it out (as just described). Alternatively, if banks experience withdrawals, then they loan out less and the money supply in the economy decreases. This process is referred to as "money multiplier" effects. The "multiplier" refers to the fact that if the Fed causes people to initially increase (decrease) their deposits by a certain amount, the banks will then "multiply" that change into a larger increase (decrease) in the supply of money in the economy.

Unfortunately for Homer, he won't be creating new money any time soon. For that matter, he won't be multiplying existing money either. Homer finds himself in the same situation as Bart in "I Don't Wanna Know Why the Caged Bird Sings." That episode begins with Bart writing over and over again on the chalkboard that he is not an FDIC-insured bank. *D'oh!*

Conclusion

Money is anything that is generally accepted as payment for goods and services. Historically, it arose from widely valued commodities that were also portable, divisible, and durable. (The Homers of the world were out of luck since neither donuts nor pork rinds are particularly durable—the former go stale quickly while the latter can easily end up as crumbs during transportation.) Today, dollars are deemed legal tender by government fiat. The Federal Reserve can influence the number of dollars in existence and also encourage or discourage private banks from creating new dollars through the loaning out of their deposits. Homer is shocked in "Lisa the Vegetarian" to discover that bacon, pork chops, and ham all come from the same magical creature. It may also seem unbelievable that cash, checking accounts, and certificates of deposit are valuable simply because the magical government says so. However, we have to keep in mind the historical evolution of U.S. dollars as a currency backed by gold; they were the medium of exchange long before any government fiat. Ultimately, the ability of something to serve as money rests on individuals' confidence that other individuals will accept it as payment for goods and services. That sort of confidence has never come, in the first place, from government fiat.

5

THANK YOU, COME AGAIN

The Pursuit of Profits in Springfield

Gregory M. Randolph

ONE OF THE MOST ENTERTAINING ASPECTS of *The Simpsons* involves the multitude of different careers, business ventures, and get-rich-quick schemes in which the characters participate. In addition to providing countless laughs, the endeavors of many characters provide excellent insight into the competition for profits within a market setting. In particular, Homer Simpson's constant and often clumsy pursuit of profits is a recurring theme throughout the series. Although often ill-fated, these attempts provide an excellent opportunity to examine the idea of economic profits.

While economists would generally disagree with many of Homer's methods and his rationale regarding business decisions, most of them would certainly commend Homer for his willingness to undertake new business ventures (at least those that involve voluntary transactions between Homer and other individuals). In fact, Homer Simpson held 188 different jobs during the first four hundred episodes![1] Throughout the life of *The Simpsons* television series, Homer has been constantly searching for profit opportunities. In a market economy, it is often this pursuit of profit that leads to advancements that help meet the needs and wants of individuals. Enterprising entrepreneurs attempt to satisfy the demands of consumers by providing goods and services in exchange transactions.[2] However, Homer often attempts to take shortcuts and fails to use sound economic reasoning, which leads to serious difficulties in his business ventures.

Ignore Opportunity Costs at Your Peril

One of the most important economic concepts that Homer consistently manages to ignore in his exploits is the idea of opportunity cost.[3] Opportunity cost is the next best alternative foregone when an individual decides to take action. It is extremely important to remember that every time an individual makes a decision to do something, he or she is also making a decision to forgo something else. For example, economists often highlight the opportunity cost of attending college as a prime application of the opportunity cost concept. When students choose to spend time attending college, they sacrifice valuable time that could be spent working (or doing something else). The foregone income and other benefits that students must give up in order to attend school full time represent an important opportunity cost. When we consider the opportunity cost of attending college, the true cost of college attendance is far greater than simply considering college tuition. Homer consistently seems to ignore the concept of opportunity cost in many episodes of *The Simpsons*, often to his own detriment. Fortunately, Marge, Lisa, and other characters frequently remind Homer of his failure to consider his next best option as a cost.

A prime example of the opportunity cost concept occurs when Homer and Bart find an overturned truck of sugar on the highway ("Lisa's Rival"). Homer views the accident as an opportunity to earn some easy money and proceeds to fill his car with the spilled sugar. He then takes the sugar to his home, planning to get rich by selling the sugar to individuals in Springfield. Since Homer does not physically pay money for the sugar, he views the sugar as free and does not think that he incurs any cost in his sugar scheme. However, Homer fails to consider the value of his time in the calculation of his costs. Later in the episode, Marge wisely reminds him that he lost $40 because he spent the day working on his sugar operation instead of going to work.

While Homer views any incoming revenue from the day as pure profit, it is clear to the economist that Homer is not considering all of the relevant costs of his decision. Homer could have earned $40 by simply performing his job at the nuclear power plant. While the sugar was free to Homer, valuable time and effort were expended in the sugar venture. Marge also informs Homer that, in addition to losing his wages for the day, his supervisor said he had better come in tomorrow or he shouldn't even bother coming in on Monday morning. While Homer actually celebrates this as a long weekend, we can see that he could potentially lose his job as a consequence of his failure to show up to work. These somewhat hidden costs should always be considered, as they are necessary to gauge the true economic cost of any decision.

Where Are the Profits? The True Nature of Economic Costs

To clarify the importance of the use of relevant opportunity costs in decision-making scenarios, economists often differentiate between accounting costs and economic costs. Accounting costs refer to any direct monetary costs incurred by the firm during the course of any business decision. These costs include inputs used to produce a product, wages paid to employees, and generally anything for which the firm incurs a monetary cost. While accounting costs are certainly important in the decision-making process and the calculation of profits, economists also stress the significance of the inclusion of opportunity costs, as our previous example concerning Homer highlights. Economic costs include any relevant opportunity costs incurred as the result of any decision in addition to the monetary costs. To calculate economic costs, the opportunity costs are added to the accounting costs. Therefore, economic costs will always outweigh accounting costs.

While many of Homer's business ideas involve suspect calculation of economic costs, his attempt at creating a grease-selling business provides perhaps the best example ("Lard of the Dance"). Bart and Homer fry up all the bacon in the house in order to get $0.63 from the grease buyer. While Homer is happy, Bart points out that the bacon cost $27. Instead of realizing that he lost over $26, Homer is happy, since Marge pays for the bacon (out of Homer's paycheck)!

In this example, Homer is actually completely ignoring all economic costs! For the sake of simplicity, we can assume that the $27 cost of the bacon is the only accounting cost involved in the production of the grease (although he likely incurred other monetary costs, such as the cost of the electricity used to cook the bacon, the cost of the gasoline used to transport the grease, and numerous other related monetary costs). In addition to the accounting costs, Homer also incurs an opportunity cost. The time spent cooking, transporting, and selling grease could have been used for some other productive activity. In addition, there may be other opportunity costs associated with his grease operation, as each input and resource employed in the production process could have been used for something else.

In addition to all relevant costs, it is necessary to calculate revenue in order to determine whether a firm is earning a profit or a loss. Revenue is simply the total amount of money received from the sale of goods or services. To determine revenue, we can multiply the number of goods or services sold by their price. In the case of Homer's grease production, he received $0.63 in revenues. We can then compare costs to revenues in order to determine profit or loss. Since Homer earned $0.63 but experienced accounting costs of $27, the accounting loss for his grease operation was −$26.37. When we employ the economic costs (which include the opportunity costs) in the profit calculation, we find that his economic loss is greater than the accounting loss.

The Role of Profits and Losses in a Market Economy

The concept of economic profits (and economic losses) serves an extremely important function in a market economy.[4] The realization of economic profits or economic losses sends a strong signal to the firm regarding its production decisions. When the firm finds that it is earning economic profits through its business activities, this suggests that the firm is increasing the value of resources, as consumers are willing to pay a price above the economic cost of production. Economic profits provide the firm with an incentive to continue to enhance the value of resources through production. On the other hand, economic losses suggest that a firm is decreasing the value of resources through the production process. This implies that the firm must make changes in order to provide goods or services that consumers want at prices that they are willing to pay. If the firm is unable to make the necessary changes to earn profits, the firm should consider closing permanently, as the resources employed in its production process could be better used elsewhere. For this reason, it is essential for firms to calculate and consider the true economic costs and economic profits associated with any decisions.

Furthermore, economic profits also provide an important incentive and signal to potential entrants. Individuals and firms constantly search for profit opportunities, and when economic profits are present in an industry, potential competitors may view that industry as a possible source of new profits. If the potential entrants believe that they can provide a good or service at a price that consumers want more than the good or service provided by the current producers, they may decide to enter the industry and compete with the existing firms. To convince consumers to purchase their product or service, the new firm must outperform the other firms in terms of quality or price, or by some other means.

While there are a number of examples of this type of competition in *The Simpsons*, one of the best illustrations of the profit motive and the resulting competition for profits occurs when Homer opens a snow-plowing business

called Mr. Plow ("Mr. Plow"). Once consumers learn of Homer's plow business through a television commercial accompanied by a catchy Mr. Plow jingle,
Homer's business venture becomes extremely successful. Residents of Springfield continuously call Homer to plow their driveways through the winter, as
Homer seems to provide an excellent service at a price that the consumers are
willing to pay. Homer's Mr. Plow business initially results in economic profits
and earns him the respect of the town. However, Homer's friend Barney recognizes the profitability and admiration that Homer receives from Mr. Plow
shortly after the start of Homer's success. Barney, searching for a profitable
venture himself, opens a competing firm called The Plow King. After buying a
larger plow and running a commercial campaign, Barney is able to earn economic profits by capturing most of the snow plow market in Springfield.

This episode of *The Simpsons* helps to highlight the process by which firms
compete for economic profits.[5] If Homer and Barney were to continue their
plow operations, we can imagine how they might act going forward. They may
compete with each other in terms of price, services, and other related issues.
If they continue earning profits, other competitors may be attracted to the
industry. If they begin earning losses, we can imagine one or both of them
leaving the business. For competition of this magnitude to arise in a particular industry, economists would stress the importance of low entry barriers to
the business.[6] Entry barriers include any potential obstructions to entering a
particular industry. There are many possible barriers that can make it difficult
and sometimes even impossible to enter a particular market segment. In the
plow business in Springfield, there appears to be very little stopping a potential
competitor from entering the market. While a new firm would need to acquire
a snow plow, find someone to operate the plow, and meet any legal requirements, it seems that the entry barriers to the snow-plow business in Springfield
are relatively low.

When entry barriers are low, economists generally do not expect economic
profits or economic losses to persist indefinitely.[7] When economic profits attract additional firms to the market, the expanded market supply and the
associated declining market price are likely to decrease revenues for the previously profitable firms. The declining revenues result in decreasing economic
profits. Eventually, economic profits tend to approach zero as the market price
decreases, eliminating the incentive for additional firms to enter the market. A
similar process tends to occur when economic losses are present in a particular
industry. Some firms will exit the market when economic losses are present,

which generally decreases the market supply of the good or service. As price tends to rise when supply declines, revenues will increase and tend to eliminate economic losses. Once economic losses are eliminated, firms will no longer have the incentive to exit the market. Economists refer to the point at which firms no longer have the incentive to enter or exit the market as normal returns (also known as normal profits or zero economic profit). At this point, revenues equal economic costs. While it may seem that a firm earning normal returns is not performing well, it is important to remember that the firm is covering all of its opportunity costs in addition to the accounting costs. This suggests that it is earning as high of a return on its efforts as it could earn elsewhere.

An excellent example of this process occurs when Marge purchases her own snack franchise, called the Pretzel Wagon ("The Twisted World of Marge Simpson"). Marge decides to set up her mobile snack cart at the nuclear power plan to sell pretzels to the workers at lunch. At first, Marge's pretzels are extremely popular and she seems to experience economic profits. However, Marge's success does not last long, as entry barriers to the industry are relatively low. A group of women from Springfield called the Investorettes, who recently expelled Marge from their organization for being too frugal, purchase a franchise called the Fleet-A-Pita. After noticing Marge's successful sales at the power plant, the Investorettes decide to compete with Marge for lunch sales. As often occurs, the entrance of the competitor substantially decreases the economic profit-earning ability of the first firm. If economic profits were to persist, we might see even more entrants to the market. If economic losses were to occur, we would likely see one or even both firms leave. The combination of competitive forces and low entry barriers tends to drive market participants toward normal returns over time.

The lunch market at the nuclear power plant proved too small to support both the pretzel and pita firms, as Marge's revenues declined substantially. At one point Agnes from the Investorettes refers to Marge's business as Gimbels, a failed former department store. By comparing Marge's pretzel business to the failed Gimbels, Agnes unconsciously highlights the process by which competitive markets with low entry barriers tend toward normal returns.

Keeping the Competition at Bay: High Barriers to Entry

The expectation of normal returns regarding profit opportunities only applies to firms that operate in competitive industries with low entry barriers. On the other hand, the presence of high entry barriers can completely alter the profit opportunities for the firm in a given industry over time. When entry barriers to a particular market are relatively high, it may be difficult for new firms to enter the market. A firm in a given industry with high entry barriers may be able to earn positive economic profits over time as competitors are unable to enter the market and compete. For example, after Homer learns of Marge's failed pretzel business, he hires members of the mafia in Springfield to harass Marge's competitors. While this type of behavior is completely illegal, it is clear that the harassment of the mob creates a significant entry barrier, as competitors face a host of difficulties if they attempt to compete. This type of entry barrier provides an opportunity for Marge's pretzel firm to earn economic profits (although she was indebted to the mafia for their assistance). While the mafia activities certainly make it difficult for firms to enter the market, it may still be possible to compete if firms are willing and able to deal with the mafia.

While there are a number of different entry barriers that may limit competition in various industries in reality, economists often focus on several key barriers to entry that may prevent competitors from entering the market. One important category of entry barriers involves government intervention into various industries. In some cases, the government provides a good or service directly to consumers and prevents private firms from competing through legal restrictions. The United States Postal Service is an excellent example of a government-granted monopoly, as private firms are unable to deliver first class mail by law. In general, the rationale for government control of mail delivery is to ensure postal services to citizens throughout the United States. However, some economists dispute the notion that postal services would not be provided through a competitive market for mail delivery.[8]

Government licenses and restrictions may also provide limitations on competition. If a new firm is unable to secure permission and meet all government requirements, potential competitors cannot enter the market. To enter numerous businesses and gain employment in many fields, market participants often must obtain licenses and permits at the local, state, and federal levels. While the stated goal of the license process is often to help ensure safety for consumers, the practice also tends to restrict competition to differing degrees depending on the difficulty of obtaining the necessary license. For example, Marge must pass an exam to get a license when she decides to become a real estate agent ("Realty Bites"). Initially, Marge doesn't know what a dwelling is. However, she studies hard, passes the test, and becomes a licensed real estate agent. The real estate licensure process may help ensure that licensed real estate agents have some real estate training, although the process restricts entry into the industry to some extent, as it is illegal to facilitate real estate exchanges without a license.

While the real estate license certainly provides an entry barrier, the licensure process provides much greater restrictions on competition in other industries. Medicine is often considered as a career with relatively high entry barriers because of licensing. Fans of *The Simpsons* will recall the running joke of the credentials and license of Dr. Nick Riviera, a questionable doctor in Springfield (the certificates on his office wall include "Club Med School").[9] In reality, an ignorant doctor can cause serious injury or death to patients. Therefore, the licensure requirements to the field are extremely high, as potential entrants must complete college and medical school before facing a medical licensing board. However, the high entry barriers also make it relatively difficult to become a doctor and restrict competition to a greater extent.[10] A consequence of higher restrictions is that wages in a restricted occupation might be higher than they otherwise would be.[11]

In addition, the complete ownership of an essential resource for a particular industry can restrict the threat of competition. Economists often cite the diamond industry through most of the 1900s as a prime example of this type of entry barrier. While firms and individuals may be interested in entering the industry, it is very difficult to enter the diamond trade without access to diamond mines.[12] Furthermore, economies of scale may prevent the entrance of competing firms. In some cases, average total costs can be reduced substantially by expanding output. This may prevent other firms from entering the market, as they are unable to cover the startup costs. The Springfield Nuclear Power Plant may provide an example of economies of scale in *The Simpsons*. While the owner, Mr. Burns, is seemingly able to earn profits in the energy business in Springfield, it may be difficult for a second competitor to enter the industry due to the large costs of constructing a power plant and installing a power distribution grid. In addition, even if a competitor is able to cover the startup costs, there may not be enough customers in Springfield to allow two firms to coexist.[13]

When entry barriers to a particular industry are high, a firm may be able to earn economic profits over time. While the entrance of competitors in industries with low entry barriers tends to eliminate economic profits, firms in high entry barrier markets do not necessarily experience the same competitive pressures. The lack of competitive pressures is evident at the Springfield Nuclear Power Plant in *The Simpsons*. In addition to the previously discussed economies of scale that restrict competition in the energy market in Springfield, Mr. Burns has also consistently attempted to restrict competition through any means possible throughout the life of the show. He even goes so far as to attempt to block the sun from shining in Springfield, which he views as his last competitor because it provides light and heat to the residents ("Who Shot Mr. Burns? [Parts One and Two]"). Although extreme, the presence of such tremendous entry barriers and lack of substitutes can allow for economic profits to persist over time.

Conclusion

Due to a vast array of character careers and business ventures, *The Simpsons* provides an excellent medium to examine economic costs, competition, and the pursuit of profits. Economic principles (or a lack of their understanding by specific characters) are often a prime source of plots and laughs in the series. Although Homer Simpson in particular seems to have a serious deficiency of economic comprehension, particularly in terms of opportunity costs (D'oh!), we are fortunate he continues his search for economic profits, as it provides us with both an excellent source of entertainment and interesting economic discussion opportunities.[14]

6

THEY HAVE THE INTERNET ON COMPUTERS NOW?

Entrepreneurship in *The Simpsons*

Per L. Bylund, Christopher M. Holbrook, and Peter G. Klein

WHO OR WHAT IS AN ENTREPRENEUR? He may be someone who starts a company and quickly makes a fortune. He can also be someone who builds great wealth—or even an empire—over many, many years of hard work. Perhaps he is an innovator with an ingenious invention, such as the oddball genius Professor Frink. Or maybe he simply runs his own business, much like Apu struggles with the Kwik-E-Mart.

In any case, we usually think of money as the motive power, the goal, and—most likely—an important part of what makes an entrepreneur. But the fact is that entrepreneurship is as much about the "D'oh!" as the dough. Entrepreneurs make plenty of mistakes. Of course, some entrepreneurs make a lot of money and get rich, but others make no money at all—or even lose their invested capital. (They may have a lot of fun doing it, though.)

What, then, defines this elusive character? What *is* an entrepreneur? We usually think of people with exceptional drive, charisma, independence, and creativity, people who like to try new things, are not afraid to take risks, and like to be in charge of their own lives. Some of them build large corporate empires, like the great industrialists of the nineteenth century. Often we think of younger, innovative companies such as Apple or Google. Indeed, researchers, journalists, and practitioners use the terms *entrepreneur, entrepreneurial,* and *entrepreneurship* in many ways, not always consistently, unfortunately. We find it useful to distinguish between theories or approaches that define entrepreneurship as an *outcome* or a phenomenon (self-employment, startup companies) and those that see it as a *way of acting or thinking* (creativity, innovation, alertness, judgment, adaptation).[1]

Entrepreneurship as an Outcome

If entrepreneurship is an outcome or phenomenon such as self-employment or new-venture formation, then it can be studied using standard economics terms and concepts (for example, labor-economics models of occupational choice, psychological studies of firm founders' characteristics, analysis of discounted cash flows, and so on). Economists have studied these phenomena for a long time, and know a lot about them. For instance, we know that self-employed people generally earn less than employed people, suggesting that they do what they do for love, not money; there is no particular "entrepreneurial" personality type; and new ventures are often difficult to finance, suggesting reliance on the "three Fs": friends, families, and fools.

Self-employment is the most common "occupational" concept of entrepreneurship.[2] Moe Szyslak and Apu Nahasapeemapetilon are obvious occupational entrepreneurs through running Moe's Tavern and the Kwik-E-Mart, respectively. What is typical for this sort of entrepreneur is not the dough.[3] Neither Moe nor Apu are rich—but they get by and they do their thing. (On the other hand, wouldn't Apu qualify as a successful business owner managing to raise eight children and care for a wife with only a convenience-store income?) What is important in this conception of entrepreneurship is not so much who or how, but in what form. If you have a firm of your own, you are an entrepreneur. Period.

The neighborhood schoolboy who mows lawns is as much of an entrepreneur as Kentucky Fried Chicken founder Colonel Harland Sanders. In the Simpsons' world, however, entrepreneurship takes on a more comedic quality. Turning grease into cash provides a very Homerian example of entrepreneurship ("Lard of the Dance"). He learns from Apu that there's a market for leftover cooking grease. Unfortunately for Homer, it took $27 worth of bacon to produce $0.63 of grease. Homer then turned toward more profitable grease opportunities, such as infiltrating the school cafeteria during a dance.

Had Homer turned his grease-producing enterprise into a firm, he would have made the entrepreneurship rolls. Note that business ownership tends to be the favorite definition of entrepreneurship among empirical researchers, not because it is obviously right, but because it is easy to measure. Like the drunk who searches for his missing car keys under the lamppost because that's where the light is, empirical researchers tend to focus on the available data, even if those data don't map easily to the dominant theories. Recall, for example, when Ned Flanders opened the "Leftorium" in the Springfield Mall ("When Flanders Failed"). It turns out that he had found a new market niche that had not yet been exploited—a great entrepreneurial insight. With Homer's help, Ned finds and gets in touch with the market for stuff specifically made for left-handed people. The substance of his accomplishment—new niches found and exploited, customers satisfied, lives improved, and so on—is hard to quantify. But it is easy to tell that Ned started a business firm—and perhaps that he made a profit (and how big).

Unfortunately, studies of occupational entrepreneurship cannot necessarily identify the essence of entrepreneurship, the links between entrepreneurship, innovation, economic growth, and so on. It seems unlikely, for example, that Mom-and-Pop stores are the unique engines of innovation and economic prosperity in the modern capitalist economy.

Another outcome- or phenomenon-based approach to entrepreneurship looks at whole firms, industries, or societies, defining some as "entrepreneurial." In this view, an entrepreneurial firm is a new or small firm, and an entrepreneurial industry or society is one with a lot of new or small firms. Presumably, these kinds of firms grow faster, innovate more, and generate more employment and economic value than larger, more established firms.[4] Though these things can be difficult to measure, they are in principle quantifiable.

One could imagine an analysis, for example, of the entrepreneurial structure of the Springfield Nuclear Power Plant. Montgomery Burns does not seem like an entrepreneurial or innovative leader, and he seems to frown upon employees who take initiative, attempt to find new solutions, and so on. On the contrary, entrepreneurship seems to be suppressed. This should have consequences that can be identified when comparing this power plant with more successful ones. Indeed, finding ways to distribute or delegate entrepreneur-like characteristics and behavior throughout the organization is often a key to firm success.[5]

On the other hand, who can blame Montgomery Burns for his authoritative style in running his power plant? With employees such as Homer, Carl, and Lenny, a hierarchical structure with managerial control may be simply a strategy for survival—a way of constraining "destructive" entrepreneurship among employees.[6] If all power plants have as lazy and disinterested workers, then this too would show in a comparative study. Perhaps Burns is right in making full use of the stick while hiding the carrots.

Entrepreneurship as a Way of Acting or Thinking

Historically, entrepreneurship has had deeper meaning in the study of economics. It is conceived as a generalized, abstract function, a way of acting or
thinking. Being "entrepreneurial" does not, then, necessarily mean being self-
employed or creating a new venture. It means acting or thinking in a certain
way—being creative, innovating, being alert to opportunities, exercising sound
business judgment, adapting to changing circumstances, and so on. In this
sense, functional entrepreneurship is not a specific formal arrangement like occupational entrepreneurship and is also not dependent on whether the structure itself is entrepreneurial or not. An entrepreneur does not need a firm[7] to
provide an entrepreneurial function to the market, and he is equally independent of whether he acts in an entrepreneurial environment—in fact, perhaps
a less entrepreneurial environment makes it easier to be a successful entrepreneur in the end.[8]

Judgment

The story of Ned Flanders' "Leftorium" is better told through thinking of entrepreneurship as a function in the marketplace. Granted, Flanders started a
business firm and got space in the mall to get closer to his market segment. But
what it was really about was Flanders' judgment.[9] He believed there were plenty
of southpaws out there utterly frustrated with all the stuff made only for right-
handed people. He alone imagined this potential opportunity and was willing
and able to bet on his judgment. In this case, his judgment turned out to be
right, and he is celebrated as a hero in the left-handed community. People with
"superior judgment" and a willingness to act on the opportunities they imagine are entrepreneurs and provide the function of pushing the market toward
greater satisfaction of consumer wants.[10]

Just as the neighborhood lawn-mowing schoolboy makes a judgment as to
the demand for lawn services, Harland Sanders' belief that people would like a
restaurant devoted to serving only fried chicken demonstrates entrepreneurial
judgment. By standardizing his recipe, Sanders was able to instill consumer
confidence in his product. Maybe even more important, however, people could
now eat fried chicken without the smelly mess associated with its preparation.

Similar to Flanders' "Leftorium," Homer's escapade as "Mr. Plow" is a matter
of superior judgment. Granted, Homer is not making the original judgment but
rather is semi-bamboozled by the truck salesman. But he carries out the idea of
plowing people's driveways and has the good judgment to advertise on televi-

sion and come up with the unpredictably unbeatable slogan. Consequently, the business is a success—at least until Barney's "Plow King" takes over the market.

But Barney's enterprise fits equally well as entrepreneurial behavior. He was of the judgment that he could be better than Homer and make more money through offering better services. Perhaps more important, he was alert to the opportunity that existed thanks to the new market created by Homer.[11]

Alertness

Alertness describes the ability of the entrepreneur to identify superior processes, new products, or other gaps in the market before others.[12] Amazon's book-reading software and hardware, named Kindle, enables one to read books on a small electronic display. The entrepreneurial alertness represented on Amazon's part was the identification of a more convenient way to read published works. With the Kindle, one can avoid the cumbersome task of carrying heavy books with them while traveling. Apple Inc., seeing the success of the Kindle, introduced the iPad to compete in the digital media market. Exploiting opportunities may generate new opportunities, however; Amazon responded by developing Kindle software for Apple's iPad.

The Simpsons provides a more humorous backdrop for alertness. With a little help from a car salesman, Homer identified the need for Springfield snow removal. By starting his Mr. Plow business, he provided a new service that was in tacit demand. Homer's alertness to this demand did not go unnoticed. Like Apple's response to Amazon's Kindle, Barney was attracted to Homer's successful business. Barney, however, identified a superior method of snow removal: a bigger truck. His entrance into the market with superior capital enabled him to dominate the market. The larger truck was not the only element of entrepreneurial alertness displayed by Barney, though. He also woke up earlier than Homer did. By doing this, Barney gained previous "Mr. Plow" customers.

In frustration, Homer tricks Barney into plowing a mountain road, thereby regaining his previous customers. Unfortunately, Barney is trapped in an avalanche and Homer goes to rescue him. The two become friends again and vow to work together because not even God can stop best friends. God, "alert" to the blasphemy, teaches them both a lesson in supply and demand by melting all the snow. This effectively puts Homer and Barney out of business.

Seeing profit opportunities in the most comedic situations, Homer provides many more examples of entrepreneurial alertness. When Bart wins a radio call-in contest, he chooses to receive an elephant in lieu of a monetary prize ("Bart

Gets an Elephant"). Care for the elephant places strain on the Simpson household finances. With a little help from Bart, Homer begins to sell elephant rides for $2 and the right to view it for $1. Unfortunately, the $2 price is too low to cover expenses for the elephant, such as shots and chains. After raising the price to $500, and seeing the elephant for $100, Homer instantly loses his customers. At the end of the episode, Homer donates the elephant to a wildlife preserve. Homer also demonstrates alertness when he comes upon a sugar truck accident ("Lisa's Rival"). Seeing pounds of sugar on the road, Homer immediately identifies a profit opportunity. With the help of Bart, he takes the sugar home and begins to sell it door to door.

Innovation

Schumpeter discussed a different kind of entrepreneurship: the innovation type.[13] Here, the entrepreneur is primarily an innovator who pushes the market out of equilibrium through new ways of organization. These new methods lower costs and force the other market players to keep up. Examples of innovation include the simple relocation of car audio controls to the steering wheel and electronic check-in at airports.

Ray Kroc demonstrated entrepreneurial innovation when he implemented the assembly line in McDonald's restaurants. As an effect, fast food truly became *fast* food. His insistence on standardization is also an example of innovation. When traveling, customers are able to rely on a certain degree of quality: a Big Mac in California should taste the same as a Big Mac in Missouri. Kroc's attention to food quality standardization gave McDonald's a competitive advantage. Travelers unfamiliar with a location, and therefore unfamiliar with the quality of local restaurants, could feel comfortable ordering at McDonald's.

Quite a few episodes introduce the viewer to Simpsonesque innovation. In "Homer vs. the Eighteenth Amendment," Springfield bans alcohol after Bart is intoxicated at a town parade. After Springfield's mob boss Fat Tony fails to smuggle alcohol, Homer develops an innovative alcohol delivery system to Moe's Tavern. Dubbed the Beer Baron, Homer supplies beer to the Springfield residents by filling bowling balls with beer he and Bart found at the dump. By their rolling the balls into a gutter at the Bowl-a-Rama, the beer is fed through an intricate piping system that leads to Moe's "pet shop." On a side note, the beer is much more expensive. Moe charges $45 per glass.

Innovation need not be so extravagant, though. In "Das Bus," Homer starts an Internet business, called Compu-Global-Hyper-Mega-Net—he's the "Internet King"—after listening to Flanders describe his home business, Flancrest Enterprises. When Marge discovers Homer setting up his office desk (the dining room table), she finds that Homer used her good butter to hold his pens and pencils. Homer's innovation allows him to write delicious memos.

Note that entrepreneurship does not have to be big business in order to provide an important function in the market. Entrepreneurs may also have more modest ambitions, simply responding to their own frustrations with existing conditions. When Marge started the gym "Shapes" for regular ladies, it was a direct response to her unhappiness with the overly exhibitionist environment at regular gyms ("Husbands and Knives"). The real-life fitness centers Curves, which have successfully created the niche of providing a women-only workout atmosphere, may have been the inspiration for the authors of this episode. In another episode, Marge created a pretzel wagon franchise to show she had guts after having been voted out of the Springfield Investorettes for being too conservative ("The Twisted World of Marge Simpson"). Marge's entrepreneurial adventures were not necessary to her financial well-being, as in other cases of "necessity entrepreneurship." (Classic joke: "What made you decide to start your own business?" "It was something my boss said to me once." "What's that?" "'You're fired.'") Still, Marge's activities were necessary for her own social and moral well-being.

Adaptation

Another important aspect of entrepreneurship is the ability to adapt to changing circumstances.[14] The neighborhood lawn-care boy may adapt to the loss of mowing business in the winter by switching to snow removal, just as Microsoft adapted to the quickly increasing popularity of the web, and the failure to establish its own Microsoft Network, by launching its own browser software. In the same vein, McDonald's noted the popularity of Starbucks and Dunkin' Donuts coffee and adapted to the increased demand of everyday premium coffee by changing its formula and adding espresso-based drinks. Long considered typically poor fast food coffee, McDonald's new brewed coffee beat Starbucks and Dunkin' Donuts in a 2007 *Consumer Reports* taste test.

In "Das Bus," Homer does not want to miss the income opportunities mentioned by Flanders, so he starts his "Internet King" business providing faster Internet service. Unfortunately for his only customer, it is revealed that Homer has no real way of providing anything. All Homer had was an Internet advertisement offering faster service. Reminiscent of the 1990s dotcom phenomenon, Bill Gates visits Homer and offers to buy him out, even though Gates can't figure out what Homer's company does. Here too, Gates adapts to the changing circumstances brought about by Homer's Internet business. In true Simpsonian comedic style, however, Gates' "buyout" amounts to his companions trashing Homer's office.

Coordination or Leadership

Whereas entrepreneurship is often the function of one person acting in a certain way or in response to certain events, it may also be in the form of leadership or coordination. In contrast to intuition, Montgomery Burns may here be a good example of entrepreneurial leadership. At least, he has successfully created a shared perception within the power plant of him as the indisputable leader.

The fact is that in order to establish and run a successful business venture, the entrepreneur combines complementary factors of production through establishing a shared framework of goals (what Casson calls a mental model of reality[15]) within the organization.[16] Theoretically speaking, entrepreneurship as coordination is about finding better (more efficient) ways of combining knowledge, labor factors, and resources, thereby establishing a comparatively advantageous position.[17]

Entrepreneurship—Productive or Destructive?

Montgomery Burns as a successful entrepreneur? That image certainly raises some questions regarding the value and function of entrepreneurship—is the entrepreneur really a productive force in the economy? Generally speaking, the answer must be a resounding "yes." The entrepreneur is what causes and catalyzes the market process toward greater satisfaction of consumer wants. As such, the entrepreneur is the agent of change in the market and hence the reason for the overall prosperity and ongoing wealth creation.[18]

Yet some entrepreneurial behavior can be unproductive in the sense that it does not create value but only redirects it. Such entrepreneurship often involves the use of the political apparatus to extract rents from other parties or organized crime—no value is here created (as it would be were the parties to engage in trade), but money still changes hands. Such behavior may even turn into destructive entrepreneurship, say, through market actors lobbying Congress to have competitors or entire competing industries shut down.

The episode in which Homer finds the wreckage of a truckload of sugar ("Lisa's Rival") demonstrates the difference between productive and unproductive entrepreneurship.[19] While his attempt to sell the sugar door to door is a productive enterprise, his difficulty in protecting his sugar stock, which is a pile in his backyard, creates an unproductive profit opportunity—it begins to attract bees from a nearby beekeeping facility. The facility owners are forced to buy their own bees back from Homer. Unfortunately for Homer, and fortunately for the beekeepers, a downpour of rain dissolves the sugar.

It can, at least with some imagination, be argued that Homer's career as the Internet King may not have been entirely productive, since he did not really offer any goods or services but only surfed the wave of market interest in Internet-based businesses. Yet one can hardly say he was unproductive (and especially not destructive), since he somehow supported himself. However, the appearance of Bill Gates with two goons wrecking Homer's home office in a very physical attempt at a hostile takeover is certainly destructive. The question one might ask, however, is whether this attack was truly entrepreneurial. Are goons with baseball bats what we think of when we think of the entrepreneur?

Probably not. The term *entrepreneurship* may have been inflated lately to encompass all sorts of behavior in all sorts of situations. That is certainly neither a scientific nor a constructive use of the word. Yet it is important to distinguish between entrepreneurship that is productive for the individual entrepreneur as well as his milieu, and that which is productive only for the entrepreneur himself while others may suffer.

Conclusion

Real-life entrepreneurs are seldom as goofy, clumsy, and idiotic as Homer Simpson, but he and his friends in *The Simpsons* still manage to perfectly illustrate everything entrepreneurship is about. Entrepreneurs exercise judgment, innovate, and scan the horizon for perceived opportunities. They establish new ventures, dissolve old ones, and keep existing businesses going. They are, in Mises's words, the "driving force" of the market economy.[20]

Note also that the world of the Simpsons—noisy, chaotic, unpredictable— is far from the quiet, stable, and calm world of mainstream economic models. Entrepreneurship is an inherently dynamic phenomenon, the force that controls and directs productive resources to satisfy consumer's needs and wants in an ever-changing world. As Lachmann put it, "We are living in a world of unexpected change; hence capital combinations . . . will be ever changing, will be dissolved and reformed. In this activity, we find the real function of the entrepreneur."[21] Even in Springfield!

7

I'VE GOT A MONOPOLY TO MAINTAIN!

Market Failure in *The Simpsons*

Diana W. Thomas

IN HIS MAGNUM OPUS, *An Inquiry into the Nature and Causes of the Wealth of Nations,* Adam Smith points out, "It is not from the benevolence of the butcher, the brewer, or the baker, that we expect our dinner, but from their regard to their own interest."[1] According to Smith, self-interested men when they exchange their goods in a private marketplace are led to serve others because the market rewards the production of goods and services that make others better off. Smith calls this the invisible hand of the market. The individual producer "intends only his own gain" but is "led by an invisible hand to promote an end which was no part of his intention."[2]

Modern economists have interpreted Smith's statement to mean that, in Hirshleifer's words, "under perfect competition, utility-maximizing behavior by individuals together with profit-maximizing behavior by firms, leads to a Pareto-efficient outcome."[3] Sounds complicated, but it really isn't! What it means is that uninhibited exchange in a free market will produce an outcome that cannot be improved upon without making at least one person in the world worse off.

Markets are considered efficient if they allocate resources to their highest-valued uses. This means that only those buyers who value a good more than its price buy the good, and only those sellers who can produce the good at the lowest possible price sell the good. All potential buyers who do not value a good more than its price remain empty-handed; all sellers who can only produce a good at a cost that is greater than the price of the good go out of business. For the last good that is sold, or as economists say, "at the margin," the value the buyer places on the good is exactly equal to the cost of making the good and to the market price of the good.[4] If this condition holds, the market is considered to be in equilibrium and Pareto efficient.

As the Hirshleifer quote suggests, there are a number of other conditions that have to hold for the market to produce this outcome. He mentions the first one in his version of the modern invisible hand quote: consumers have to be utility maximizers and producers have to be profit maximizers, or more simply put, consumers and producers have to have their own well-being at heart. If consumers did not care to make themselves as happy as possible, in other words, maximize their utility, they would not have an incentive to seek out the producer who sells the good they want at the lowest price. Similarly, if producers did not care about their profit, they would not constantly try to improve their product to make it more attractive to consumers, and they also would not try to lower their cost of production to increase their profit margin.

But there are three other conditions that are hidden in the words *perfectly competitive*.[5] When economists say "perfect competition," they mean something very specific. Usually, they will assume that the following three conditions hold. First, there have to be many producers and many consumers. This condition is important because consumers have to be able to walk away from a producer if he or she tries to charge them more than they are willing to pay. The same has to be true for producers; they have to be able to sell to more than one person, or else that person might be able to force them to sell at a price that is lower than they would otherwise be willing to accept. No individual producer or consumer can have the power to alter the market outcome.

Second, producers and consumers have perfect information about the product's quality and price. If a Wolverine comic Bart wants to purchase is cheaper at the comic book store around the corner than at the Android's Dungeon, Bart will know. Third, products are homogenous. This means that the Wolverine comic at the Android's Dungeon is of exactly the same quality as the Wolverine comic at the comic book store around the corner.

As you might have already guessed, these three conditions are a tough call for both *The Simpsons* and reality. As every fifth grader knows, used comic books are never of exactly the same quality, and the Android's Dungeon is the only supplier of comic books in Springfield for most of the series. It is not until season 19 that a guy named Milo opens up a competing comic book store named Coolsville Comics across the street ("Husbands and Knives").

Although it remains doubtful that the perfectly competitive marketplace described by modern economists is the same market that Adam Smith had in mind, modern economists have stuck with it. Because the three assumptions for a perfectly competitive marketplace are so stringent, however, modern economists have had to acknowledge that their perfectly efficient marketplace fails, at least sometimes. They have identified four main categories of market failure: monopoly, public goods, asymmetric information, and externalities. In this chapter, I will discuss monopoly, public goods, and asymmetric information as market failures in more detail using examples from *The Simpsons*. Justin Ross discusses externalities in more detail in Chapter 9.

Monopoly as Market Failure

When the proprietor of the Android's Dungeon comic book store, the Comic Book Guy, tries to charge Milhouse $25 for a Wolverine comic, Bart laments that the Comic Book Guy is always mean to kids ("Husbands and Knives"). In response, the storeowner points out that he can be mean to the boys because there is no competition for his comic book store in town. The Comic Book Guy knows that he is the only supplier of comic books to Springfield's kids. Since they have no choice in where to buy, he can charge high prices. Economists call the Comic Book Guy a price maker or monopolist. Strictly speaking, economists define a monopoly as a situation in which one single producer carries out the production of a specific good or service for which no close substitutes exist. However, we also speak of monopoly or monopolistic competition when one seller has enough market power to influence the market price of a good even though other producers exist.

When a monopolist reduces the amount of a good he or she produces, the price of the good increases, because consumers now compete for fewer goods. A good example from the real world of competition between consumers that bids up prices is new releases of gaming consoles. If you have never camped out at Best Buy to get your hands on one of the first new PlayStations, you probably have a friend who has. In fact, many people buy those consoles just to turn around and resell them on eBay for a higher price. In doing so, they drive up the price of the gaming consoles.

As the price of the good rises, the monopolist (or the smart consumer) can make a greater profit than he or she otherwise would. Economists speak of the monopolist as price maker, while they call the producer in perfect competition a price taker, because the producer cannot charge more than the market price. As you might expect, the story of the Android's Dungeon and its mean proprietor who acts like a monopolist takes a good turn. The days of the Android's Dungeon as a monopoly for comics in Springfield are limited, since this is the episode in which a competing book store, Coolsville Comics, opens across the street.

This episode of *The Simpsons* illustrates well that monopoly profits, when they exist, are usually short-lived because they create an incentive for other producers to enter the industry. Additional producers, offering the same good at a slightly lower price or at a better quality compete with the incumbent until the industries' profits are bid down to zero. Coolsville Comics does just that: it offers free candy and all kinds of other attractions that keep the customers coming. Unable to attract his old customers back to the Android's Dungeon, the Comic Book Guy has to close his shop, which now leaves Coolsville as the only comic book store in town.

A special kind of monopoly is one based on what economists call a *natural monopoly*. Natural monopolies are situations in which economies of scale leave the market unfit for many producers to exist side by side. If the average cost of producing a good decreases as output increases, it makes sense for a producer to sell more because his profit margin increases for each additional unit sold. When the average cost per unit of a good is decreasing like this, we call that *economies of scale*. In most industries, economies of scale exist over some range, but once the firm hits a certain level of output its average cost will rise again because of diseconomies of scale. For example, the ice cream cart industry is an industry in which diseconomies of scale are reached at rather low levels of output. The owner of an ice cream cart can only supply ice cream to so many people before he has to expand and buy a bigger ice cream truck. Buying an ice cream truck will make his average cost of making ice cream go up, however, which makes it harder to compete with other ice cream carts in the area. Because diseconomies of scale are reached rather quickly, many ice cream carts can sell ice cream side by side.

When an industry is characterized by economies of scale for large levels of output, on the other hand, a producer can increase her output without facing increasing cost. The producer actually becomes more profitable as she increases output and takes advantage of economies of scale. In an industry like that, larger producers are more efficient and profitable than small producers. It is therefore possible for one producer to continue to grow until she serves the whole market by herself. Entering such an industry is very difficult because new entrants start out with low levels of production, which are more costly to

produce than bigger quantities. In such a situation, a monopoly is the most efficient way to produce, and we therefore call it a natural monopoly. In Springfield, Monty Burns' power plant is the ideal example of a natural monopoly.
Once an atomic power plant is built, it can increase its output of power at a
very low cost; that is, it has economies of scale in production.[6]

There is another reason why Monty's power plant is a natural monopoly,
however. It also has economies of scale in distribution. Burns distributes his
power through a network of power lines. Once a distribution network has
reached a certain size, it is easy and cheap to expand it to neighboring areas. If
an alternative producer of power were to try to compete with Monty Burns, he
would have to set up a network that he could reach all his potential customers
with first, which is prohibitively expensive. Natural monopolies can therefore
also be based on distribution.

Because monopolists (both natural as well as others) do not have to compete with anyone, they often behave badly. They can raise their price at the
expense of consumers, because no one can offer the product they sell at a lower
price. For similar reasons, they can sell a low-quality product, and their production processes are often inefficient and wasteful. In the case of the Springfield
Nuclear Power Plant, that is pretty clear even to the casual *Simpsons* watcher:
dangerous conditions for workers at the power plant; atomic waste polluting
Springfield's rivers to the point at which the three-eyed fish, Blinky, can be seen
in many episodes; and a more-than-comfortable income for the owner of the
monopoly privilege, Mr. Burns.

Because of their tendency to behave badly, monopolies have a pretty bad
reputation, and governments are often called to intervene in defense of the
consumer. In the United States, the Sherman and Clayton Antitrust acts were
passed at the turn of the nineteenth century to promote and maintain market
competition. They made it illegal for anyone to "conspire, in restraint of trade
or commerce" or to monopolize an industry. The Clayton act furthermore
charged the Federal Trade Commission with oversight over any mergers and
acquisitions that might create a monopoly. In addition to overseeing mergers
and acquisitions, governments can also break up existing monopolies, to promote competition and lower prices. Natural monopolies such as power plants,
water providers, or wastewater treatment plants are usually regulated to prevent them from abusing their power to raise prices and lower quality.

In "Two Cars in Every Garage and Three Eyes on Every Fish," we find out
that the Springfield Nuclear Power Plant is an example of a regulated natural

monopoly. When the story about Bart catching a three-eyed fish out of a river downstream from the nuclear plant makes the newspaper headlines, regulators come to inspect the plant and find a number of drastic violations. To prevent his plant from being shut down, Monty Burns decides to run for governor. His campaign ends unsuccessfully, however, after Burns spits out a bite of the three-eyed fish that Marge serves him for a televised dinner on the night before the election.

Natural monopolies, whether regulated or not, often persist despite producing low-quality products and selling them at a high price, because new entrants with lower levels of output cannot compete with them. Other types of monopolies, on the other hand, usually cannot persist in the long run unless they offer a high-quality product at a competitive price. If a monopolist without a natural monopoly were to increase the price or lower the quality of the product being sold, it would be profitable for new producers to enter the market and offer a better-quality product at a lower price. In the absence of large economies of scale, the monopolist's behavior is therefore kept in check by the threat of new entry.

Monopolies that are not natural monopolies can only take advantage of their situation if barriers to entry keep potential competitors out. Often, such barriers to entry are put in place by governments to protect specific producers. In that case, the protected monopolist can misbehave just like the natural monopolist.

Even natural monopolies are not completely free from the threat of competition, however. Consider the case of telephone service. Before cell phones, phone services used to be natural monopolies because they had economies of scale in distribution. Unless you were hooked up to a cable network in the ground that connected your phone through the phone company to all other phone users in the world, your phone was worthless. Because networks come with large economies of scale, it was inefficient to have more than one phone service provider. The invention of cell phones provided a technical solution to the network problem by making hardwired networks obsolete. Today the market for phone services is much more competitive than it used to be. Moreover, just as you might expect, the new competition came with lots of quality improvements and price decreases that benefited consumers. Technological innovation has also resulted in the destruction of many other monopolies that used to be considered natural monopolies, for example, cable services.[7]

In conclusion, monopolies are indeed imperfect market outcomes. They leave consumers worse off and allow producers to earn supra-normal profits while offering an often mediocre product. Monopolies, however, do not usually persist for long because the market itself has a remedy for them: the profit motive. It lures other producers to enter the industry and compete with the monopolist until prices are lower and products are of higher quality. This is the case even for natural monopolies; the short-run profits of monopolists often provide the economic incentive to create technological solutions to the natural monopoly problem.

That leaves us with two other market failures to discuss, public goods and asymmetric information. The next section takes a closer look at public goods and their market and nonmarket remedies.

Public Goods as Market Failure

In "Marge vs. the Monorail," Springfield receives $3 million in damages from Monty Burns, who has been dumping his toxic waste in a public park. In a town hall meeting that is called to decide on how to spend the money, Marge points out that Springfield's roads are in a state of disrepair because of all the pot-holes caused by poor maintenance, heavy loads, and tire chains. Main Street is a public good suffering from what economists call the commons problem. The residents of Springfield pay a tax for the construction and maintenance of the road, but they do not have to pay for their specific use of it. Since they pay the same tax whether they drive a tank or a motorcycle, they do not pay attention to how much wear their different driving activities put on the road. Without an incentive to keep the road in good condition, everyone leaves on winter chains and carries too much weight in their car, increasing the wear on the road.

A good is considered a public good if it has the following two character-istics: (1) people cannot be excluded from using it (economists say it is non-excludable), and (2) one person's use of the good does not reduce another person's ability to use it (economists say it is nonrival). The most common ex-ample of a public good is national defense. National defense is non-excludable because every person in a country benefits from the protection that a national military provides. No resident of Springfield can be excluded from the benefits the U.S. military provides, even if they do not pay taxes. National defense is also nonrival because the protection the military provides for the Simpson family does not diminish the amount of protection the Flanders receive.

Public goods suffer from two problems: the free-rider problem and the tragedy of the commons.[8] Individuals can free ride, that is, not pay for a good, and still enjoy the benefits of it, because they cannot be excluded from the consumption of it. When individuals cannot be excluded from the consumption of a good they did not pay for, the supply of the good will be smaller than what it otherwise would be. This is because producers will only provide a good if they can profit from selling it. As long as people can use a product without paying for it, profits will be limited, which means fewer potential producers will be interested in supplying or producing the good. Overall, the good will be underprovided.

Similarly, when a good is commonly owned and individuals do not pay for their use of it, they do not have an incentive to conserve the good and may use it until it is destroyed. Economists call this excess free riding the tragedy of the commons. The economist's first reaction to a commons problem is to suggest privatization. This solution works well for goods that are not true public goods because they are not non-excludable; that is, there is a way to exclude non-payers. Successful examples of privatization abound; they range from telecoms and airlines to toll roads and local trash removal or recycling. What happens when a good is truly non-excludable, however? Many people suggest that in such cases government intervention is required to solve the problem.

When a good is truly a public good, that is, it is really non-excludable and nonrival, one way of still ensuring provision of the good is to task a government agency or a publicly owned company with its production and to finance its provision through taxes. This is the preferred solution for military services as well as for national and public parks.

However, Elinor Ostrom, who was the 2009 Nobel Prize winner in economics, has found in many years of fieldwork that even when goods are truly non-excludable and commons problems emerge, people often find local solutions to those problems without government intervention. Her examples range from Turkish fisheries to California water basins, and she concludes that in many instances of commons problems local public entrepreneurs have found private self-governance solutions to the commons problems they faced. In the example of the California water basin, the problem was the over-extraction of ground-water by water producers in the basin area. As groundwater levels in the basin were falling, salt water from the bordering ocean started to intrude, which threatened to destroy the precious common resource. Over a period of more than twenty years, the major water producers of the area litigated, fought, and finally cooperated with each other to reach a solution. In the end, they were able to reduce the amount of water extracted from the basin below the level of natural water replenishment.[9] They solved the problem on their own through local self-governance, and central government intervention was not required.

For most of the commons problems Ostrom presents, local public entre-preneurs were able to find a way to create something akin to private property rights over part of the common pool resource. In doing so, they turned a non-excludable commons into an excludable private good and thereby resolved the initial market failure problem.

Asymmetric Information as Market Failure

The third type of market failure economists have identified is asymmetric in-formation. Information is asymmetric when either party to an exchange knows more about the exchanged product than the other.

One problem that arises because of asymmetric information is called moral hazard. Moral hazard is usually associated with problems of asymmetric in-formation between employer and employee. When Bart needs money to buy a new video console, he gets a job hanging menus on doors for the restaurant You Thai Now ("Lisa the Tree Hugger"). Bart quickly learns that people do not like menus on their doors when Moe, in response to a menu on his door, threatens to cut Bart like a box. Instead of continuing his work as the restaurant owner intended, Bart dumps the remaining menus in a back-alley dumpster. Because the Thai restaurant owner cannot perfectly monitor his work, Bart puts in less effort than what is desirable from the employer's perspective.[10] In the episode, his shirking is quickly discovered. The story nevertheless well illustrates the problem of adverse selection.[11]

The most commonly cited solution for moral hazard problems in labor mar-kets is efficiency wages.[12] Employers will pay their employees slightly more than the market clearing wage to incentivize them to be more productive and to shirk less. Without efficiency wages, the choice for the employee is between working hard to keep the job that pays the market wage, or shirking and, in case he or she is caught, having to find a new job that pays the same. With efficiency wages, on the other hand, the employee is incentivized to be more productive. Getting paid a slightly higher (efficiency) wage, the employee now faces the choice be-tween being as productive as possible to keep the higher-paying job or having to find a new job that will most likely pay less because he or she shirked. Voila, the asymmetric information problem is overcome and your workers stay busy.

Efficiency wages might be a lesson for Monty Burns to consider: just as Bart would have been more diligent hanging Thai restaurant menus on people's doors if the restaurant owner had paid him a higher wage, Homer might sleep less at work and cause fewer problems if Mr. Burns paid him a slightly higher wage.

The second problem that arises when information is asymmetric is called adverse selection. Consider the case of beer. Sellers of beer know what ingredients they used in the production of their beer; they have technology, which can help them determine the alcohol content of their beer; and they know when the beer was brewed. Potential buyers of beer generally have less information and can only rely on labels to help them determine what to buy. Bad beer should sell at a lower price than good beer, but because it is hard for consumers to distinguish good from bad without tasting, good and bad beer sell at the same price.[13] That is the essence of the problem of adverse selection. In extreme cases of adverse selection, high-quality products are driven out of the market because consumers' average quality expectations are so low that they are not willing to pay enough to cover the cost of producing good beer. Economists call situations like that a lemons problem.

Just as with the previous two types of market failures, governments also attempt to provide solutions for problems of asymmetric information through consumer protection. In the United States, the Pure Food and Drug Act was passed in 1906 to provide for federal inspection of meat products, and the Food and Drug Administration (FDA), as the oldest existing consumer protection agency, monitors the production of food and pharmaceutical products to enforce health and safety standards.

Government intervention is not the only way to protect consumers from problems of asymmetric information, however. As with the previous two types of market failures, market entrepreneurs have found effective ways of avoiding the problems associated with asymmetric information and adverse selection. Daniel B. Klein illustrates various ways the free enterprise system has found to supply assurance of quality to buyers when information about quality is asymmetric.[14] His examples include local gossip about the quality of plumbers, painters, electricians, and even piano tuners. When you do not know how to choose a good mechanic for your Volvo, you ask around among colleagues and neighbors to find out about the reputation of local mechanics.

Klein also suggests that brand names provide assurance in extended dealings that go beyond your local neighborhood. When you are unable to distinguish low-quality from high-quality beer, you buy Duff because you know exactly what you get. The Duff brand is well known in Springfield, and even though the beer is of low quality, it has a reputation for consistency and customers know what to expect when they buy it.[15]

Conclusion

Modern economics has placed assumptions on Adam Smith's invisible hand that are often unable to stand the test of reality. When real-world markets violate these unrealistic assumptions, people are quick to suggest market failure. In both the real world and Springfield, however, private entrepreneurs have found ways to overcome at least some of these market failure problems. They don't require assistance from central planners or local governments. Whether it is brands such as Duff Beer, or competition in the form of the Coolsville Comics store, market failure problems in Springfield are often solved by the free enterprise system, not by "corruptus in extremis" mayor Joe Quimby.[16]

8

WILL YOU STOP
THAT INFERNAL RACKET!?!

Externalities and *The Simpsons*

Justin M. Ross

SINCE ITS ESTABLISHMENT IN 1989, the Springfield tire fire has featured prominently in the opening credits of news anchor Kent Brockman's *Eye on Springfield* to illustrate the ignorance and indifference of Springfield citizens. Though the fire perpetually produces cancerous toxins, the tire yard owner apparently does not find it in their interest to extinguish it. Similarly, nuclear plant owner C. Montgomery Burns refuses to let proper radioactive waste disposal costs eat into his profits, instead preferring to deposit the waste in a neighborhood park, where it causes laser-eye-beam mutations in squirrels. Economics as a discipline has never been particularly interested in profits *per se*, but rather the role profits play in incentivizing socially beneficial behavior through competition. After all, it is not from the benevolence of Apu that the Simpsons expect their dinner, but from Apu's regard to his own self-interest.[1] However, as the Springfield tire fire and Mr. Burns demonstrate, the self-interest motive requires qualification if it is expected to maximize social net benefits. So how does economic theory explain three-eyed fish, eternal tire fires, and mutant squirrels caused by profit-seeking when so much of the science emphasizes an unintentional alignment between private self-interest with the greater social interest?

The answer can be found in the study of *externalities*, a concept conventionally defined as spillover effects from an action or exchange on a nonparticipating party that causes a change in the amount of a real good or service being provided. When these spillovers confer benefits on others they are considered positive externalities, and they are negative when they impose costs on others. Whether the externality is positive or negative might be subjective to the party on the receiving end of the spillover. In "Milhouse of Sand and Fog," Maggie gets the chicken pox and immediately becomes a serious health threat to Homer, who never had the pox as a child. However, Homer quickly learns from Ned Flanders that her contagiousness is a positive externality for other children who can more safely develop immunity early on by catching the illness now. Homer finds that he is even able to charge other parents for their children to attend a "pox party" with Maggie. Likewise, in "Two Cars in Every Garage and Three Eyes on Every Fish," Montgomery Burns would successfully spin a three-eyed flounder found in the waters surrounding his nuclear power plant as a desirable evolutionary advancement during his campaign for governor. Regardless, we can proceed by thinking about externalities as definitively "positive" or "negative" occurrences for the purposes of understanding their role in affecting collective well-being.

So how do economists incorporate externalities in the context of market exchange? What is their underlying cause? Are all spillover effects viewed this way? Finally, in what ways can they be corrected?[2]

Market Exchange Externalities

Despite its relatively simple definition, externalities is a rather complex idea. When economists refer to "externalities," they are actually referring to only a subset of spillover effects. There is another type of spillover, known as *pecuniary externalities*, which are nothing short of vital to the ability of markets to create social benefits. The competitive process constantly generates pecuniary externalities that raise the standard of living.

Consider the Flaming Moe, an alcoholic drink Moe the Bartender found to be extremely profitable to serve. In "Flaming Moe's," he initially is able to sell a large quantity of this drink at a high price, earning himself a monopoly rent.[3] After Homer reveals to everyone that the secret ingredient of the drink is children's cough syrup, the streets are quickly filled with independent vendors serving their own knock-off version of the drink. Moe's monopoly profit margin disappears as the new wider availability of the drink causes prices to fall. A drink that people enjoy becomes more widely available and affordable to them, precisely the social benefits of competition that economists predict.

Notice that when the independent vendors decided to enter into the business of selling knock-off Flaming Moes at competitive prices, they did so because it was profitable for them, not because it would reduce Moe's profits. Nevertheless, their decision to compete in this market was harmful to Moe, just like any of the other negative externalities described earlier.[4] Similarly, when unemployed workers from Ogdenville immigrate to Springfield in "Coming to Homerica," businesses such as Moe's accommodate them to some extent by displacing the original Springfielders' preference, Duff Beer, with Akvait, which is popular among the Ogdenvillians. From the standpoint of economics, this displacement reflected the rationing of resources to those who valued them the most, but the change left some Springfield residents worse off. This mechanism is illustrated in Figure 8.1 using supply and demand for bar service. Prior to the Ogdenville immigrants' arrival, market output and price (Q_1 and P^*) were determined solely by demand from Springfield residents (D_1). A new, higher demand curve (D_2) came into effect after the immigrants arrived, driving up both market output and price along the supply curve to Q_3 and P^{**}. However, the original Springfield residents' demand curve is unchanged, as they do not value bar service any less than before, so their demand remains at D_1, but they nevertheless experience an increase in price to P^{**}. The effect on Springfield residents is that they get less market output, Q_2 instead of Q_1, and they pay a higher price, P^{**} instead of P^*.

Again, though it was not of the Ogdenvillians' intention, these kinds of spill-over effects were transmitted through the market process in the form of prices and thus serve to ration resources to those who value them most. What does strike the concern of economists are those extra-market spillovers that actually cause a misallocation of resources. These externalities are considered in the remainder of the chapter.

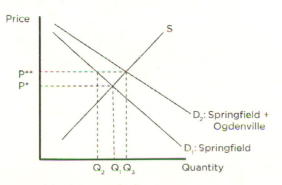

FIGURE 8.1. Demand displacement for bar service

Externalities: Misallocating Resources

In a market transaction, two or more consenting parties voluntarily agree to some type of exchange. Each party only agrees under the expectation that the exchange will leave them better off, and as a result, market transactions improve the well-being of all those involved. Furthermore, people engage in these transactions repeatedly until their own marginal benefit is equal to their marginal cost. Economics does not play favorites in considering the well-being among the parties involved in the transaction: everyone is a member of society whose well-being is important, and everyone is equally important. Though this uniform treatment of individuals has drawn the ire of many over the years, even earning it "the dismal science" label, it has held up relatively well over time as a unifying principle in the field.[5] As a result, when these market transactions improve the lives of the individuals, as a first approximation, economics treats these actions as having improved the welfare of society. In other words, the individual's marginal benefits and costs are the same as those of society. After all, as members of society, these individuals' utility (that is, happiness) counts as social utility as well. What can be surprising is that this private exchange can result in the same outcomes as those of a benevolent central planner with perfect information about people's preferences.

As an example, let's consider a case in which Homer, Lenny, and Carl are buying mugs of Duff Beer at Moe's Tavern. Table 8.1 expresses, in dollar terms, how much happier each brew makes them. If Duff sells for $5 per mug, we would expect the three to purchase each mug in which the marginal benefit was greater than or equal to its price. Therefore, we would expect Homer to buy four, Lenny to buy three, and Carl to buy two. Notice that these nine beers purchased result in a total utility of $74. Remarkably, if Moe was a benevolent friend interested in rationing nine beers to maximize the total utility of his

TABLE 8.1. Duff Consumption and Marginal Benefit Per Mug

	Marginal Benefit By Individual (in $)		
# of Duffs	Homer	Lenny	Carl
1st	12	10	8
2nd	10	8	6
3rd	8	6	4
4th	6	4	2
5th	4	2	0
6th	2	0	−2

friends and had perfect information about their preferences, he would not find another allocation of those nine beers that would yield more than $74! However, letting each customer choose their quantity according to a given price resulted in a socially optimal allocation of Duff without Moe being anything other than a selfish bartender.

Now suppose that Duff Beer consumption, as it does in "Homer vs. the Eighteenth Amendment," causes lewd behavior that draws the wrath of a group of Springfield women concerned with the example it sets for children. Suppose that this lewd behavior requires parents to place extra emphasis on character and morality while raising their children, an effort which they value at $2 per Duff per person. At a price of $5 per mug, Table 8.2 presents the marginal social benefits by group, which for the three friends privately is still $74 in total, but is −$18 for the children, so total social welfare is just $56. From the standpoint of economic theory, too many resources are being devoted to Duff Beer because its consumers do not imbibe its full social cost. This does not imply that Duff should not be consumed, merely that less of it should be. If, for instance, a $2 payment to a parent support group had to be made with each Duff purchase, each of the individuals in Table 8.1 would drink one less beer for just six in total. The private benefits would now be $56 to the three friends, while the $2 payment could be used to cancel out the damaging effects on the children.[6] Under this scheme, the $2 payment would internalize the damages they were occurring on others, causing them to consume a socially optimal amount of Duff. Again, notice that as long as the externality exists, social welfare is $56 at its maximum, but it can be achieved with fewer resources devoted to Duff when the $2 fee is in place, resulting in a more socially efficient outcome.

TABLE 8.2. Marginal Social Benefits of Duff by Group at $5 Per Mug.

# of Duffs	Marginal Benefit By Individual (in $)	
	Homer, Lenny & Carl	The Children
1st	30	−6
2nd	24	−6
3rd	14	−4
4th	6	−2
5th	0	0
6th	0	0
Total	74	−18

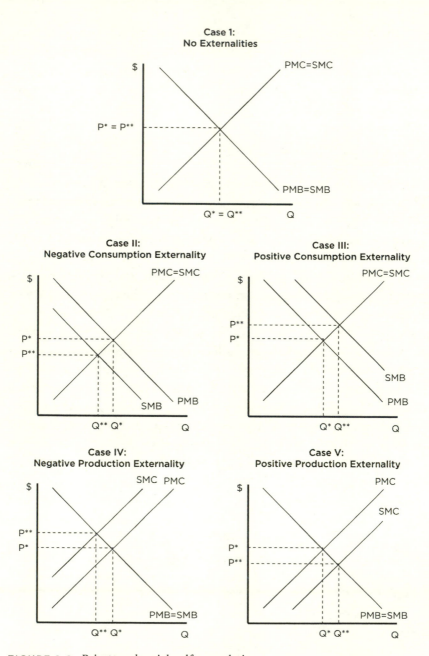

FIGURE 8.2. Private and social welfare analysis

NOTE: * indicates private outcome; ** indicates social ideal outcome; PMC and SMC indicate private and social marginal cost; PMB and SMB represent private and social marginal benefits.

Depending on where the externality occurs (in consumption or production) as well as its nature (positive or negative), the social welfare analysis will differ slightly.[7] Figure 8.2 presents each of these cases and compares it with a market in which there are no externalities (Case I), causing private and social marginal analysis to align. The previous example of Duff consumption causing external damages through lewd behavior is referred to as a negative consumption externality (Case II). When the Duff Brewing Company determined its level of production, it presumably considered only the price its customers were willing to pay. If its customers are indifferent to the concerns of these women, then the price they are willing to pay (P^*) will be higher than the true "social price" (P^{**}) of Duff. The consumers' neglect of their negative externalities will cause their private marginal benefits (PMB) to exceed the social marginal benefits (SMB), leading Duff to *overproduce* its beer relative to its socially optimal level ($Q^{**} < Q^*$). A critical point here is that the externality exists in that consumers neglect the risk or damages they post to others, not damage they risk to themselves. The externality in Bart risking zombiism by eating a tainted Krusty Burger in "Treehouse of Horror XX" occurred when he seemingly disregarded the risk his zombiism would pose to others, and not the risk he posed to himself.

A positive consumption externality (Case III) occurs in the opposite case, when individuals do not consider that there may be benefits conferred to others. This is on display in a scene from "Bart-Mangled Banner," when Dr. Hibbert is forced to actually chase Bart through town for a vaccination. While Hibbert finally does successfully trick Bart into an inoculation, the young menace never seems to acknowledge that he has reduced the likelihood that others will get sick as well. Because people like Bart neglect benefits conferred on others from their consumption, their willingness to undertake that consumption is lower than what would be socially optimal.

If a production process incurs some costs that are not borne by the supplier, economists refer to this process as having a negative production externality (Case IV). In "Marge vs. Singles, Seniors, Childless Couples and Teens, and Gays," an anti-child advocacy group led by Lindsay Naegel finds sympathy among the public for eliminating child-friendly things in Springfield after babies riot at an oversold Roofi concert. Naegel and her group quite explicitly argue that the town "breeders" have too many children in part because they do not bear the full cost of having them. Homer even summarizes the textbook economic analysis of this case when he frets that he would not have had Bart,

Maggie, and Lisa if he thought he was going to have to pay for all their costs. In other words, negative externalities in production result in an oversupply because the private costs do not encompass the full social cost.[8]

In the real world, the construction of a golf course often results in a qualitative improvement in the look and feel of a community. These benefits imply that golf course construction carries a positive externality in the production process (Case V), and thus the true social cost of its development is below that of the cost incurred by the developer. Examples of positive production externalities (Case V) are less common in *The Simpsons*, but are occasionally alluded to throughout the series. Lisa Simpson points out the positive externalities of allowing snakes in gardening during "Whacking Day," and for honeybees in "The Burns and the Bees." In "Papa's Got a Brand New Badge," Homer's private security force, SpringShield, places signs outside of stores under their protection, which likely deters crime in the locations surrounding it as well. Finally, before its sinister purpose was discovered, Montgomery Burns' recycling factory was a model of positive externalities generated by using recycled inputs. Such situations result in too little of the final market output, as the true social costs are actually lower than the private costs incurred during production.

Bubble Domes and Other Ways of Dealing with Externalities

In the examples of the previous section, it becomes apparent that externalities drive a wedge between the socially optimal price of a market and the privately incurred price, and that one way to deal with this is to nudge that price. Since Homer, Lenny, and Carl pay $2 less than the true price of their action, levying a $2 tax per Duff would rectify the problem. This approach is known as Pigouvian taxation, and the rule of thumb is to tax negative externalities according to the damage they create while subsidizing positive externalities according to the amount of the benefits.[9] However, another approach that has gotten a lot of attention in the policy world is rooted in addressing the problem through private property rights.[10]

Private property rights are the fundamental underpinning of markets transactions, not to mention liberal democracies. For individuals to hold private property rights over something, it must be said that they have

- The right to exclusive use of the property
- Legal protection
- The right to transfer[11]

Upon closer inspection of the examples in the previous section, one can see that externalities take place because some element of private property rights is missing. One policy solution then is to establish private property rights, or whichever element of it that is missing, to create the appropriate incentives for them to internalize the full social costs and benefits. Consider the decision-making process of purchasing a Canyonero, the sports utility vehicle featured prominently during the episode "Marge Simpson in: 'Screaming Yellow Honkers.'" In addition to being ruled unsafe for city or highway driving by the Federal Highway Commission, the theme song for the SUV reveals that it experiences unexplained spontaneous fires. Marge further reveals that it flips over during sharp turns and that the gas tank explodes unexpectedly.

Now knowing all this, any individual who wishes to drive a Canyonero at his or her personal risk is fine from an economics perspective since it is a voluntary action, but such a vehicle puts others at risk as well. Another way to view this negative externality is to treat the Canyonero as a threat to the property rights of other drivers, but which can be removed if (1) Canyoneros are taken off the road or (2) the other drivers are taken off the road. After all, both parties value driving their respective vehicles on the road, and preventing either from doing so would make them worse off.[12] The task of economics is to determine which party values being on the road more, or at least devise a mechanism that would get the parties to truthfully reveal who values it most.

A way to identify the value of being on the road would be to consider the respective amounts that each party would have to be compensated in order for them to surrender their rights to the road.[13] Suppose we knew that Canyonero drivers value having the road at $1,000, while other drivers value it at $300. From a social welfare perspective, if we were going to ban one party from the road, it would make the most sense to ban other drivers and allow Canyonero drivers full reign over the road. The result is that Canyonero drivers gain $1,000 while other drivers lose $300, for a net social gain of $700. *The Simpsons* has used this type of policy approach as a comic device several times. In "Homer vs. the Eighteenth Amendment," alcohol is banned from Springfield, as is sugar in "Sweets and Sour Marge." In the most drastic example, the plot of *The Simpson's Movie* was set around isolating the always polluting Springfield from the rest of the planet using a gigantic dome.

Though this sounds rather simple, it is often quite difficult in practice to actually determine who values such resources the most, especially since both parties would have a considerable interest in exaggerating the value they place on obtaining the right. As it turns out, if the parties in question can effectively bargain with each other, it will not matter who is initially assigned the property right. For the sake of argument, in the case of the Canyonero, suppose each party can organize amongst themselves and enter into negotiations. The negotiations will take different courses depending on which party is initially assigned the right to the road, and these courses are depicted on a Kaldor-Hicks tableau in Table 8.3. For example, in scenario A of Table 8.3, the property right to the road is assigned to the Canyonero drivers. If they enter into negotiations with other drivers, they will not accept a payment less than $1,000, while the other drivers will not be willing to pay more than $300 to the Canyonero drivers in exchange for their exit. As a result, no bargain will be achieved, Canyoneros will take their rights to the road, and net social welfare will be $700 as per the analysis in the previous paragraph. On the other hand, if we were to assign the property rights to the other drivers as in scenario B, a bargain can now be reached. After all, Canyonero drivers will be willing to pay up to $1,000 to get on the road, while other drivers would leave for as little as $300. Some mutually agreeable payment should be feasible, say $500 from Canyonero drivers to the others. Canyonero drivers will gain $1,000 in value, but lose $500 in the transfer for a net gain of $500. The other drivers will gain the $500 transfer, but lose $300 in value, for a $200 net. The social net gain is the sum of the net gains for a total of $700. Notice that in both scenarios Canyonero drivers ended up on the road, and that the net social gain was $700 (as it would be for any agreed transfer payment).

Now, in reality, it seems unlikely that these parties could effectively organize and engage in such bargaining. Economists frequently refer to these

TABLE 8.3. Kaldor-Hicks tableau of negotiations for rights to the road

Scenario A- Rights to Canyonero (in $)

	Canyonero	Others	Net
Road	1000	−300	700
Transfer	0	0	0
Net	1000	−300	700

Scenario B- Rights to Others (in $)

	Canyonero	Others	Net
Road	1000	−300	700
Transfer	−500	500	0
Net	500	200	700

situations as having "transaction costs" that are significant enough to derail effective bargaining. After all, the negotiation process can be time consuming and expensive, especially if a larger number of parties are involved.[14] These costs may result in a situation in which an inefficient outcome may persist if these types of transaction costs outweigh the expected benefits of bargaining.[15] Still, a mix of traffic and vehicular insurance laws has established a set of well-defined and -enforced property rights that result in drivers of high-risk vehicles (like those of the Canyonero) internalizing the risks they pose to others. A person who has been unduly harmed by another driver has legal recourse through the judicial system. As a result, insurance companies price this added risk into their premiums. As long as those premiums are reflective of the expected damages, the externality is internalized so that private and social marginal benefits come into alignment, as in Case I in Figure 8.2.

Mr. Stigler Goes to Springfield:
Is Government Intervention the Answer to Externalities?

If we start with the assumption that government is run by socially benevolent and well-informed central planners, then we would be rather indifferent between Pigouvian taxation, regulation, and the assignment of property rights as policy alternatives to correcting externalities. In reality, politicians and bureaucrats are every bit as self-interested as the rest of us human beings, and our judicial system might handle certain industries even more poorly than regulators. This requires us to consider the case-specific practical difficulties of implementing policies.[16] On *The Simpsons*, "Mr. Spitz Goes to Washington" provides one such case study of the difficulties involved.

In the episode, a change in the landing patterns at the local airport results in the planes touching down just beyond the Simpson house. The noise and vibration are intolerable for the family, who find themselves unable to sleep or sell the house. It turns out the landing patterns were changed to accommodate the mating habits of local indigenous wildlife. After failing to negotiate a solution with a government bureaucrat, as a last resort they convince Krusty the Clown to run for Congress. Once in Congress, Krusty and the family are able to blackmail a senior congressman to let a change in the flight pattern pass as a rider to a bill intended to give orphans American flags.

That the airplanes created a negative production externality is of no question, but whether or not any of these solutions approximated an economically efficient outcome is unsettled. The difficulty in answering this question lies in the various practical and political difficulties that become apparent when examining the case. First, the problem lies in a lack of clearly defined private property rights: nobody owns the airspace. Presently, there is no clear institutional solution to dealing with this issue beyond assigning custody to the government, or nobody at all. (Presumably, this also allowed Burns to block out the sun in "Who Shot Mr. Burns?") It would appear to be incredibly burdensome for property owners to extend their rights indefinitely into airspace, requiring airlines to obtain the permission from any property owners they had to navigate over.[17] Assigning the airspace rights to the government also proves to be difficult, albeit for different reasons. Attempts at bargaining with government bureaucrats fall on deaf ears because there is no institutional incentive to partake in the negotiations, as it is already established that the government owns the right to undertake this change and there is no benefit for bureaucrats to find improvements.

The ultimate theme of the episode, from an economics perspective, is that government intervention results in the property rights being distributed to the most politically powerful group. The episode at least alludes to the idea that the initial allocation of flight paths was close to the social optimum, because they took place over a mostly deserted area. Viewers are clued in that the local indigenous wildlife whose mating habits were being disturbed by the original flight paths were actually those of Springfield mayor Joe Quimby, who prefers to undertake his extramarital affairs at a remote hotel in the area. The wealthy elites of Springfield finance Krusty's congressional campaign, while Krusty tailors his policy interests to those of middle-working-class families like the Simpsons. At the end of the episode, Homer notes that the planes are no longer landing over their house and instead are landing over the homes of poor people. Indeed, it seems likely that poor people would have the least amount of political power.

However, since airports tend to depress property values that make them more attractive to lower-income households anyway, it is not entirely clear that Homer's observation implies economic inefficiency. Whether or not political power will result in inefficient outcomes is an open subject of debate in political economy. The Chicago School, led by notable economists such as George Stigler, Gary Becker, and Donald Wittman, tends to view the political process as resulting in economically efficient allocations of rights, at least under certain conditions.[18] In regulatory capture theory, the development of which helped earn Stigler a Nobel Prize in economics, the group with the largest financial stake in regulatory outcomes is the one with the most incentive to capture any regulatory agency.[19] This can be desirable to the extent that the group with the largest financial stake may correspond to the group with the highest value of the right in question. The Virginia School, perhaps most identified with the likes of James Buchanan and Gordon Tullock, tends to view this process as less likely to result in efficient outcomes. For instance, regulatory agencies may be created for political opportunism, to undermine competitors, or to avoid correcting one's own negative externalities at all. This view might be best characterized in "Two Cars in Every Garage and Three Eyes on Every Fish," in which a three-eyed fish causes the launch of a regulatory inspection that turns up many safety and environmental violations (plutonium rods used as paperweights, chewing gum used as cooling tower sealant, and so on). After the regulators turn down a bribe, Burns runs for governor so that *he* can decide what's safe.

Many, perhaps most, externalities are addressed without government interventions. Undoubtedly, some interventions are worse than the externality they intend to correct. In these cases, private entities often find it in their interest to find ways to internalize positive externalities. As mentioned earlier, Homer Simpson did exactly this when he realized that people wanted their children to get chicken pox from Maggie in "Milhouse of Sand and Fog." Though some, like Ned Flanders, might find this act distasteful, many others might not willingly otherwise undertake the effort. However, much of the comedy in *The Simpsons* is derived from Homer's unresponsiveness to social norms that each of us follow to regulate negative externalities every day.

Conclusion

Conflict is the heart of comedy, and the writers of the *The Simpsons* often find externalities to be an excellent comedic device for their plot lines. Perhaps the best lesson of economics is that no solution is without its trade-offs, and we might simply be stuck looking for the alternative with the least significant failures. *The Simpsons* teaches us that we should try to enjoy the irony and humor of the process when we look anyway. Milton Friedman may have popularized the old economics axiom "There ain't no such thing as a free lunch," but it is Homer Simpson who popularized the response, "Mmm . . . free lunch."

MAYORS, MONORAILS, AND MORONS

Government Failure in *The Simpsons*

John Considine

IN A SCENE REMINISCENT of the sinking of the *RMS Titanic*, the barge on which Green Day are performing their concert is destroyed by pollution in Lake Springfield (*The Simpsons Movie*). Only Lisa seems concerned about the pollution, and her concerns are heightened later when she observes the dumping of waste products into the lake. Eventually, Lisa convinces the citizens of the importance of the issue, and they come together to clean up the mess. This is done on a voluntary basis.

At this stage, Mayor Quimby erects a superfluous three-foot concrete barrier around the lake. A short period later Homer is in a line at the Hazardous Waste Treatment Center, where he intends to dump a silo full of the "leavings" generated by himself and Spider Pig. He then gets a call from Carl to say they are giving out a limited number of free donuts at the donut store. Unable to control himself, Homer leaves the line and dumps the silo in Lake Springfield, with disastrous environmental effects. By his action, Homer brings about the intervention of President Schwarzenegger. The presidential solution is to enclose Springfield in a dome, and when the dome solution turns out to be less than effective, the head of the EPA decides on a nuclear wipeout of Springfield.

The Simpsons Movie illustrates what economics classifies as the three "failures"—market failure, government failure, and individual failure.[1] Market failure occurred because those dumping in the lake did not take into account the effects of their actions on others.[2] Government failure occurred because, among other things, the head of the EPA owned the company that made the dome.[3] Individual failure occurred because Homer could not resist the short-term temptation of free donuts and, therefore, damaged his longer-term best interests.[4] *The Simpsons Movie* also demonstrates that there is no reason why the government solution to market failure is better than the market failure itself. Few would argue that the three-foot concrete barrier was an effective solution. Even fewer would argue that the dome or a nuclear wipeout is unambiguously better than a polluted Lake Springfield. In *The Simpsons* there is never a presumption in favor of government activity as a solution to any market imperfection.

This chapter presents the government failure (or public choice) perspective in *The Simpsons*. Prior to the public choice research program, there was an implicit assumption in favor of government intervention as a solution to market failure. Then, fifty years ago James M. Buchanan and the public choice school argued that government should be evaluated on the same basis as the market.[5] This, they suggested, should be done by application of the principles of economics to the analysis of government just as these principle are applied to the market. The application of a logically consistent methodological framework demonstrates that "public and private choice processes differ, not because the motivations of actors are different, but because of stark differences in the incentives and constraints that channel the pursuit of self-interest in the two settings."[6]

Choice in a public setting is channeled through political institutions. If these institutions ensured that pursuit of private interest served the public interest then there would be no government failure. In such circumstances, the public interest would be best served when citizens voted for the candidates or policies that best suited them, bureaucrats could maximize their departmental budgets, and politicians could focus on policies that would get them reelected.[7] Unfortunately, this is not always the case, and the filtering of choice through the political process means that private interests are not always aligned with public interest.

It is impossible to devise a voting system that perfectly captures the "public interest" and is immune to manipulation by the strategic actions of those involved. For example, if a politician had to act in the public interest to ensure reelection, then there would be no government failure. However, with majority rule the politician needs to only act in the interest of just over 50 percent of the electorate.[8] The percentage could approximate 25 percent for legislative decisions, because success of a policy proposal requires support of just over 50 percent of the legislators, each of whom could be elected with just over 50 percent electoral support. Of course, the politician may not need to keep such a large proportion of the electorate happy because they may not all vote. The rational, self-interested citizen will weigh the costs of voting against the benefits of voting and will be unlikely to vote because the benefits will be smaller than the costs. The benefits of voting are usually miniscule, because one's vote is unlikely to be decisive and the benefits of any particular outcome are likely to be widely dispersed.[9]

Such a system can be manipulated by the strategic choices of the participants. Small, well-organized groups of voters can take advantage of the situation to get special-interest legislation passed. The costs and benefits of such activity mean that only small groups with narrow sectional interests will engage in such activity—this is known as the logic of collective action.[10] Public officials can manipulate the choices that the electorate are given such that the electorate vote for an outcome that provides a private return to the public official over and above the public interest. For example, suppose 100 percent of the electorate agree on public funding of a sports stadium with fifty thousand capacity, but the support drops by 1 percent with every two hundred seats more, or less, than this figure. A public official with a desire for a larger stadium can hold a referendum on the taxpayers funding a fifty-nine thousand capacity stadium, and it will be supported by 55 percent of the electorate.[11] Alternatively, the electorate could be presented with a proposal for a fifty thousand capacity stadium combined with a "small" pay increase for public officials. There is no shortage of ways an enterprising agenda-setter could manipulate the choices presented to the electorate.

The preceding examples are just some of the ways that choice in a public setting can produce suboptimal outcomes, or government failure. In what follows, government activity is examined using some principles of economics and *The Simpsons*. As a result, government does not get favorable treatment by comparisons with nongovernment activity. The next two sections examine the extent to which the behavior of government officials and voters in *The Simpsons* is consistent with the self-interested aspect of *homo economicus*. The treatments of public expenditure and taxation in *The Simpsons* are then examined.

Mr. Lisa Goes to Washington: Self-Interest Versus Public Interest
Given the amount of cultural references in *The Simpsons*, it was only a matter of time before it got around to a parody of the 1939 classic *Mr. Smith Goes to Washington*, which was directed by Frank Capra and starred James Stewart. And so it came to pass that in the show's third season, "Mr. Lisa Goes to Washington" was aired.[12] Lisa wins an all-expenses-paid trip to Washington to represent

her state in the national final of the *Reading Digest* Young Patriot essay-writing competition. Like Jefferson Smith from the film, Lisa is also shocked by what she observes in Washington. She sees Congressman Bob Arnold accepting a bribe from a logging company in return for destroying Springfield Forest.[13] When visiting Capitol Hill, all she can see is fat cats scratching each others' backs and pigs eating dollar bills from barrels while wiping their snouts in the flag. As a result she changes her essay to "Cesspool on the Potomac."[14] For all but two minutes of this episode we are treated to a situation in which those involved in politics are driven by private rather than public interest. Then, for the final two minutes of the episode, the alternative is presented. The alternative has public officials acting in the public interest. Bob Arnold is arrested in a sting operation. The arresting FBI agent claims to work for Uncle Sam. When a senator proposes they tack on a pay raise to the bill dealing with the expulsion of Bob Arnold there is a unanimous no. In signing the bill into law, President Bush says that doing so should make all 250 million of his bosses glad.

It is no coincidence that it is only for a small proportion of "Mr. Lisa Goes to Washington" that public officials act in the public interest rather than their own private interest. For over twenty seasons of the series, it has been rare to see public officials act in the public interest when it conflicts with their private interest. The norm is for public officials to act in their private interest, with the exception to the rule coming in the behavior of lesser-known characters.[15] Mayor Quimby goes beyond self-interest and is actually corrupt. Chief Wiggum is also corrupt and incompetent. This portrait of self-serving public officials serves to warn against the normal presumption that public officials act in the public interest. Public choice scholars have always argued that the evaluation of government and market alternatives was biased in favor of government because of the logical inconsistency of assuming that individuals were motivated differently in government and market settings. Because there is no difference in how individuals are motivated in private and public spheres in *The Simpsons*, the show accurately presents the public choice view.

Importantly, there is no presumption in either *The Simpsons* or public choice that any one group of individuals is any better than any other group. The Democratic Mayor Quimby is an individual who engages in tax cheating, is linked to the mob via Fat Tony, and pays bribes to Chief Wiggum. However, the alternative mayor is the Republican Sideshow Bob, who was twice convicted of attempted murder as well as electoral fraud.[16] Nor is Chief Clancy Wiggum exactly a paragon of virtue, and his competence is questionable. He is replaced when he is unable to stop Fat Tony from supplying Moe with alcohol during a brief period of prohibition ("Homer vs. the Eighteenth Amendment"). Eventually, Homer and the citizens of Springfield decide they do not want his replacement, Rex Banner. Wiggum is reinstated, and Quimby immediately gets Fat Tony to supply the town with alcohol.[17]

If the alternatives to Quimby and Wiggum are no better than the incumbents, then the same can be said about the democratic system itself. One alternative to democratically elected government is presented in "They Saved Lisa's Brain." In this episode the Mensa chapter attempts to confront Quimby because its members believe the town's civic institutions are run by the least intelligent citizens. Quimby flees town before the meeting, and it is discovered in the town's constitution that in such circumstances the town is to be run by a "council of learned citizens." The other citizens do not like the new laws of their arrogant leaders, which include banning contact sports and limiting procreation to once every seven years. As a result, the town is returned to the control of the democratically elected mayor.

The Simpsons invites us to consider the alternatives to existing market and government arrangements. It highlights the concept that the alternative to the failings of one group of individuals (or system) is another group (or system) with other failings. The important lesson from public choice "is that changing the identities of the people who hold public office will not produce major changes in policy outcomes. Electing better people will not, by itself, lead to much better government."[18] Scholars of government failure have argued that those who favor government solutions to market failure may not evaluate government alternatives consistently. In particular, they contend that there is a logical inconsistency in the presumption that individuals behave in a self-interested fashion in their private roles and in a publicly interested fashion in their public roles.[19] Scholars of government failure say that the assumed motivational force should be a consistent one, and that for economists, it should be the self-interested *homo economicus*. In other words, scholars of government failure believe we should model human behavior in a government setting as we find it in *The Simpsons*.

Electing Sideshow Bob as Mayor and Homer as Sanitation Commissioner

Public officials are not the only ones to behave in a self-interested fashion. When Major Quimby and Sideshow Bob canvass the old folks in Springfield

Retirement Castle, it is clear that the senior citizens of Springfield view voting as an exchange ("Sideshow Bob Roberts"). It is also clear that the old folks are a special-interest group, who because of their organization and likelihood to vote, are likely to see the candidates try to meet their demands. Grandpa even tells Quimby to give the elderly what they want or they'll send him packing. Quimby asks them what they want and eventually agrees to name the new expressway "the Matlock Expressway." When Sideshow Bob arrives, Grandpa asks him to top Quimby's offer. Bob does so by building the expressway *and* spending all afternoon listening to their neverending stories.

This exchange view of voting is also present in "Trash of the Titans," in which Homer succeeds in beating Ray Patterson for the post of sanitation commissioner by making outlandish promises such as twenty-four-hour trash pickup, car washing, and shower scrubbing. Homer realizes that he needs to promise the citizens something in return for their votes after his earlier failed attempt to persuade patrons at a U2 concert to vote for him.[20]

Further evidence that the citizens take an economic approach to voting can be seen by the number of voters who do not vote. Failure to vote can be rational in an economic sense. A rational individual might think as follows: there are substantial time and travel costs to voting; I'll still get the benefits if my preferred option is selected even if I do not vote; the chances of my vote making a difference are miniscule; therefore, I will not vote. Of course, if everyone thought the same way then very few would vote. Such free-riding behavior is exactly what happened when Bart got two votes for class president and was beaten by Martin Prince—Bart beat Martin comprehensively in the class debate by telling jokes rather than discussing policy ("Lisa's Substitute").

When an individual does vote, then it may be rational to be less than fully informed about the candidates or issues. Information is costly to acquire, and rational individuals should only inform themselves up to the point that the value of the last piece of information gathered is equal to the cost of acquiring that information. Therefore, it is rational to remain ignorant of some information. There is plenty of evidence that the citizens of Springfield are less than fully informed (although it is less clear if this is a deliberate rational choice). For example, the debate between Homer and Ray Patterson is hosted by "The League of Uniformed Voters," Lisa has to remind the town meeting that Burns paid a $3 million fine rather than a $2 million fine that Quimby claims is available for spending ("Marge vs. the Monorail"), and there is the belief that Proposition 24 is about immigrants causing high taxes ("Much Apu About Nothing").

Those who claim government failure is greater than market failure argue that rational ignorance is greater in the public setting because of the wider distribution of costs and benefits. They also argue that the choice faced by individuals in the ballot box is narrower than in a food market, since politics is like getting to choose between two different grocery stores but having to purchase everything offered inside. Nowhere is this clearer than in "Sideshow Bob Roberts," in which Lisa attempts to get people to vote for Quimby on the grounds that he is the lesser of two evils. Later in the same episode, she questions the legality of the outcome, and by implication the choice offered to the electorate, when she notes being surprised that one convicted felon can get so many more votes than another. This lack of choice is further illustrated by the comments of Homer when he enters the ballot box. Homer is in favor of Sideshow Bob's Selma-killing policy, but against his Bart-killing policy.

In a market setting, with wider choice, Homer might have purchased only the Selma-killing policy! It is probable that government failure might be greater than market failure because the rational ignorance is greater in a public setting and the number of choices open to the electorate is smaller. The implication of these two possibilities can be seen when it comes to public expenditure in *The Simpsons*.

Public Expenditure on Monorails and Bear Patrols

A car hitting a tree in Evergreen Terrace, in the opening scene of an episode, is the signal for questionable public expenditure. In "Marge vs. the Monorail," Homer is driving home from work when he hits a chestnut tree. The EPA then catches Burns and Smithers dumping nuclear waste, Burns is released after payment of a fine, and Lyle Lanley persuades the townsfolk to spend the money on a monorail. In "Much Apu About Nothing," Flanders is driving home when he panics and crashes his car into a tree after seeing a bear on the road. Homer then leads a march on town hall looking for a solution to the bear problem, Quimby obliges with excessive expenditure on bear patrols and raises taxes to fund the expenditure, Homer is outraged by the tax increase and leads another march on town hall, and Quimby blames the high taxes on the immigrants and promises a referendum on immigration, to be called Proposition 24.

It would be an understatement to say that the public expenditure just described was inefficient. So why do the citizens of Springfield select an inefficient option? They do so because they are less than fully informed, and in some cases they are strategically misinformed, about the costs and benefits of the options under consideration. In "Marge vs. the Monorail," the citizens get carried away on a wave of irrational optimism about the potential benefits of the monorail. In "Much Apu About Nothing," it is irrational pessimism about the potential for bear attacks. The result in each case is that the citizens select an inefficient option.

The citizens are misinformed about the benefits of the monorail by Lyle Lanley. Lanley is the monorail salesman who sees the opportunity provided by the town meeting called to discuss how to spend the $3 million revenue from the fine on Burns.[21] Langley persuades the meeting that the monorail would put Springfield on the map just like it had Ogdenville, North Haverbrook, and Brockway. He also claimed it would generate employment for brain-dead slobs!

In the face of such promises, Marge's proposal to fix Main Street never stood a chance. The monorail ends up like previously ill-conceived expenditures in Springfield such as the popsicle stick skyscraper, the giant magnifying glass, and the escalator to nowhere—monuments to government failure. Lyle Lanley knew how to take advantage of the way in which choice in the public setting is filtered through political institutions. (He also knew how to appeal to the less rational side of human nature.)[22]

The citizens are also ill-informed about the need for bear patrols, the cost of bear patrols, and the benefits of bear patrols in "Much Apu About Nothing." Again, public opinion is easily swayed by rhetoric to seek expenditure that would otherwise be deemed unwise. Homer distorts the nature and frequency of the bear intrusions by saying that the frequent (one) bear attacks are scaring their children and salmon.

To the background shrieks of Helen Lovejoy about the safety of children, Homer leads a march on town hall, where he secures a promise from Quimby for decisive action.[23] As a response to this one bear visit to Springfield, Mayor Quimby delivers the Bear Patrol, which includes ground patrols and flyovers by B-2 stealth bombers. The resulting tax increase produces a classic scene in which Lisa attempts, in vain, to explain to Homer the concept of causation and the link between expenditure and taxation.

Homer: Woo-hoo! A perfect day. Zero bears and one big fat hairy paycheck. Hey! How come my pay is so low? Bear patrol tax. This is an outrage! It's the biggest tax increase in history.

Lisa: Actually, Dad, it's the smallest tax increase in history.

Homer: Let the bears pay the bear tax. I pay the Homer tax.

Lisa: That's home-owner tax.

Homer: Well, anyway, I'm still outraged.

Crowd: Down with taxes! Down with taxes! Down with taxes!

Helen Lovejoy: Won't you think of the children?

Quimby: Are these morons getting louder or dumber?

Aide: Dumber, sir. They won't give up the Bear Patrol but they won't pay taxes for it either.

Quimby: Ducking this issue calls for real leadership. . . . People, your taxes are high because of illegal immigrants. That's right, illegal immigrants. We need to get rid of them.

The crowd seems content to believe Quimby. There are two reasons public expenditure is probably less efficient than private expenditure. First, individuals are more informed about the link between income and expenditure in their private dealings than in the government budget. Second, given the limited choice for mayor, there is little they can do if they do not agree with the tax-and-spend policies of Mayor Quimby.

Some might say that the treatment of public expenditure in both *The Simpsons* and the government failure literature displays a similar bias. Both tend to focus on too much public expenditure as a result of poor decision making, and there is little emphasis on the possibility that there is too little public expenditure. Moreover, the bias is exaggerated when one considers the combined tax-and-spend decisions because when it comes to taxation, both the literature and *The Simpsons* focus on taxes being "too high."

Taxation: The Trouble with Trillions

With the exception of Lisa, and possibly Ned Flanders, those who want greater public expenditure don't understand that they have to pay taxes for it. Those who understand the link between spending and taxes are those who don't want to pay higher taxes. Both Homer and Mr. Burns, however, grudgingly come to an appreciation for some level of taxation in "The Trouble with Trillions" after visiting Cuba. The implicit government failure is in having taxes that are too high. That said, there is a comparison of the alternatives and a grudging acceptance of some level of taxation. The episode follows the standard structure, in which much of the episode is spent finding fault with the existing system before the realization that things could be worse in an alternative scenario. In this case the majority of the episode is spent finding fault with the tax system before the grudging endorsement of it by Homer and Burns.

It is interesting to contrast the views of Flanders and Burns on taxation from the episode. Flanders seems happy to pay taxes for a range of questionable items such as trees, sunshine, and people who don't want to work, whereas Burns objects to paying taxes for what seems to be a more reasonable set of items such as nuclear missiles and to polish the Tomb of the Unknown Soldier.

There is less "failure" identified on the tax side in the academic literature on government failure. This is possibly because the only failure is deemed to be where taxes are too high (as in Cuba). Indeed, it seems that some of the literature excuses tax "avoidance and evasion" on the grounds that they keep tax rates down.[24]

Conclusion

Government fails for the same reasons markets fail, that is, information problems. In addition, government is deemed to fail when individuals make decisions in their private interests when those private interests are not aligned with the interests of the public. Public officials get away with such decisions because of failures in the political market, for example, a choice limited to Quimby or Sideshow Bob. For over a half a century government failure scholars believed that there was a bias in favor of government intervention as a solution to market failure. *The Simpsons* addresses this bias—even if the show is possibly biased in the other direction. Even if we do not accept the perspective of *The Simpsons* on government, there is no getting away from the way in which it invites us to consider the alternative to any proposed government intervention in the economy.

PART III
APPLIED MICROECONOMICS

10

COMING TO HOMERICA

The Economics of Immigration

Seth R. Gitter and Robert J. Gitter

Q: Why did the chicken cross the road?

A: The discounted present value of migration exceeded the discounted present value of staying added to the cost of migration.

ECONOMISTS USE THEIR TOOLKIT to answer a wide variety of questions revolving around the choices people make when their resources are limited. (Although some might argue we should add a joke book to our toolkit.) Migrating, that is, moving to a different place, is a choice people make, and you will not be surprised to learn that it is a decision studied by economists.[1] We begin by discussing how economists think about the decision to migrate. In the case of the United States, we can also examine if migrants cause unemployment for native-born workers as well as the effect of migrants on tax revenues and government expenditures. We will use a fairly typical migrant in this section: Apu Nahasapeemapetilon, or for ease of exposition, A. Nahasapeemapetilon.

A Model of Migration: Should I Stay or Should I Go Now?

Economists view the decision to migrate as one in which an individual compares the costs of staying and migrating. A person considering migrating would most likely reason as follows:

Value of Migration = Benefit of Migration − Benefit from Staying − Cost of Migration[2]

This is a decision that people make each year, or if you prefer, every so often. They compare the benefits of leaving their home for a new place to what they would have if they stayed as well as the cost of moving. The benefits can be financial, or, to paraphrase Homer Simpson, "mmm . . . money." In the United

States, many immigrants earn higher wages than they would have at home.[3] For example, in the year 2000 the average wage for Mexicans living in Mexico was around $10 a day.[4] The benefits of migration can also be nonmonetary. Both the Pilgrims and the Amish came to America in part for religious freedom, and many people nowadays move to Florida, Arizona, and California to escape winter.

There are certain benefits to be had from remaining in one's home country. First, there might be some income that could be earned if someone does not migrate. So if one leaves, one must give up his or her current earnings, or what economists call an opportunity cost. (How far did you think we could get before we mentioned opportunity cost?) The benefits of staying also involve nonmonetary benefits. Staying means one will be in closer proximity to family and community (although, depending on your family it might not be a good thing to be closer). Finally, there is a cost associated with migrating. Although this might involve purchasing a plane ticket, these costs can also include the cost of a hired guide, sometimes called a "coyote," if one is attempting to illegally cross into the United States from Mexico. Coyotes charge several thousand dollars per person to guide people into the United States. Crossing the U.S.-Mexico border is also dangerous, and hundreds of people die each year attempting the passage.[5] These costs must also be taken into account. Migrants take similar risks to cross other borders throughout the world. In addition, some people will be caught by the border patrol and sent back. A more complex analysis would also consider the probability of being sent back.

In terms of the earlier equation, if the value of migration is positive, then the person will choose to migrate, and if it is not, the person will choose to stay. One should think of this as a decision that is made again and again at various time periods. If a person is migrating to raise sufficient funds to build a home or start a business back home, then when enough money has been saved he or she might return. It may surprise you, but until recently nearly half of Mexican immigrants to the United States returned home after only a few years.[6] Also, as the joke at the beginning noted, we sometimes discount benefits that might come to us in the future.[7] So we can look at benefits in the future from migrating or staying and discount them appropriately.

The Case of Apu
The model described in the preceding section does a good job of explaining Apu's journey to America from India. As we saw in "Much Apu About Nothing,"

he came to America after graduating first (out of seven million) in his class at Cal(cutta) Tech. Economists have noted that people from the bottom of the income distribution tend to be the ones to come to America when the income distribution in their homeland is dispersed.[8] (Think of one Mr. Burns and many Homers.) The reason is that life is hard for them back home, so they migrate. If things are more equal, it is the better off who are more likely to leave and go where the skills will be better rewarded. Although the distribution of income in India is more equal than that of the United States, the reason that a better off, well-educated person such as Apu immigrates is that he can afford the cost of migrating, the last term in our equation.

In the episode, Apu comes to the Springfield Heights Institute of Technology[9] and earns his Ph.D. in computer science. He finds that he must earn money to pay for his education and takes a job as a manager at the Kwik-E-Mart. His experience actually illustrates several very real aspects of migration. First, some people do in fact migrate to the United States illegally or as undocumented migrants. Some cross over the border to avoid detection, but a sizeable share overstay a temporary work or student visa like Apu. Also, each year the United States admits approximately just over one million migrants. As shown in Table 10.1, in 2009 1.1 million migrants were given visas making them legal residents. Two-thirds of such people are allowed in for family reunification. A limited number qualify because they possess special talents. Other immigrants come to the United States for political asylum, and there is even a lottery.

Although careful watchers of *The Simpsons* might recall that Apu's younger brother Sanjay also came to the United States and works at the Kwik-E-Mart, Apu would not have had to take a citizenship test if he had been admitted to the United States as part of family reunification.[10] Having a relative in the place one is going to makes migration easier and reduces the cost. After Apu becomes

TABLE 10.1. Visas issued by the U.S. government in 2009

Relatives and Family	747,413
Employment Preferences	140,903
Refugees and Asylees	177,308
Lottery	47,879
Other	14,124
Total Visas	1,130,818

SOURCE: U.S. Department of Homeland Security (2010).

a citizen he marries Manjula, and she migrates to the United States. Following where family, friends, and people from one's hometown have already gone is common and is called social capital.

Apu also has apparent nonmonetary benefits associated with migrating to the United States. In the "The Two Mrs. Nahasapeemapetilons," Apu enjoys the freedom of being a bachelor in the United States dating many of Springfield's most eligible bachelorettes. However, in "Much Apu About Nothing" he clearly misses his homeland and parents. In addition, Apu must deal with the lack of knowledge about Hinduism that leads people like Homer to try to feed his sacred statue of Ganeesh a peanut.

Migration and Jobs

So what effect do migrants have on the job market? As "Coming to Homerica" illustrated, many migrants come to America to work, and some of those born in the United States (native born) fear a fall in their wages. The wage rate is what economists call the price of labor. One must always remember that every price reflects both a buyer and a seller. A low price is neither a good nor a bad thing. It depends to a large extent on whether you are a buyer or a seller of the good, in this case, labor. Low wage rates are great if you are hiring someone to do something (like plow your driveway after it snows) and not so good if you are getting paid to do the job (being a snow plow operator like Homer as Mr. Plow).

In "Coming to Homerica," we saw the result of this increase in the supply of labor due to the influx of immigrants when the barley farmers from nearby Ogdenville migrated to Springfield. At the start of the episode, the Krusty Burger was declared the unhealthiest fast-food item in the world. In response, Krusty developed the Mother Earth Burger, made with barley and packaged in a green wrapper. (It must have been good for the environment, as Homer declared it eco-licious!) The early orders were good for Ogdenville, as they likely caused more barley to be sold at a higher price (from a shift to the right of the demand). Unfortunately, due to rats getting stuck in the combines the new barley burgers caused people to line up for the bathroom instead of at Krusty Burger. After a hard-hitting news story by local anchor Kent Brockman publicized the problem, barley prices and demand fell (a shift of the demand curve to the left), and Ogdenvillians had no other economic options but to make their way to Springfield.[11]

The Simpson family hired Ogdenvillian immigrants to help with home repairs, to do landscaping, and to be baby Maggie's nanny. This was great for the

Simpsons, since Homer and Marge could spend more time on other activities, but why would some of the residents of Springfield oppose this?

In Figure 10.1 we can see a normal supply-and-demand curve. The only difference is that we are looking at the market for labor in Springfield, and the price is the wage rate, that is, how much workers get paid per hour. The quantity here is the number of people working. When a large number of Ogdenvillians migrated to Springfield, the supply curve shifted to the right and the wage rate fell. This is great if you are Mr. Burns[12] or Homer and hiring people for home repairs, but not if you are a native-born Springfield roofer and your wage rate declines, that is, you get paid less.[13]

So the result of the increased number of workers is that more people are being employed but at a wage of $8 an hour rather than $10. Some of these people will be migrants, and some the native-born workers. This is in fact what does happen. Many of the migrants arriving in the United States have lower levels of education and compete with the lower-wage and less-skilled native-born population. By far, the United States receives more immigrants from Latin American and Asia than from Europe. The typical Latin American migrant has approximately a ninth grade education, while American's average education is high school plus a little college.[14] The native born U.S. citizens with only a high school diploma or less see their wages fall with the increased competition, but

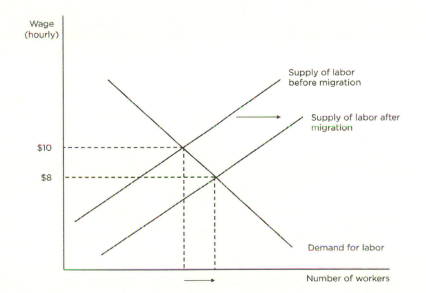

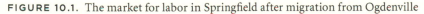

FIGURE 10.1. The market for labor in Springfield after migration from Ogdenville

the more educated portion of the population enjoys lower prices for services such as roofing, landscaping, and child care.[15] Recent work suggests that the impact of migration on average wages is about a negative 1 or 2 percent.[16] Since a large share of immigrants have lower levels of formal education, their impact on less-educated Americans is greater and might be causing their wages to be about 5 percent lower for the native-born, less-educated American workers.[17]

One argument that some people make in favor of immigration is that migrants do jobs that Americans don't want to do. In this example, we might see that Springfield residents don't want to work on roofs for $8 an hour and perhaps the Ogdenville folks will. But we have to remember that if there were no immigration, then the wage would be $10 and some Springfield roofers would want to work for that.[18]

What Can We Thank Immigrants For?

Immigrants get blamed for many problems, but of course there are many benefits to having immigrants in the United States. They increase productivity through innovation, provide us tasty food, and may even lower crime. Typically, when some people think about the jobs that immigrants perform they think of jobs that require physical labor and limited formal education (like the ones the migrants from Ogdenville performed). However, some immigrants such as Apu have advanced degrees, and many of those degrees were earned at U.S. universities. Immigrants such as Albert Einstein or Sergey Brin (Google's cofounder) help improve productivity, increasing wages for all by helping the United States innovate new ideas and technologies.[19]

Like many American cities, Springfield enjoys a large selection of international cuisine, including Italian, Japanese, Thai, and French restaurants run by immigrants. Homer, however, must go to New York to enjoy Klauh Kalesh.[20] A growing body of literature suggests that immigrants may decrease crime in the United States.[21] One explanation for this result might be that illegal immigrants want to avoid getting in trouble for fear of getting deported. Further, migrants tend to be less likely to be criminals in the first place.

Immigration, Taxes, and Government Spending

When Apu became a citizen in "Much Apu About Nothing," he jokingly asked for directions to the welfare office. The possibility of Apu going on welfare demonstrates the concerns about the impact of migration on government expenditures and, as a result, taxes on others to pay for these expenditures. In fact, this sentiment against illegal immigration often increases when governments are financially strapped. In the episode "Much Apu About Nothing," it is the tax created to fund the Bear Patrol that creates the anti-immigrant sentiment.

If people are working without the proper papers, they might be getting paid under the table. With no formal record of their employment, they will not be paying income taxes or social security taxes. When they buy items at the store, though, they will be paying sales tax.[22] In "Much Apu About Nothing," Apu purchased fake papers to stay in the United States.[23] In such a case Apu or other immigrants might pay taxes under their fake identities. One of the interesting aspects of the issue of government finances is government expenditures. In the United States we only require that a student live in the area of a public school district. Citizenship is not required to attend school, and in fact schools are not permitted under federal law from inquiring if students and their families are legally in the country.[24] One can imagine that the taxes Apu pays for his earnings from the Kwik-E-Mart probably do not cover the cost of educating his octuplets.

In looking at health care expenditures, we see that in "Coming to Homerica" Bart attempts to show the Ogdenville kids how to skateboard and breaks his arm in the process. A visit to the hospital results in a long wait, and the only forms available are in Norwegian, the native language of the Ogdenvillians. In reality, hospital emergency rooms are required to treat those with a life-threatening condition regardless of citizenship. As others in this book have noted, economists love to say "people respond to incentives." If people cannot afford regular health care, they have an incentive to not treat a condition until it becomes more serious and hence can be treated for free in an emergency room. This is a rather expensive way to provide health care. Since hospitals cannot ask an emergency room patient about his or her citizenship, we do not know the extent to which undocumented migrants are actually using emergency rooms. Therefore, the amount of care provided to Ogdenvillians and other migrants without proper papers might be substantial or not.

In reality, though, it is difficult to estimate the total impact of immigrants on tax revenues and the cost of the benefits they receive from government programs. First, many immigrants are illegal and therefore not particularly interested in answering surveys, for which question one might be "Are you an illegal immigrant?" A further complicating factor is that political bias can influence assumptions and have an impact on the conclusion.

Borjas provides a review of several studies that attempt to estimate the impact of immigrants on tax revenue and government spending.[25] Most studies start by estimating the amount of taxes paid and the welfare payments received and government services used by immigrants. However, as Borjas points out it is extremely difficult to calculate the cost of providing services such as roads, national defense, or other public goods to immigrants. A more recent study by the nonpolitical government organization called the Congressional Budget Office summarized several studies of the total impact of immigrants on government revenues and expenditures.[26] The study concludes that according to federal revenues and expenditures, illegal and legal immigrants contribute more in taxes than they receive in benefits. At the state and local levels, illegal immigrants may receive more in benefits than they pay in taxes, because state and local governments fund schools and health, two of the main benefits illegal immigrants receive. In total, combining federal, state, and local taxes, the tax revenues of immigrants probably exceed the cost of the government benefits they receive.

Conclusion

We have tried to use *The Simpsons* to help you better understand the issues surrounding migration. Economic models help us better understand why people choose to migrate or remain in their home countries. Clearly, there are benefits to migration. The migrants would not come to a new land and leave home and family if they did not feel it was improvement. A nation that receives migrants enjoys lower prices for many things, a greater variety of products (Klauh Kalesh?), and increased energy and cultural diversity. But, as with most things, there is a cost. An increased supply of labor does reduce wages a bit on average and more so for less-skilled and lower-paid Americans. It appears, however, when all is said and done, that immigrants pay more into the government in taxes than they receive in benefits.

Immigration debates in the United States go back even before Grandpa Simpson was born in "the old country," although he can't remember which one is the old country. You might ask, Is it fair for the citizens of Springfield or the United States to limit migration? Economists generally do not address questions of fairness. Economists do however calculate the cost and benefits to help citizens decide what they think is best.[27] There are many options for the United States in terms of an immigration policy, from closing off our borders to completely open borders. Politically and economically wise policies, however, most likely lie somewhere in between.

For further reading we suggest George Borjas' book *Heaven's Door: Immigration Policy and the American Economy.*[28] Like most other economists, Borjas considers potential U.S. immigration policies by weighing the various factors, including the impacts on people who don't migrate, U.S. workers, the U.S. economy, and government budgets. One possible change in the immigration policy that almost all economists support is increasing the number of visas for educated immigrants and programs that bring in temporary workers, especially in areas where there is a need. It is up to you as a citizen and voter to decide if our government's policies should promote immigration from India and Ogdenville or if you would rather the United States and Springfield live in a bubble like in *The Simpsons Movie*.

11

DONUT AND DIMED

Labor Markets in Springfield

David T. Mitchell

WORK, NOT THE BOY, is Homer Simpson's real bane.[1] Homer hates work and has tried (nearly) every job known to man. He still needs a job to pay for his family and lifestyle, however, and he needs one that pays well enough to have made Frank Grimes jealous. There are two main worries people have about jobs: How available are they? and, What do they pay? In Homer's case, how does he earn enough to pay for his big house? Why is his job at the power plant always awaiting him when he's done working for the city, being Mr. Plow, impersonating Krusty the Clown, or serving as an astronaut? These are questions that economists can help to answer on the basis of their study of labor markets.

Homer lives in a nice house and supports a family of five. In some episodes Maggie has her own room. When added to the master bedroom and Bart and Lisa's rooms, this implies a house with four bedrooms, three bathrooms, and a two-car garage. Marge only occasionally works outside the home for pay. (Probably because taking care of Bart and Homer is equivalent to two full-time jobs!) Given the family's high consumption on only one income, it would seem that Homer isn't doing badly with just his high school diploma. Perhaps Springfield is a really cheap place to live; after all, a local idiot throws a uranium rod out of his car window every week, which can't be good for property values.[2]

Homer has a nice house and a nice life. However, he is the classic Joe Six-pack. He doesn't have a prestigious job, he doesn't invest, and he doesn't seem to understand that spending money on assets that appreciate instead of depreciate leads to more wealth. How does Homer avoid being nickel and dimed to death? How does he afford the good life?

Supply and Demand for Labor

When economists think about labor markets, we think about supply and demand. Most of the time individuals *demand* goods and firms *supply* goods. In labor economics firms *demand* workers and individuals *supply* labor. Workers are the suppliers. Homer supplies labor to Mr. Burns (if you can call what Homer does labor). Mr. Burns and the power plant are demanders of labor. If you think about labor markets in terms of supply and demand, you can easily answer questions about which jobs will be available and which jobs will pay well. Supply and demand can also help us figure out how Homer affords his lifestyle.

For example, thinking about labor markets from the demand side helps us to understand what employers want out of the employer-employee relationship. Why does Mr. Burns hire people to work for him, whether in his power plant or as his prank monkey ("Homer vs. Dignity")? Remember, like all people he is self-interested. Mr. Burns is also greedy and thus not so different from some other real-life employers.[3] His self-interest not only means that he has to get more value from his employees' work than he pays them, it is the very reason he hires them in the first place! After all, it is not as though Mr. Burns likes most of his employees as people—he can't even remember their names! ("Who Shot Mr. Burns?")

So Mr. Burns isn't hiring employees out of love. The more valuable skills an employee brings to an employer, the more the employer is willing to pay, other things being equal. Remember that firms want to hire workers who earn profits for the company. In Figure 11.1, we can see what happens when workers become more profitable. When workers earn more profits for firms, firms want to hire more workers. This shifts the demand curve for labor outward (to the right) from D_1 to D_2. That not only increases the number of workers that firms want to hire, but also pushes up the wage from w_1 to w_2. Firms in need of more employees have to pay higher wages in order to lure workers away from other firms.[4] Over time, these higher wages induce more workers into the industry.

This is one reason why electrical engineering majors earn more than philosophy majors. An electrical engineering major can produce products that employers can sell for a profit. Despite the intellectual value of his degree, the philosophy major may struggle to produce things that consumers will find valuable. This is also why Peyton Manning earns an estimated $27 million a year while economists and nuclear safety inspectors earn a bit less. Peyton

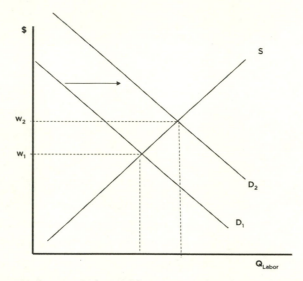

FIGURE 11.1. An increase in demand from increased worker profitability

Manning's unique set of skills helps to win a lot of football games, which helps his team to fill their expensive stadium seats. Homer Simpson's job, on the other hand, could partly be done by a mechanical pigeon ("King-Size Homer"), so his skills are quite common.[5] The more an employee can increase a firm's profits, the more that employee is going to earn.

Table 11.1 shows starting and mid-career salaries for a number of different majors. Students who major in technical fields earn much more money than those with liberal arts degrees. Though Homer easily passed nuclear physics with an A+ with some help from his friends ("Homer Goes to College"), he doesn't appear to be making a mid-career engineer's salary.[6]

People with technical skills earn good money not only because firms have a strong demand for those skills, but also because there is a lower supply of such individuals. Fewer people graduate with technical degrees than with liberal arts degrees, so those with technical degrees earn more on average. If everyone suddenly graduated with aerospace or chemical engineering degrees, average wages for aerospace or chemical engineering degree holders would fall because all the new engineers would compete against each other for jobs. Fortunately for engineers, their coursework is difficult, which limits the supply of engineers. Engineers, therefore, benefit from both sides of the market—supply and demand. There is a strong demand for their services because lots of firms need

TABLE 11.1. Starting and mid-career salaries for various majors

	Starting Median Salary (in $)	Mid-Career Median Salary (in $)
Chemical Engineering	65,700	107,000
Computer Engineering	61,700	105,000
Electrical Engineering	60,200	102,000
Aerospace Engineering	59,600	109,000
Economics	50,200	101,000
Spanish	35,600	52,600
Theology	34,800	51,500
Music	34,000	52,000
Social Work	33,400	41,600
Elementary Education	33,000	42,400

SOURCE: Payscale.com, 2010.

engineering services, and there is a limited supply since the courses are difficult and not intrinsically interesting to most people. Combined, these reasons tend to produce higher-than-average wages.

Competing with the World and Productivity

When Homer agrees to supply labor to the nuclear power plant, he has to earn more than he would elsewhere. Mr. Burns has to pay more than Homer's next best alternative (his *opportunity cost*, in econspeak). So Mr. Burns' demand is based on Homer's productivity, but Homer's supply is based on Homer's other options. The more options Homer has, the more Mr. Burns has to pay Homer to induce him to work at the power plant.[7]

If you wonder why unskilled jobs pay more in the United States than they do in other countries, the reason is that U.S. employers have to pay workers better than their other alternatives. American workers have lots of alternatives. This is why we get immigrants from developing countries such as Scotland and India. Groundskeeper Willie makes more in the United States than he could in Scotland, where there are fewer other opportunities for groundskeepers.[8] Apu makes more money working at the Kwik-E-Mart in the United States than he would as an engineer in India.

Carl Carlson makes clear the point about other options in "The Devil Wears Nada." In that episode, Carl becomes a manager and makes Homer his executive assistant. While Homer does not want to be Carl's assistant, Carl tells him that he can take the job as his assistant or go elsewhere, which isn't hiring. Given the lack of other opportunities, Homer takes the assistant job. The more options employees have, however, the more they can make and the nicer they have to be treated.

In "Kiss Kiss, Bang Bangalore," Mr. Burns tries to hire cheaper workers by moving the plant to India, where labor costs (including benefits) are lower. In the episode, the Indian workers are more productive than American workers.[9] Unfortunately for Mr. Burns, he sends Homer to train them, and Homer teaches them how to be lazy and to demand more breaks. The "retrained" workers then provide Mr. Burns with less output per dollar of wages, causing Mr. Burns to move the plant back to Springfield.

A storyline like this may seem implausible with all the U.S. headlines about jobs going to India or China for cheap labor. However, there is cheap labor in the United States, too, so why don't all the jobs in America go to Mississippi? For example, Mississippi's per capita income is under $16,000, while the U.S. average is over $21,000.[10] Why don't employers save $5,000 per worker by moving all of their jobs to Mississippi?

The reasons are simple. First, Mississippi can't fill every job. Second, what matters is the productivity relative to the wage, and productivity is related to education, willingness to try new ideas, regulations, taxes, and so on. Mississippi might win on low wages but doesn't win on everything else, which is why all the jobs in America haven't moved to Mississippi. Likewise, productivity at the nuclear power plant in India falls after Homer teaches the workers about things like early retirement and Mylar balloons on birthdays.

So skills, productivity, and even the ability to work with others are important. It isn't at all clear that Homer has the first two abilities, but at least he gets along well with his co-workers, who even voted him union head once ("Last Exit to Springfield"). Gil Gunderson, on the other hand, is too depressing to work with and shuffles through one entry-level job after another.[11] He can't sell real estate, shoes, used cars, Springfield Shopper ads, doorbells, or Amway. He can't even make it as a mascot for the WNBA ("Pray Anything")!

Kirk Van Houten is in the same boat, in that others don't want him around and he doesn't have skills that are in demand. After his divorce leads him to being fired from his father-in-law's cracker factory, Kirk can only find a job as an assistant to the person who puts fliers on car windshields ("I Am Furious (Yellow)"). That is not only a job that anyone can do, it is not a job that is crucial to the economy.

Compensating Differentials

Certain jobs are better than others. People will only work at bad jobs if these pay better than other positions they could get. We see this when Homer quits his job at the nuclear power plant to work at the bowling alley in "And Maggie Makes Three." Homer is willing to make less money at the bowling alley because he finds it to be such a pleasant job.[12] Unfortunately for Homer, his circumstances change when Marge gets pregnant with Maggie, forcing him to go back to work at the nuclear power plant in order to make enough to support another child.

When a job with some undesirable characteristic pays more than similar jobs without that characteristic, economists call the difference in pay a "compensating differential." Homer likely earns a compensating differential that takes into account the increased danger from working at a nuclear power plant compared to the Gulp 'n' Blow.[13] The higher pay is necessary for Mr. Burns to get enough workers, since most people wouldn't want to work in a place where you get a uranium rod stuck in your clothes every day or are made to eat nuclear waste as punishment for being late.[14] Once we understand the notion of compensating differentials, it is more understandable that Homer keeps working at the power plant. Not only does he need the money to support his family in their nice house, but if it weren't dangerous there would be lots of other people lining up to take the job.

Other episodes illustrate how the pleasantness of a job influences wages. In "Million Dollar Maybe," Lisa buys a Funtendo Zii Sports game for Grandpa and the other residents of the nursing home. After playing the game the patients become more active, which in turn causes the nurses to have to work harder. Apparently the nurses are only paid enough to deal with docile patients, since they ruin the Funtendo Zii by putting it in the dishwasher. The patients return to their old docile selves, and the nurses are happy with their wages relative to the effort they have to put forth. While it is wrong to treat patients this way, this episode says quite a bit about the importance of work environment as a part of compensation.

Labor Markets for Skilled and Unskilled Workers

It is important to keep in mind that in many ways there are two labor markets.[15] First, there is the labor market for skilled workers. These are the workers who have had lengthy training and bring in lots of profit for their employers. The other labor market is for unskilled workers. An illustration of the difference between the markets for skilled and unskilled labor is shown in Figure 11.2. Unskilled positions are easily replaced because employers won't have to spend

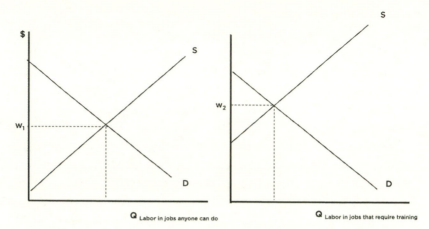

FIGURE 11.2. An increase in demand from increased worker profitability

large amounts of time and money getting new employees ready to work. Spreading tar in the hot summer sun is a horrible job, but it doesn't pay better than accounting, which mostly takes place in air-conditioned offices. The person spreading tar earns a compensating differential compared to other unskilled jobs, but not compared to skilled jobs.

An accountant is skilled labor. The accountant who works in a pleasant environment makes less than the accountant who has to go work somewhere else—Afghanistan, for instance. If the accountant in the undesirable environment didn't make a compensating differential, she would leave for a better placement. But the accountant who works in a nice environment doesn't make less than the guy spreading tar. The guy spreading tar would love to have a high-paying job in air conditioning, but it is costly and difficult to train for the better job. This is why Dr. Hibbert makes more than Groundskeeper Willie.

On the other side of the market there is demand for workers. Mr. Burns would love to have Homer, Lenny, and Carl work for nothing. However, if Springfield Nuclear Power Plant paid nothing, Mr. Burns would find himself without employees. The compensation Mr. Burns has to pay his employees is related to how easily workers can be replaced, either by other workers or by technology. For example, in "Last Exit to Springfield," the workers strike to keep a dental plan, causing Mr. Burns to try to replace them with robots. Only when Burns realizes that the workers can't easily be replaced by robots is he willing to meet the union's demands.

Employee Benefits

Both "Kiss Kiss, Bang Bangalore" and "Last Exit to Springfield" clearly demonstrate that benefits are part of pay. They reduce profitability for firms. Employers have to pay benefits, and this makes them more reluctant to hire workers. Employers who are reluctant to hire workers can make jobs scarcer. When jobs are scarce, employees have to compete against each other more fiercely, and that leads to lower wages.

Sometimes, however, employee benefits are helpful to both employee and employer. If the employees value something that the employer can provide more cheaply in bulk, there can be a real benefit. A traditional example would be health insurance. Sometimes a firm can purchase group insurance at a lower rate than an individual could buy it at. In this case it makes sense for the employer to provide insurance to employees. Keep in mind that employees are still paying for the insurance in lower wages. Just think about what happens when insurance rates go up. Either employees have to pay a higher rate, raises get smaller, or wages go down.

In "Once Upon a Time in Springfield," the nuclear plant gets rid of donuts as one of the employee benefits. A headhunter overhears that the workers are dissatisfied and offers them more money. This is a great example of employees making their boss compete against other employers. But we also find out that Homer and his friends are willing to give up the higher pay for better donuts back at the Springfield nuclear plant.

Naturally, employers wish to keep the costs of employee benefits down, because providing the benefit at a lower cost increases profits. In "King-Size Homer," Mr. Burns starts a mandatory exercise program to keep health costs down. Unfortunately for Mr. Burns, it has unintended consequences. Homer decides that working *and* exercising is so miserable that he would rather get so fat he's disabled.[16] Mr. Burns ends up paying more money and having a nuclear meltdown. Perhaps next time he will get the incentives right, with overtime for fit workers, higher pay for fit workers, and so on.

Entrepreneurship: Another Key to Not Being Nickel and Dimed[17]

Homer avoids being nickel and dimed to death by taking a job that has some risk (radiation), getting some hard-to-get qualifications (A+ in nuclear physics), and being entrepreneurial. He doesn't like his job so he does something about it. Instead of going the traditional route of getting additional degrees, like Frank Grimes, he sometimes gets part-time jobs, such as working for Apu at the Kwik-E-Mart ("Lisa's Pony"). Homer's favorite way to deal with his misery, however, is to try starting his own business. Here are but a few examples of Homer's entrepreneurial ventures:

- Day care center operator ("Children of a Lesser Clod")
- Music agent and manager ("Colonel Homer")
- Internet entrepreneur ("Das Bus")
- Trash picker ("Days of Wine and D'oh'ses")
- Freak at a rock show ("Homerpalooza")
- Safety inspector ("Homer's Odyssey")
- Bar owner ("In the Name of the Grandfather")
- Grease collector ("Lard of the Dance")
- Snow plow operator ("Mr. Plow")
- Happiness telemarketer ("Lisa's Date with Density")
- Tow truck operator ("Midnight Towboy")
- Chicken pox infector ("Milhouse of Sand and Fog")
- Casino owner in a third world country ("Missionary Impossible")
- Pants marketer ("My Fair Laddy")
- Bail bondsman ("Sex, Pies and Idiot-Scrapes")
- Sugar smuggler ("Sweets and Sour Marge")
- Gay marriage officiate: ("There's Something About Marrying")

It is unclear how Homer is able to return to his job at the Springfield Nuclear Power Plant after leaving to start these businesses. He must be a very valuable employee, since Mr. Burns doesn't seem like the kind of boss who's interested in hiring employees out of the goodness of his heart. Maybe Homer's serial entrepreneurship creates regular reminders for Mr. Burns of how valuable Homer is to the bottom line. Or it could be that Mr. Burns just thinks that Homer is going to eventually do something right on the basis of random chance.[18]

Just the Right Amount of Searching

Jobs pay better when there is high demand because the skills in that area bring revenues to the employer. Jobs also pay better when there is low supply because no one else wants to or is able to do the job. If you want to get paid well, make sure you have valuable skills or are willing to do things no one else wants to or is able to do. If you have a job for which you are valuable and other employers want to hire you, it is important to remind your employer of how valuable your skills are. You should also be actively looking for other positions, because competing offers are an excellent way to remind your boss of your value.

The dilemma that workers face is that if you are always trying to find a new job your boss won't put you on the big important projects or send you out for training. The reasoning will be that whatever skills you have will immediately be taken elsewhere. Without the skills and experience from the big projects and new training, however, employees will be stuck at their current positions and pay levels. This means that employees need to *occasionally* remind their supervisors that there are other positions available that pay better or have better working conditions.

Signaling

Why do college graduates in general make more money than non-college graduates—in fact, nearly double?[19] In some cases, it is because some college degrees impart skills that are in demand by employers because they will help the firms satisfy customer demands. College is certainly a place where hard skills such as accounting, financial analysis, and technical writing are learned. A college education often imparts soft skills such as learning how to learn, doing research in a team, and getting along with weird roommates. In fact, much of what people learn in college is designed to broaden student horizons in order to help students see the big picture and put things in context.

Unfortunately, there are many positions for which employers don't necessarily value that knowledge. If employers don't value it, why do they pay college graduates more? One answer is that a college degree acts like a signal of what sort of person you are.[20] Everyone's resume states that they are hardworking, smart, and detail oriented.[21] However, employers know that not everyone is hard working, smart, and detail oriented.[22]

How can an employer like Mr. Burns figure out who is actually detail oriented? Anyone who makes it through the maze of college must not only be smart, but also practiced in following rules. Part of the reason that employers prefer college graduates is their skills, but part of the reason is also that a college degree says that you have intelligence and diligence. Employers prefer those qualities in employees.

This explains why a G.E.D. is not as valuable as a high school diploma. The eight-hour G.E.D. exam tests people on the general knowledge that they would have gotten in high school. Empirical research suggests that people with a G.E.D. earn significantly less on average than people with a high school diploma. Why does a high school diploma pay better? People who are able to stick out high school have more "stick with it," which employers value.[23]

Of course, sometimes people get hired not because they increase profits but because of government mandates or incentives. In "Homer Defined," we find out that Homer was part of one such program, called "Project Bootstrap." Why Homer wasn't fired when Project Bootstrap ended can only be because he is immune to radiation. Such a unique trait would not be surprising, given that Dr. Hibbert has already diagnosed him with an absolutely unique genetic condition known as "Homer Simpson Syndrome."[24] Perhaps he is also immune to radiation, which would be rare and valuable and might explain why he's kept his job so long. If so, maybe he should ask for a raise.

Conclusion

So Homer avoids being nickel and dimed by a minimum-wage lifestyle because he doesn't earn a minimum wage. Homer affords his nice house and lifestyle by earning above minimum wage. He even gets to have lobster for dinner ("Homer's Enemy"). Homer accomplishes this lifestyle by doing several things. He has a rare ability—an inability to be affected by radiation or punches to the head. He earns a compensating differential by working at a dangerous nuclear power plant. He also isn't afraid to try new things. By leaving his job for other positions both within his industry and outside his industry, he lets his boss know that his skills are valuable. That, or Operation Bootstrap could still be in effect.

12

PAGING DR. HIBBERT

What *The Simpsons* Can Teach Us About Health Economics

Lauren Heller

WITH THE RISE IN HEALTH CARE COSTS over the past few decades and the recent passage of health care legislation, issues in health economics have been on the minds of many Americans. What we may not realize, however, is that *The Simpsons* has been trying to teach us health economics for years. Through a satirical and witty view of the world, the town of Springfield has poked fun at many of the main issues in health and health care that are being debated in cities and towns throughout the United States today.

Most of the major issues in the economics of health care provision can be related back to two main concepts: asymmetric information and the role of third-party payers for health services. One of the fundamental assumptions common to most basic economic theories is the idea of perfect information. Economists typically assume that all parties in a transaction know all of the pertinent facts necessary in order to make an informed decision. Usually, this assumption works pretty well and allows us to focus on the aspects of an economic problem that are most relevant to its solution. This assumption is invalid, however, when we look at the current structure of health care provision in most countries. Doctors tend to know more about available treatments than patients do, and patients usually know more about their own health status than insurance companies do. This is further complicated by a complex system of government regulations and third-party payers that prevent any of these parties in a health care transaction (doctors, patients, and insurance companies) from knowing the true costs and consumer valuations for health services.

Matt Groening and the other creators of *The Simpsons* have not been oblivious to the increasing complexities of health care provision that have evolved over the years. In fact, scenes from many episodes centrally focus on such information problems, causing a great deal of discussion about health care policy over dinner tables and around water coolers across America. Indeed, the Simpson family can teach us a great deal about health economics, and in this chapter we will discuss these lessons in detail.

The Demand for Health and Health Care
The demand for health care services is a derived demand: we do not usually derive happiness from visiting the doctor, but from the increased level of health that visiting the doctor promotes. We demand most other types of goods, such as movie tickets, because we expect to directly enjoy the benefits that those goods provide. In contrast, it is unlikely that many of us enjoy visiting the doctor because we receive a high level of enjoyment from the experience of the visit itself. Instead, we visit the doctor because we anticipate that the visit will result in an increased level of health, which will make us happier in the future. In addition, because the choices we make in life can directly affect our health status later on, we as people are both consumers and producers of good (or bad) health.

The Simpsons teaches us about the health impacts of lifestyle choices in almost every episode. Every time Homer eats a donut, he is sacrificing the health benefits of reduced weight and cardiovascular fitness later on for the joys of sprinkles and frosting today. An economist would say that when it comes to donuts, Homer has an increased rate of time preference: he values the "here and now" more heavily than he values potential gains that he could realize in the future.[1] Homer isn't the only resident of Springfield who discounts the future in this way. For example, when Krusty the Clown visits Homer in the hospital before a heart bypass operation, he attempts to assuage Homer's fears by telling him that he's also in the zipper club ("Homer's Triple Bypass"). Krusty then pulls open his shirt, exposing a heart surgery scar, and promptly begins to smoke a cigarette. It's evident that Krusty values the nicotine from his cigarette more highly than the prevention of pain from a future operation.[2]

A person's rate of time preference matters greatly in the production of individual health and well-being, because in most cases, healthy lives are built over time rather than through a single hospital visit. The choices we make every day with regard to diet, exercise, and other habits affect the probability that we will demand health care services in the future. A prominent health economist named Michael Grossman created a model to explain this phenomenon.[3] In Grossman's model, an individual receives an initial "stock" of health at birth, which can vary according to genetics or other factors. The individual can then make investments in his or her health stock over time, either through the consumption of health services (such as doctor visits) or through time spent in health-producing activities (such as exercise). As people in the model get older, their health depreciates, which increases the cost of maintaining a given level of health. People make choices over their lifetimes in order to maximize utility (happiness), taking into account their ability to produce health, their budget, and the limited amount of time they have available.

The Grossman model is important because it teaches us that health is an investment good, requiring a steady stream of inputs over time. When our health fails and we require medical services to restore our health stock, usually our demand for those services is relatively inelastic. This is especially true if an adverse health event is life-threatening. Once again, *The Simpsons* can be relied upon to illustrate this concept. When Homer has a heart attack and requires a bypass operation, Marge tells Dr. Hibbert that they'll do anything necessary to get Homer healthy ("Homer's Triple Bypass"). When Dr. Hibbert warns them that the bypass will cost $30,000, Homer has a second heart attack, raising the price to $40,000.

When people will pay almost anything to obtain a given good or service, it means that their demand for that service is inelastic: as the market price of the good or service rises, people only reduce the quantity they will consume by a small amount. This implies that as the price for the good rises, so does the total amount spent on that good by consumers. If the demand for health care services is inelastic, it means that, all else equal, an increase in the price for those services will result in a corresponding increase in total expenditures for health care. This is one way that we can begin to understand the rise in health expenditures over time, as shown in Figure 12.1.

Asymmetric Information and Physician Agency

The inelastic demand for health services is very much complicated by the fact that there are vast differences in access to information both within and across various health care markets. In most health care transactions, the distribution of information relevant to the transaction is asymmetric: one party has more information than another. In the case of doctor-patient relationships, it is often true that doctors know more about a given illness and its treatment than

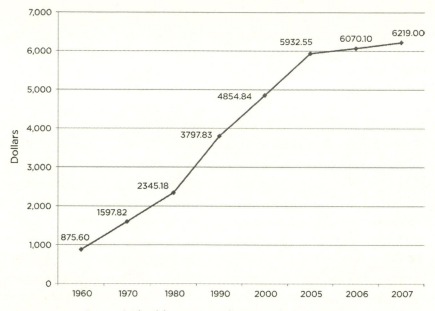

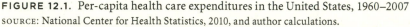

FIGURE 12.1. Per-capita health care expenditures in the United States, 1960–2007
SOURCE: National Center for Health Statistics, 2010, and author calculations.

patients do. After all, a doctor's skills and medical knowledge are a main reason
for visiting him or her in the first place. In many ways a doctor can resemble
an auto mechanic: both know more about the item they are repairing than the
consumer, and both can use this information to their advantage in some way.[4]
In addition, the markets for both car repairs and medical procedures involve
what economists would call "supplier-induced demand," in which the supplier
of the good or service facilitates the consumer's demand for the same good.

Doctors may be able to use this information to exaggerate the need for surgeries or to overprescribe medication. This tendency is illustrated nicely by an
episode of *The Simpsons* in which an orthodontist tells the family that Lisa will
need braces by showing them increasingly disturbing pictures of Lisa as she ages
without braces ("Last Exit to Springfield"). The final picture the doctor displays
is of Lisa with massively crooked teeth, with one tooth emerging through the
top of her skull. In other words, the incentive exists for doctors to motivate patients to undergo procedures that they might not otherwise demand.

Though laws regarding informed consent exist in the United States and
other countries as a protection mechanism for patients, patients are severely

limited in their abilities to be truly informed regarding medical procedures. Even if a doctor makes the best attempts to explain a given procedure to a patient, the patient may never be able to fully comprehend all of the relative risks and benefits of a procedure without completing medical training. In the episode "Homer's Triple Bypass," Dr. Hibbert tries valiantly to dumb things down for Homer when he explains to Homer that he has to undergo a coronary bypass operation. Even at its simplest, however, Homer still asked for it to be dumbed down some more.

Some who have read this chapter up to this point may be tempted to blame all of the recent increases in health care costs on overutilization on the part of physicians. It is important to recognize, however, that there are a variety of incentives, other than a physician's desire for additional income, that motivate doctors and other prescribers to recommend additional surgeries and medications to patients. Some of these incentives stem from the supply side of the health care market—namely, pharmaceutical companies and other suppliers of medical tools and equipment. As with any other firm, it is in a pharmaceutical company's best interest to increase the demand for the goods it produces among individuals who decide whether or not to purchase its products. In the case of prescription drugs, it is doctors who choose the medications that their patients consume. Encouraging doctors to prescribe their medications, then, is one way for pharmaceutical companies to increase profits.

This is illustrated quite humorously in an episode of *The Simpsons* titled "Midnight Rx," in which Kent Brockman (Springfield's most famous news anchor) reports on the lengths to which citizens of Springfield will go to obtain cheap prescriptions. Brockman follows up with a commentary, noting that more reasonable drug prices would eliminate the need for such efforts. As the newscast cuts to a video feed of Dr. Hibbert wearing a hat that says Allegra and large pieces of "bling" in the shape of the names Celebrex and Prilosec, Brockman asks him if he agrees. Hibbert not only disagrees, he introduces viewers to the dancing Pfizer girls while Sir Mix-A-Lot's song "Baby Got Back" plays.

In addition to the pressure exerted on them by pharmaceutical companies, doctors in today's world face an even more daunting challenge: the risk of lawsuits for medical malpractice. Most doctors carry large malpractice insurance policies to guard against lawsuits, but the premiums for these policies have become increasingly expensive, adding substantially to a physician's costs of doing business. Dr. Nick is Springfield's prime example of a physician who needs to worry about malpractice suits. In an episode from the fourth season, he calls out to the observers seated in the operating theater as he begins surgery to not get the police involved if something goes awry ("Homer's Triple Bypass"). Most credible physicians aren't like Dr. Nick, however, and take a variety of steps to ensure that they provide quality care to their patients. One of the easiest ways to do this is to recommend any procedure that has the potential to provide a marginal benefit to their patient, regardless of marginal costs. A doctor could potentially be sued if he or she does not recommend a procedure and the patient experiences complications as a result. If there is any doubt as to whether a procedure is necessary, in an environment of high litigation costs it is in a doctor's best interest to err on the side of recommending that procedure at the margin.[5]

Doctors may take other steps to reduce their lawsuit risk, including having patients sign detailed waivers and other paperwork to limit their potential liability in the event that something goes wrong. In an episode in which Homer decides to donate a kidney to Grampa Simpson, he reaches the front desk of the hospital and is promptly handed a liability waiver ("Homer Simpson in: Kidney Trouble").

It's not just patients who are faced with a level of uncertainty regarding medical procedures. Doctors face uncertainty as well, and can never be sure that they are presented with a full medical history for each patient. In a particularly comical *Simpsons* episode in which Homer cuts off his thumb, Marge is taking Homer to the hospital when he asks her to lie about how the thumb got cut off ("Trilogy of Error"). He wants her to tell the doctor that she cut it off because she caught him in bed with four women. Though the origin of Homer's thumb amputation may not be particularly useful to the doctor in this case, there are many cases in which a doctor will not know the full "story" behind a patient's injuries. Without full information, a doctor may decide to "play it safe" and recommend additional tests or procedures. Given this and the other incentives discussed earlier, it is no wonder that a doctor's best interest is to prescribe additional treatments at the margin.

The Role of Information, Third-Party Payers, and the Demand for Health Insurance

To complicate the situation even further, health insurance markets in the United States make it such that most people do not actually face the true prices of the health care services that they receive. Unlike other types of insurance, such as homeowner and car insurance, a large percentage of the U.S. population receives health care benefits through their employers. These health insurance benefits are exempt from federal income tax, giving an implicit subsidy to employers to reallocate a portion of the wages that they otherwise would pay employees toward insurance premiums.[6] As marginal tax rates have increased over time, this incentive has become increasingly pronounced.[7] This implicit subsidy has caused consumers to purchase more health care than they otherwise would in a free market. As Figures 12.2 and 12.3 indicate, the role of "third-party payers," including government and private health insurance, has become increasingly pronounced in the United States over time. Meanwhile, the share that individuals actually pay for health services has decreased substantially.[8] This overprovision of health insurance creates increased distance between the price faced by a consumer and the true price of health services.

Asymmetric information plays an even more pivotal role in the case of health insurance. Suppose for the moment that a person is perfectly healthy and does not expect to face high health expenses in the future. This person would likely have a reduced willingness to pay for health insurance, because he or she does not expect to accrue very many benefits from the policy. Conversely, a sick person who thinks that he or she will face higher health costs in the future will have a much greater desire to obtain health insurance than a healthy person.

Unfortunately for health insurance companies, the ability to figure out which applicants for health insurance will incur high health costs in the future is limited. In most cases, applicants know a great deal more about their own health status than health insurance companies. For example, Homer Simpson applies for insurance with the Merry Widow Insurance Company shortly after having a heart attack ("Homer's Triple Bypass"):

Agent: Now, before we give you health insurance, I have to ask you a few questions.

Homer: Questions? Questions?! D'oh, my whole scheme down the . . . I mean, ask away.

Agent: Well good. Now, under heart attacks, you crossed out three, and wrote zero.

Homer: [laughing] Oh, I thought that said brain hemorrhages.

Agent: Ah ha. And do you drink?

Homer: I do enjoy a snifter of port at Christmas.

Agent: All right. Here's your policy.

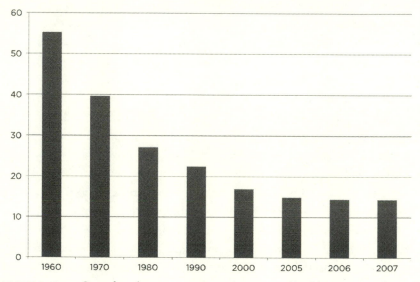

FIGURE 12.2. Out-of-pocket payments as a percentage of health care expenditures, 1960–2007
SOURCE: National Center for Health Statistics, 2010.

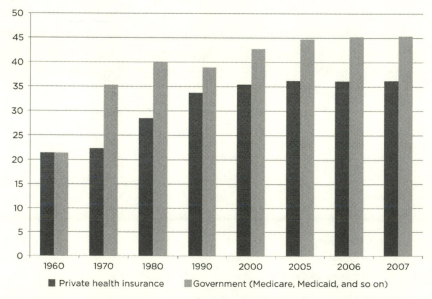

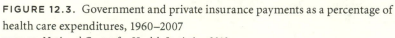

FIGURE 12.3. Government and private insurance payments as a percentage of health care expenditures, 1960–2007
SOURCE: National Center for Health Statistics, 2010.

Homer: Now let me tell you something, Mr. Sucker. I just. . . .

Agent: Oh, hold on there, you still have to sign it.

Homer: Oh . . .

[*Homer* picks up a pen and then has a heart attack in front of the agent]

Homer: Must. Sign. Policy.

Agent: Sir, I'm sorry, we can't insure you.

Homer: I made an H.

Agent: No, that doesn't count.

Homer: It's like an X. [collapses].

Agent: We'd better get you to a hospital.

Homer: Can I have a free calendar?

Agent: Okay.

Most applicants for insurance aren't quite as obvious as Homer, but the principle remains the same. The propensity for sick patients to purchase health insurance more often than healthy patients is an example of what economists call "adverse selection." When high-cost patients demand insurance at an increased rate, this increases insurance premiums for everyone in the pool of insurance applicants.

Information problems don't cease to exist once consumers obtain health care coverage. In fact, in some cases these problems can become even more pronounced. For example, health insurance serves to decrease the costs that consumers face when they purchase health care goods. Basic economic theory tells us that when the price of an item decreases, people tend to consume more of that item. This law of demand applies to everything from movie tickets to sports cars to even the most basic health services, such as visits to a primary care physician. When coinsurance rates for health coverage are low, the effective price of a medical visit is also correspondingly low. Rational people, following economic incentives, will tend to consume more of these services than they would without insurance. This tendency is known as "moral hazard" to economists who study insurance markets.

Again, the town of Springfield comes to the rescue to show us that people make different choices regarding the use of medical services when they face different levels of insurance coverage. In "Midnight Rx," a large number of local companies follow the lead of the Springfield Nuclear Power Plant and cancel their prescription drug plans. This causes the citizens of Springfield to seek alternative sources of prescription drugs or alternative treatments. Krusty the Clown asks his viewers to raid their parent's medicine cabinets for lithium dibromide to help treat his bipolar disorder, while Chief Wiggum uses pills from the evidence locker to medicate Ralph.

Why is the town of Springfield willing to go to such great lengths to obtain medications at a reduced price when their prescription coverage is cancelled? One answer to this question can be found using economics. The subsidization of medical treatment through insurance leads not only to an increased number of services purchased but to increased prices for the drugs and medical procedures themselves. When patients are induced to consume health services by artificially low prices, the pharmaceutical companies and other suppliers of medical services face an elevated demand for their products: at every price charged by the producers of health-related goods, people are willing to consume more of these goods. In response, the "market" price of these goods increases.

The increased utilization of health services due to moral hazard is not a costless phenomenon in society. Economists are famous for saying that "there's no such thing as a free lunch," and this unequivocally applies to the health insurance industry. Insurance companies are well aware of the incentives facing consumers who purchase their policies and adjust the premiums that they charge for these policies accordingly. Every time a person receives an unnecessary medical test or procedure that he or she would not pay for if facing 100 percent of the cost, this raises the overall cost of doing business for the insurance company by raising the expected amount that insurance companies anticipate that they will pay out to policyholders. The increase in market prices for health care goods exacerbates this problem. In this way, elevated charges for medical care raise the costs of insurance policies in general.

The Supply Side: Government Regulation and Licensing

If providing health-related goods and services is such a lucrative business, why don't more people become doctors? If prescription drugs sell for such high prices, why don't more firms produce them? One of the ways we can begin answering these questions is to look at the obstacles facing potential suppliers in health care markets, otherwise known as "barriers to entry."

It's not easy to obtain a medical degree in the United States. Aspiring physicians must complete four years of medical school and usually three to four years of training in the field, known as "residency." After that, many of them decide to complete additional years of training to become specialists. Before they can do any of this, college graduates face one of the biggest barriers to entry in the health field: getting into medical school. Several economists have argued that physicians restrict entry into their own field by exerting control over medical school admissions and physician licensure through the American Medical Association. In addition, medical schools are in large part funded by outside donors, including government agencies, and receive a relatively smaller portion of revenue from student tuition. For this reason, medical schools have fewer incentives to increase enrollments. This shortage of medical school slots restricts the number of practicing physicians that are able to enter the field each year.[9]

One might ask, however, whether it might be a good thing that becoming a doctor is so difficult. After all, not many patients want to see a physician as incompetent as Springfield's Dr. Nick, who repeatedly botches medical procedures and offers a free Chinese finger trap with every brain surgery. Regardless of one's beliefs about whether or not physicians like Dr. Nick should be permitted to remain in business, the fact remains that there are fewer doctors treating patients in the United States today because of the barriers to entry that potential doctors face. This shortage can be at least partially explained by the large investments required for medical education and the licensing of physicians by state governments.

When restrictions exist on the sale of a product or service, it's almost inevitable that black markets will develop to provide that service outside of such restrictions. We see this phenomenon repeatedly in episodes of *The Simpsons*, often in reference to black markets for medical care. When Homer has a crayon removed from his brain and loses his subnormal intelligence, he becomes increasingly unhappy with the world around him ("HOMR"). When he attempts to get the crayon reinserted into his brain, no licensed physician will perform the procedure, but a doctor gives him the business card of Moe Szyslak (Homer's bartender), who performs the surgery instead. In another episode, when Homer loses a thumb and his HMO won't cover surgery, one of Fat Tony's henchmen performs the procedure ("Trilogy of Error"). When we look at potential restrictions on the provision of medical care, we can rely on *The Simpsons* to show us that market mechanisms will develop to provide such services despite these regulations.[10]

Conclusion

We can observe a great deal about the world of health care by watching the Simpson family as they go about their daily lives. If we learn a few lessons from their adventures, what might they be? With their help, we might be able to explain the rise in health care costs in the United States with increased clarity. They have shown us that health markets are fraught with information asymmetries, and that these asymmetries lead to increased costs for patients, doctors, and insurance companies. We also know that the subsidization of health insurance in our tax system leads to increases in both the amount of insurance coverage for health services and the quantity of health services demanded. Other regulations affecting physician training and licensure limit the supply of doctors to the market, further contributing to cost increases. Perhaps the most important lesson that they can teach us, though, is that the system of health care in the United States is much more complicated than it seems at first glance, and that we must carefully account for all of the competing incentives and unintended consequences of our actions whenever we think about health care policy.

13

AT FIRST I THOUGHT PROHIBITION WAS A GOOD THING

The Economics of Alcohol Control

Mark Thornton

HOMER SIMPSON CAN BE CHARACTERIZED as many things, but in terms of casual political economy he is a representative member of the drinking class.[1] This class is very large and diverse. It reaches down to include the lowest wretches on the income distribution scale, up through the middle class, and on up to the highest levels of achievement and wealth. It includes males and females; young and old; and all races, nationalities, and most religions.

The drinking class is not generally to be admired, and the best we can typically offer them is our pity and acceptance. On occasion we can root for them and celebrate their successes, even if these are only the result of dumb luck. More frequently, however, the drinking class is offered scorn and hostility for its lifestyle and its seeming disinterest in the more sophisticated aspects of life such as hygiene, nutrition, rules of the road, and parental responsibilities. Nonetheless, economic science must remain objective regarding individual choices if it ever hopes to understand human action and contribute anything to the betterment of society.

Among other such "classes" in society are the zealots and the stars. The zealots include priests, ministers, rabbis, mullahs, shamans, witch doctors, fortune tellers, evangelicals, fundamentalists, and hermits. The star class includes movie stars, sports heroes, and politicians, as well as those who reach the pinnacle of success in their professions. There are star musicians, artists, explorers, scientists, writers, chefs, and even economists.

The big difference between the drinking class on the one hand, and the zealots and stars on the other, is that zealots and stars are defined by their "goodness." In contrast, members of the drinking class are defined by their character flaws and their general mediocrity in terms of ability and performance. Zealots lose membership to their class when a flaw is discovered. For example, recall the infidelity and "falls from grace" of such luminary zealots as the Reverends Jimmy Swaggart, Ted Haggard, and Jim Baker. Zealots can be "reborn," but their reputations often remain tarnished.

Stars must also be "good," though typically not as good as zealots. As Tiger Woods and Britney Spears have demonstrated, bad behavior can create the risk of becoming "fallen stars." Politicians—especially the zealous ones—seem to have a particularly hard time maintaining their "class." For example, New York Attorney General Elliott Spitzer, Senators Larry Craig and David Vitter, Congressmen Mark Foley and Newt Gingrich, and even President Clinton have all lost public approval, at least temporarily, due to their bad behavior. Zealous media stars such as Bill O'Reilly and Rush Limbaugh have also faced the possibility of losing their star status when they seemed to be preaching one lifestyle but living another.

The appeal of Homer Simpson and the citizens of Springfield is that regular people can identify with them. Like the customers of *Cheers*, Homer seems for most people to be a closer representation of reality than the zealots and stars. People are by their nature imperfect; we "fall from grace" on a regular basis. It often seems impossible for us to stick by our decisions regarding even the most simple of daily activities such as dieting, exercise, and entertainment choices. The challenge for economic science then is to construct economic theory that can be successfully applied to real people who are not robots, but who are nonetheless keen to follow their self-interest.

Ironically, one of the reasons for the enduring success of this fictional cartoon TV series has been its close alignment with "reality." Episodes have been based on zealots such as Homer's neighbor Ned Flanders, or on stars such as Alec Baldwin and Joe Namath, but all the *real* action revolves around the comical everyday life of the Simpson family. It is this reality that makes the economics and politics of the show flow so naturally and realistically. In the episode "Homer vs. The Eighteenth Amendment," Springfield becomes the stage for a reenactment of America's "Noble Experiment" with alcohol prohibition, with Homer playing the role of hero.[2]

Bootleggers and Baptists: The Politics of Prohibition

The episode opens with a riot breaking out during the St. Patrick's Day parade in Springfield. Bart accidentally becomes intoxicated, and as he staggers down Main Street, Channel 6 newscaster Kent Brockman calls for a return to the "antiquated notion" of Prohibition. While Marge is busy feeling guilty and considering herself the world's worst mom, a mob of angry women marches on City Hall demanding that the government "think of the children" and enact a law prohibiting alcohol. Government officials offer a feeble defense of alcohol that includes arguments such as alcohol makes women appear more attractive and virtually all of their heroes were either drunks or drug addicts.

Economics offers an explanation for the persistence of failed policies such as prohibition. "Bootleggers and Baptists" is the title of a political model first suggested by Bruce Yandle to explain how unpopular legislation is enacted.[3] When it comes to prohibition and blue laws (which prevent the sale of alcohol on Sundays), Yandle shows how opposites can sometimes attract. Both the Baptist minister and the bootlegger support the continuation of prohibition; the first does so in order to keep his congregation sober while the latter does it to keep booze prices high and to keep out legal competitors.[4] The Baptist and Bootlegger model has also been applied to other regulations such as environmental laws.[5] For example, it is in the interest of both environmental groups and some big oil companies to limit the amount of oil drilling. The environmental groups want to protect the environment while the big oil companies want to keep the price of oil high.

But how does a law as discriminatory and unpopular as Prohibition get passed in the first place? There certainly were many Baptists and other Protestants in favor of it. And there were also a substantial number of bootleggers, thanks to state- and county-level prohibitions already in existence.[6] Yet a policy such as alcohol prohibition requires a tremendous amount of support and political effort to become successful on the national level, and it is difficult to imagine that these two groups alone could have sufficed to mobilize such a campaign.

Both the Baptist and the bootlegger, along with other elements related to the adoption of prohibition, are portrayed in the opening scenes of this episode. The targeting of minority groups is another such element. In this episode of *The Simpsons*, it is the Irish Americans who are stereotyped as drunks that pose a danger to society. In American history, German, Irish, and Italian immigrant groups were the actual targets of Prohibition, while Native Americans,

Chinese immigrants, African Americans, and Mexican immigrants were the targets of various other prohibitions.[7]

In addition to discrimination against minority groups, Prohibition required other elements as well, including a "muckraking" media, ideological interest groups, and an "easy target." Linking Springfield with Prohibition, we find newscaster Kent Brockman filling the role of the muckraking media. In the real era of Prohibition, the muckrakers were socialist-leaning journalists and writers of the Progressive Era who supported political reforms such as Prohibition. The angry women in Springfield's City Hall represent the Women's Christian Temperance Union (WCTU)—an ideological, single-issue organization that had several hundred thousand members during the Prohibition years. The WCTU is comparable to today's pro- and anti-abortion rights groups or Mothers Against Drunk Driving (MADD). The members of the WCTU marched in the streets, disrupted saloons, and worked in political campaigns to pass Prohibition. Last, alcohol is made an "easy target," given the lame arguments offered by politicians and law enforcement officials.[8]

The actual adoption of Prohibition was a long and messy process. In fact, it took more than a century to achieve a national prohibition on alcohol. The writers of *The Simpsons* simplified matters by assuming that the prohibition was already in place. Here, the city clerk discovers that alcohol was prohibited in Springfield two hundred years ago. The historical reality was that while some Americans had always wanted to prohibit alcohol, alcohol taxes had long been an important source of government revenues since the beginning of the nation. The passage of the Sixteenth Amendment—the income tax—provided an alternative to alcohol taxes and thus made Prohibition financially feasible. When the Great Depression hit in 1929, the revenue from the income tax declined and created a strong incentive to repeal Prohibition and bring back alcohol taxes.[9]

The Economics of Prohibition

America has been experimenting with prohibitions—particularly alcohol prohibition—since the early colonial period. The United States is the world leader in the "War on Drugs," and we have prohibitions on gambling, prostitution, insider trading, and much more. So far, all the experiments have failed. Yet the biggest failure of all was the Eighteenth Amendment to the U.S. Constitution. Beginning in 1920 it instituted a complete ban on the production, distribution, and sale of alcoholic beverages.[10] The experiment was finally called off in 1933 with the passage of the Twenty-First Amendment to the Constitution. When people use the word *prohibition* today, this is usually what they are referring to.[11]

This episode of *The Simpsons* nicely encapsulates and summarizes much of what took place during America's Prohibition. With the right to consume alcohol in jeopardy we find Homer and the writers of *The Simpsons* at the top of their comedic game. Yet an economic analysis provides the real reasons for all the consequences of prohibition that Matt Groening and other writers for *The Simpsons* so cleverly lampoon. Economics also allows us to take these lessons regarding cause and effect and apply them to other instances of prohibition, such as the so-called War on Drugs.

The economic analysis of prohibition begins with the idea that prohibition decreases the legal supply of the product, as shown in Figure 13.1.[12] With alcohol prohibition this can be shown on a graph as a leftward shift of the supply curve from S_0 to S_1. This will result in an increased price, as shown by the movement of price along the vertical axis from P_0 to P_1. The basic results are that suppliers lose most of their producer surplus (in other words, their comparative advantage and profits) and demanders lose most of their consumer surplus (that is, satisfaction or utility from alcohol consumption). Add to that the cost of enforcing prohibition (such as cost of police, courts, and prisons), and it becomes clear that it imposes a large cost on society.

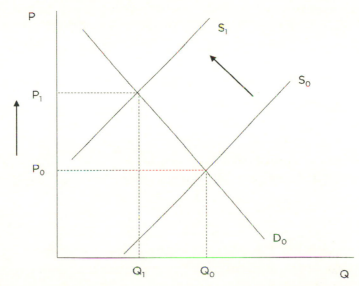

FIGURE 13.1. A decrease in the legal supply of alcohol due to Prohibition

In contrast to these large costs, the economic benefits of prohibition are relatively small or nonexistent. The idea behind prohibition is that reducing consumption will reduce the harms associated with alcohol. These harms include negative health consequences associated with alcohol consumption, crime, violence, automobile and industrial accidents, poverty, absenteeism at work, political corruption, and disrespect for the law. There are several problems with this analysis. First, most of these costs are born by the individual consumer, not the rest of society. Second, most of these harms are more directly controlled in society by incentives, specific laws, and institutions. Third, this analysis neglects important benefits of alcohol consumption.[13] For example, people like to consume alcohol because of the physical satisfaction and social interaction it provides. Also, moderate alcohol consumption is thought by many researchers to improve health and longevity and is even associated with higher income. Finally, the alcohol business provides numerous jobs and profit opportunities that can help alleviate unemployment and poverty.

Yet most significantly, this analysis neglects to consider the unintended consequences of prohibition that often aggravate some or all of the problems that prohibitionists typically associate with alcohol. Most important, prohibitions often lead to large increases in crime that go far beyond the selling of the prohibited product, and they even lead to the production of more potent or dangerous versions of the banned product. Price is certainly an important component of economic analysis, but with prohibition not only does price rise, everything else related to the market for the product is radically changed. Virtually all aspects of the production, distribution, and consumption of alcohol, for example, are distorted by prohibition. These changes are the result of profit opportunities and changes in legal constraints that emerge when prohibition eliminates the free market for a product.

What filled the void of legal alcohol during the Prohibition years? With the legal supply of alcohol suppressed, prices rose and an illegal market emerged consisting of bootleggers, rum runners, moonshiners, and speakeasies. These illegal businesses arose due to profit opportunities presented by prohibition. Beyond the illegal alcohol business, it created widespread increases in crime, corruption, and violence. All of this crime was the result of profit opportunities and the changes in legal constraints brought about by prohibition. These results actually made worse the social problems that prohibitionists hoped to address. The effectiveness of this episode of *The Simpsons* is that it correctly depicts how all these changes follow immediately and obviously after prohibition is imposed. By contrast, the War on Drugs has been around for as long as many of us have been alive, and thus most people tend to associate all the violence and crime with the drugs themselves rather than with the prohibition that makes them illegal.

These results of prohibition are often classified as unintended consequences because they were not the explicit reasons that motivated people to vote for prohibition legislation. However, just because these results were "unintended" does not mean they are unpredictable or random. Each of these consequences is driven by prices and profit opportunities and is therefore potentially predictable and should even be considered as expected features of prohibition, especially for those with a basic understanding of economics. Furthermore, we should expect that as the enforcement of prohibition is intensified—by either adding more resources or increasing penalties—the unintended consequences will become more significant. We can see these results historically during the Prohibition years, in today's War on Drugs, and in this chapter in the comical world of *The Simpsons*.

Prohibition and Crime

As word spreads around Springfield about alcohol prohibition, it causes people to faint. The inventory of Duff Beer is taken to the Springfield Dump and buried to the cheers of the optimistic crowd. The owner of Duff Brewery confidently predicts that he will be able to sell even more non-alcoholic beer. However, not unlike during Prohibition, the surprise and optimism in Springfield quickly vanish to reveal the reality of black markets. The demand for non-alcoholic beer is very small, and Duff Brewery is out of business in thirty minutes. While there are no official figures on the number of businesses negatively affected by Prohibition, we do know that hundreds of wineries and distilleries closed due to Prohibition as well as more than two thousand breweries and thousands of bars, taverns, and saloons.

By the end of the day the black market has gone to work in Springfield. The lack of alcoholic beer creates profit opportunities for people willing to risk being caught and punished for smuggling beer. In Springfield it is the "gangsters" or mafia who smuggle beer in by truck. They pay the police bribes in order to avoid being arrested for violating the prohibition. In reality, the mafia uses bribery, corruption, violence, and threats to become "organized crime." They corrupt politicians and law enforcement with bribes to protect themselves and to have law enforcement target their competitors. In this manner people in government sell the gangsters a kind of monopoly over the distribution of an illegal product in which they face less risk and can increase price because of a lack of competition.[14]

Corruption was rampant during Prohibition, and the enforcement bureaucracy had to be "reorganized" in an attempt to remove corrupt law enforcement officials. Things were so bad that people feared that the rampant disrespect for Prohibition would lead to a general disrespect for all law. Even the commissioner of Prohibition, Henry Anderson, concluded that "the fruitless efforts at enforcement are creating public disregard not only for this law but for all laws. Public corruption through the purchase of official protection for this illegal traffic is widespread and notorious. The courts are cluttered with prohibition cases to an extent which seriously affects the entire administration of justice."[15]

Moe's Tavern is turned into Moe's Pet Shop, a "speakeasy" where alcohol is sold illegally to consumers. To protect the bartenders and customers from going to jail, the speakeasy is designed to look like a pet shop instead of a bar, and customers must knock on the door and ask permission or provide a password to enter. Despite the risks and higher prices, Moe has even more customers, including Mr. Burns and Smithers. There is a jazz band playing raucous jazz music from the Prohibition Era. People are dancing and partying like never before. Making something illegal can reduce the demand (shift the demand curve to the left) of risk-averse people, but it mostly increases the demand of risk takers and may therefore actually tend to increase overall consumption. The evidence from Prohibition suggests that average per capita consumption declined but that various forms of problem drinking increased, such as binge drinking and public intoxication.

The angry women of Springfield burst into Moe's speakeasy and find a big crowd—including Police Chief Clancy Wiggum—dancing and partying. The women put political pressure on Mayor Quimby to replace Wiggum. Prohibitionists have long believed that if they could just have the right type of laws and penalties as well as the right people in charge, then prohibition would work. However, in the real world prohibitionists have tried various combinations of laws, penalties, and administrators over the centuries and nothing has been truly effective.

Mayor Quimby eventually calls on the U.S. Treasury Department—which was in charge of enforcing Prohibition in the 1920s—to send the one man who is thought to be able to enforce prohibition, Rex Banner. Banner's character is based on Elliot Ness, the Prohibition agent who led the "Untouchables" unit of the Treasury Department in Chicago.[16] Ness and his agents could not be bribed and would stop at nothing to enforce Prohibition. However, Ness's prime target was the famous gangster Al Capone, and Capone was not convicted on charges of violating Prohibition but on charges of income tax evasion. Needless to say, alcohol was widely available in Chicago throughout Prohibition just as drugs are available today.

Rex Banner eventually kicks Wiggum out of office, shapes up the police department, and employs extraordinary and violent means to prevent smugglers from bringing alcohol into Springfield. This reflects another long-held view of the prohibitionists: they think that if we could only use violent and unconstitutional means, we could make prohibition work. With Banner stopping the open smuggling of the mafia and unwilling to accept bribes, the mafia boss Fat Tony concedes and vows to return to smuggling heroin instead.

With the mafia gone and the city running dry, Homer laments the early days of prohibition when people were drinking more. Then, to underscore his status as a role model for the drinking class, Homer chastises Police Chief Wiggum for giving in to the good guys. With Bart at his side, Homer gets the idea to retrieve the kegs of Duff Beer buried at the Springfield Dump. After successfully recovering the beer, Homer is shot at by Banner and is involved in a dangerous high-speed chase that nearly destroys his car. In these scenes the writers of *The Simpsons* have correctly introduced elements that are the natural consequences of prohibition, such as risk, danger, violence, deceit, and secrecy.

To deal with the risks of bootlegging and to conceal his illegal beer business, Homer develops the clever idea of hiding the beer in bowling balls. He then throws the balls into the gutter at the bowling alley, where they next go through an overly complicated network of pipes that ultimately ends up behind the bar at Moe's. Real-world smugglers often invent complicated ways to conceal their operations, although Homer's creation is more of a Rube Goldberg machine. A *Rube Goldberg machine* is a term for anything that is excessively complicated or confusing, usually a machine or system that performs a simple task in an overly complex manner.[17]

All this risk and deception comes at a cost to the consumer. Barney finds out the hard way when Moe charges him $45 for a mug of beer. Note that with the higher prices, Moe now has a higher-income clientele. The higher prices also benefit Homer, who lectures Bart that he is wasting his time with vandalism, as bootlegging is where the money is at. The profit motive provided by prohibition has turned Homer into a hero. He is now referred to in Springfield as the "Beer Baron," and when his beer smuggling business is discovered at home, Lisa protests but Marge uncharacteristically approves of Homer's cleverness. The allure of very high monetary profits from prohibition ensures that there will be supply in order to meet the demand.

Rex Banner is unable to detect the secret of the Beer Baron and reveals his ineffectiveness to his police officers in a restaurant scene based on the famous painting *Nighthawks* by American artist Edward Hopper. Banner's incompetence at real detective work is revealed when he raids Moe's speakeasy and is convinced that it really *is* just a pet store filled with rowdy customers at one o'clock in the morning. As Banner exits the speakeasy, his "do gooder" personality flaw is revealed when he lectures the patrons against buying baby alligators. While government employees and law enforcement officers are often portrayed as innately incompetent, economics shows that government bureaucrats can simply never have the same strong incentives to produce and innovate that smugglers and entrepreneurs enjoy. In other words, it is not a matter of having an honest and competent law enforcement bureaucracy. Even the combination of honesty and competence is no match for the profit motive.

More Unintended Consequences

Homer soon runs out of the beer inventory that he retrieved from the Springfield Dump. His next plan involves making "bathtub" alcohol of various sorts, which includes beer but is mostly the higher-potency "spirits" such as whiskey and gin. Prohibition leads to higher-potency products because producers want smaller-sized products that are easier to conceal from law enforcement. Anytime you add a fixed cost such as a tax, transport charge, or risk of penalty to two competing products, you lower the relative price of the higher-priced, higher-potency product. As a result of the risk of being caught, the potency of alcohol by volume increased ten to twenty times during Prohibition, as producers, smugglers, and consumers switched from beer toward higher-potency alcohol such as whiskey. Similarly, in the War on Drugs, the potency of marijuana has increased by several hundred percent, and more potent drugs have been introduced and have grown in importance, such as cocaine and methamphetamine. At the beginning of Prohibition, expenditures on "hard liquor" products increased from 40 percent to 90 percent of total spending on alcohol. After Prohibition was repealed, spending on liquor returned to the 40 percent level.[18]

Homer is easily able to evade the incompetent Banner, but the following scenes portray two seemingly contrary implications regarding prohibition and victimless crimes in general. The black market as a whole is easily able to out-wit law enforcement; however, the people who enforce prohibition are generally successful at apprehending and imprisoning large numbers of people. This hap-pened both during Prohibition and in the War on Drugs because the economic incentives meant that there was a virtually endless supply of potential smugglers.

However, the alcohol stills that Homer uses to make the higher-potency alcohol products start exploding. He concedes the dangers of the business to Marge and decides to quit the business. Illegal and often improvised stills can explode, scald, and burn people. They can also produce alcohol with toxins and poisons that can harm the consumer. The exploding alcohol stills signify the dangerous nature of illegal black markets.

Homer makes another plan with Police Chief Wiggum to get rid of Banner and reinstate the chief by allowing Wiggum to capture him and his stills. Homer is then sentenced to be catapulted out of the city, which symbolizes the draconian punishments associated with the War on Drugs.

Conclusion

While Homer is tied up in the catapult, Marge makes the argument to the crowd that prohibition just doesn't make sense and it costs us our basic free-dom and liberty. The crowd approvingly cheers. Homer is then saved when the city clerk announces that he has discovered that the 200-year-old prohibition was repealed 199 years ago. Mayor Quimby then asks Homer to quickly pro-vide some booze, and when Homer declines the mafia agrees to flood the town in four minutes. Homer's triumphant conclusion is to make a toast to alcohol and freedom from atop a pile of beer kegs.

While Springfielders achieved the repeal of their prohibition by a bungling bureaucrat, in the real world repeal is much harder to come by. People have to realize that prohibition is unworkable and that it is actually counterproductive to the goals of the prohibitionists themselves. They have to realize that people are less safe with prohibition than with a free and open marketplace. Finally, people must realize that prohibition is an unnatural type of law that threatens freedom and can be easily replaced by the market. Ironically, true freedom is the best method of achieving the social goals of the prohibitionists.[19]

It seems clear that the writers of *The Simpsons* are decidedly anti-prohi-bitionist. They were sensitive enough to get Bart drunk "accidentally" and to give all parties (prohibitionists, government, law enforcement, and business) a hearing, but in the end they correctly saw prohibition as painfully ineffective, tragically counterproductive to the goals of prohibition, and at odds with the nature of a free society.

Economics dictates that prohibition has certain results. Prohibition does drive out the legal suppliers in a market. However, as prices rise the void is then filled by people willing to break the law. These suppliers bring products that are more potent and more dangerous to the consumer. As a result, prohibition does not improve health or make people more law abiding, but just the opposite. In fact, prohibition causes crime and corruption to increase, not decrease. This episode of *The Simpsons* ably demonstrates why the law enforcement route to temperance and sobriety backfires and that effective prohibition by government is impossible.

14

MR. BURNS' CASINO

The Economics of Casino Gambling

Douglas M. Walker and Shannon M. Kelly[1]

CASINOS HAVE BEEN LEGAL IN NEVADA since the 1930s and in Atlantic City, New Jersey, since the late 1970s. Just as casinos were beginning to spread across the United States in the early 1990s, *The Simpsons* aired an episode titled "$pringfield (Or, How I Stopped Worrying and Started to Love Legalized Gambling)" that closely reflected the economic and political debate surrounding legalized casinos. On the DVD commentary about the episode, the creators mention that the motivation for this episode came from a newspaper article published in a town in Mississippi that was considering opening a casino in order to stimulate its local economy. Interestingly, most of the issues identified in 1993 in this episode of *The Simpsons* continue to be debated as more states consider the legalization and expansion of casino gambling. In this chapter, we discuss the economic effects of Mr. Burns' Casino, as it is chronicled in the episode "$pringfield." The specific economic issues that we discuss in this chapter include (1) the economic benefits from legalized casinos, (2) the economic and social costs of casinos, and (3) problem gambling and rational behavior.

At the beginning of the episode, Abe Simpson and a friend are shown in the 1950s, enjoying a movie that discusses some current events from the '50s and declares that Springfield is one of the four hundred fastest growing cities in the United States. As a signal of the city's ability to engage in conspicuous consumption, the streets are even paved with gold. The scene moves forward to the present day, and Abe laments that things have changed. Springfield is now in the midst of a serious recession. After turning down a beggar who asks him for spare change, Abe notes how everyone seems to want something for nothing, then walks into the Social Security office.

Upon hearing of the current recession, Mr. Burns enthusiastically lays off a variety of employees from the power plant. Kent Brockman files a TV report that helps to clarify the current economic woes, noting that the unemployment office is no longer just for philosophy majors. He interviews Barney, the town drunk, who has been unemployed for six years, even though he has over ten years of modern and tap dance training. Brockman explains that the economic woes began when the government shut down the local military base, Fort Springfield. The base closing devastated the local liquor and prostitution industries.

The residents of Springfield hold a town meeting to discuss ways they can overcome their woes. Mayor Quimby proposes that he move to a more prosperous city, and once elected as Mayor, he will send for other Springfield residents. Lisa offers to donate the change in her piggy bank. But Principal Skinner proposes the only substantive proposal: legalizing gambling. The debate moves quickly in Springfield, as it does in many cities, and the discussion focuses on the economy and where the additional tax revenue will go:

Skinner: "A number of cities have rejuvenated their economies with . . . uh . . . legalized gambling."

Crowd: (interested chatter)

Skinner: "There is an added bonus. Some of the revenue can go to help our underfunded schools."

Crowd: (silence)

Crickets: (chirp chirp chirp)

Selma: "Oh well, I like the part about the gambling."

Flanders: (talking to Lovejoy) "What do you think, Reverend?"

Reverend Lovejoy: "Once something has been approved by the government, it's no longer immoral."

Crowd: (in unison) "Yay!"

Burns: "By building a casino, I could tighten my stranglehold on this dismal town!"

Crowd: (in unison) "Yay!"

Barney: (loud burp)

Crowd: (in unison) "Yay!"

Quimby: "Well now, are there any objections?"

Crowd: (soft chatter), "Marge; probably Marge . . . "

Marge: "Actually, I think it might really help our economy."

Quimby: "Very well then. Instead of fleeing this town, I'll stay here and grow fat off kick-backs and slush funds."

Crowd: (in unison) "Yay!"

With that short debate, Mr. Burns' Casino is approved to open in Springfield.[2] Oddly, the crowd approves a casino for Springfield with hardly any discussion or concern of the economic benefits and costs other than the discussion of tax revenues. So we shall explore some of those in the following.

Economic Benefits from Casino Legalization

Without exception, casinos are considered a policy option because of their potential to generate tax revenues and economic development. It is interesting to reiterate that on the DVD commentary on this *Simpsons* episode, the writers specifically mention the debate in Mississippi. The director of the Chamber of Commerce of Tunica (Mississippi) testified to Congress in 1994 about the economic effects casinos had on his community, one of the poorest counties in America:

> In January 1992, per capita income in the county was $11,865. . . . 53 percent of residents received food stamps. . . . Since casinos have been legalized, however, land once valued at $250 per acre now sells for $25,000 per acre. . . . The county's planning commission has issued more than $1 billion worth of building permits. . . . Because of the increased government revenues, property taxes have been lowered by 32 percent in recent years. . . . Unemployment has dropped to 4.9 percent. . . . The number of welfare recipients has decreased by 42 percent; the number of food stamp recipients has decreased by 13 percent. . . . In 1994, the county recorded the highest percentage increase in retail sales of all Mississippi counties, 299 percent.[3]

This is nice anecdotal evidence, but how, exactly, can casinos promote economic development? Proponents of legalization address three potential economic benefits: tax revenues, employment, and consumer surplus and increased variety. However, opponents also present viable arguments against casino legalization, including moral objections, industry cannibalization, crime, and the potential for negative externalities and problem gambling behavior. We discuss each of these potential economic impacts from casinos.

Tax Revenues

Perhaps the most common argument for casino legalization relates to state tax revenues. Tax rates on gross casino revenues range from about 7 percent in Nevada up to 55 percent in Pennsylvania. In 2009, Nevada casinos had revenues of about $10.5 billion, and state casino taxes were $832 million. Pennsylvania has one of the smallest casino markets but has the highest tax rates. In 2009 casinos in Pennsylvania earned just under $2 billion in revenues and paid about $929 million in taxes.[4] But do these data mean that casinos will certainly add to *net* state tax revenues?

If we assume that each dollar spent at a casino is not spent on some other type of consumption, then it would seem that casinos will increase net tax receipts. This is because sales taxes are usually less than 10 percent. In most states, taxes on casino revenues are higher than this, sometimes significantly higher.[5] This suggests casinos will be large revenue generators, which is why politicians typically look to casinos to help fix fiscal woes.

However, casinos may not have as large an impact on state tax revenues as casino proponents often suggest. The "substitution" of spending away from other industries means that the net impact of casino taxes is less than the absolute amount of tax revenues. One recently published study even suggests that casinos may *reduce* state tax revenues.[6] The actual impact of casinos on tax revenues in states—or in Springfield—surely varies by case.

Even if casinos do not raise the overall revenues of the state government, there could be large political benefits from legalizing casinos. First, casino tax revenues can be directed to specific purposes, such as funding public education. Principal Skinner mentions this at the town hall meeting, but only the crickets respond with enthusiasm. Perhaps more important, casino tax receipts can also be used as a substitute for other taxes, such as property taxes, as in Tunica.

Alternatively, introducing a new type of tax can be a means by which politicians can avoid cutting spending. In the current state of affairs in most state governments—and especially in the federal government—it is politically difficult to cut government spending. Legalizing a new industry that can then be taxed is a politically expedient way of reducing budget deficits, increasing spending, or not reducing spending. In Mayor Quimby's case in Springfield, it is a way for him to get more political donations and kickbacks.

Employment

As discussed previously, the casino debate centers on economic development. Increased employment is one aspect of the purported economic development benefits of casinos. Although casinos can be expected to increase employment within a particular region that introduces casinos, the estimates for job creation from casinos may be overly optimistic. For example, the American Gaming Association reports that the U.S. casino industry employed over 328,000 people in 2009.[7] But this is not necessarily a good estimate of the *net* jobs created by casinos. The explanation follows the tax substitution issue discussed previously.

While a new casino may create a large number of new jobs in a time of high unemployment, if workers simply switch from their current jobs to the casino jobs, then there is less of an impact on net employment. For example, Homer quit working at the power plant in order to achieve one of his life-long dreams: to work at the casino.[8] Nevertheless, if individual workers choose to work at the casino, it must be the best option available to them; otherwise they wouldn't take the casino job.

One additional employment impact of casinos comes through related industries. Certainly casinos compete with other entertainment industries, and some employment may be reallocated among them. But other industries, such as bars and restaurants, are complementary to casinos. In these industries we may expect to see increased employment due to casino openings.

There are several possible impacts of casinos on employment. On net, empirical evidence suggests that casinos have a positive impact on employment and wages.[9]

Consumer Choice and Increased Variety

Although it rarely comes up in political debate over casinos, one of the potentially largest economic benefits from legalizing casinos accrues to the consumers who enjoy visiting the casinos. Economists are concerned with economic efficiency. One aspect of this from a social perspective is the maximization of "total surplus," which is the sum of consumer and producer surplus.[10] One avenue for increasing total surplus is by increasing consumer surplus. The addition of a casino to a region—or adding any new form of entertainment—creates more choices, which increases consumer surplus. This happens either because there is simply a new good available for consumers, or because the presence of the new consumption option increases competition and lowers prices. The additional option allows consumers who would prefer to spend their discretionary income in casinos to do so conveniently.

Another potential benefit of introducing casinos arises simply from the greater variety. Consumers benefit from having different producers of a particular product, as well as from having more consumption choices. Such variety is an important aspect of standard of living, which is typically neglected in political debate over casinos. In *The Simpsons* debate, at least one person in the crowd alluded to this issue.

The economic benefits from legalized casinos are not clear or easily measurable, even years after *The Simpsons* first debated the issue. But there is good reason to believe that casinos can have a positive impact on tax revenues, employment, and consumer choice. In general, casinos increase economic activity in a region; they increase the number of mutually beneficial voluntary transactions. This is a key source of economic growth. Importantly, it does not really matter whether the transactions are for "services" such as casino games or attending sporting events, or for tangible goods such as cars or computers. What matters is that the consumers value what is being produced.

Economist Joseph Schumpeter lists five primary sources of economic development, the first of which is "the introduction of a new good—that is one with which consumers are not yet familiar—or of a new quality of a good."[11] The casino in Springfield would clearly fall into this category.

Economic and Social Costs from Casinos

There are several arguments common in opposition to legalizing casinos. Many of these center on economic and social costs. We discuss four of these: moral objections, industry cannibalization, crime, and negative externalities from problem gambling.

Moral Objections to Gambling

One common objection to casinos comes from religious organizations or others concerned with the morality of gambling. Indeed, this was the single concern raised against Mr. Burns' Casino. In *The Simpsons*, however, Reverend Lovejoy defended the morality of gambling on the grounds that government approval of an activity makes it moral. In reality, religious figures often have a strong opinion against casinos. A primary concern is that legalized gambling sends a message that one doesn't need to work hard to earn a living—that "luck" can take care of it.[12]

Industry Cannibalization

An economic argument typically raised against casinos is that they will "cannibalize" other businesses. Suppose consumers have only a set amount of discretionary income, and any dollar spent in a casino is one dollar that is not spent on other forms of entertainment. Basically, opponents argue that casino revenues can only come from revenues lost by other industries. This also implies lost jobs in competing industries. While this may happen, it is odd to raise this concern as an argument to prevent a new industry from opening. After all, any new firm opening may create greater competition for existing businesses. Of course competing firms will not be happy about the casino opening, but consumers still benefit. Why not let the consumers "vote with their dollars" and determine which firms and industries should continue to produce? This is the point behind "allocative efficiency." Markets tend to be efficient because they produce what consumers want.

Crime

Casinos are often portrayed as attracting unsavory people. Since casinos also host numerous customers who sometimes carry large sums of cash, casinos may be popular hangouts for criminals. Why not go where the money is, after all? One very common concern with casinos is that they generate crime.

Overall, the research relating casinos and crime has returned mixed results. Although some studies show an increase in the crime rate following the opening of casinos, these studies are fundamentally flawed. When determining the crime rate, researchers measure the number of crimes with relation to the total population (both local and visiting population) of a region.[13] But many researchers fail to account for the increase in visiting population following the introduction of a casino. When they account for increases in visiting population, studies generally do *not* show an increase in crime, and sometimes even show a decrease.[14] A more general concern with legalizing casinos, albeit one overlooked in *The Simpsons*, is that casinos may generate any number of negative externalities other than crime.

Negative Externalities and Problem Gambling

Casinos can completely change the personality of a neighborhood or region. They are usually large structures that increase traffic flow, put additional strain on infrastructure, and may be associated with other negative impacts. The NIMBY argument—"not in my back yard"—entails many different impacts. One can expect that some individuals simply won't want to live near a casino. For those neighbors who do not like a casino, the casino can represent a negative externality.

Another externality issue related to casinos is "problem gambling." Marge demonstrates classic problem gambling behavior. She is consumed with gambling, and it becomes more important to her than her home, family, and friends. (It might have been more important than her career if she had steady work other than as a homemaker.) So-called problem gamblers have trouble controlling their gambling, and gambling often has a negative impact on the person's career, family, or finances.[15] In addition, problem gamblers often engage in crime, fail to pay back debts, and otherwise generate costs that are ultimately borne by others in society. Such externalities can be seen as social costs of gambling.

Social costs exist when the entire cost of a transaction is not borne by the parties to the transaction; the overall wealth of society is reduced as a result. Thus wealth transfers do not count as "social costs."[16] Walker lists eleven of these alleged "social costs" and places them into two separate groups.[17] The first four costs often mentioned cannot be considered social costs as these costs are "internalized" or fully borne by the gambler. Income lost from missing work, decreased work productivity, depression and illness stemming from gambling-related stress, and increased suicide attempts are all costs borne by the gambler. The next seven costs are simply "wealth transfers" in which the overall wealth of society is not reduced. Bailout costs, unrecovered gambling loans, unpaid debts and bankruptcies, higher insurance premiums from gambling-related fraud, public corruption, public service strain, and cannibalization of other industries just transfer resources from one person in society to another. Although many of these effects may be judged to be "bad," they are not social costs.

The actual social costs from problem gambling would include treatment expenses and incarceration and court expenses for problem gamblers engaging in crime, as well as anguish on the part of the gambler and his or her family who may also suffer. Unfortunately, these social costs are not easy to measure in monetary terms. But they do exist.

An additional problem with trying to estimate the costs attributed to pathological gamblers is that these people typically have other disorders such as alcohol abuse problems, drug abuse, or depression.[18] One cannot simply blame gambling for all the social costs caused by the person's behavior. Nevertheless, there is some agreement among economists that legalized gambling can exacerbate some social costs that might not otherwise exist.[19]

Problem Gambling and Rational Behavior

One of the most interesting aspects of *The Simpsons* episode on casino gambling is watching Marge descend into gambling addiction. She even skips Lisa's state pageant to gamble at the casino. Economics is largely based on the assumption that individuals tend to be "rational." This basically just means that people are goal-oriented—in other words, they want to make themselves better off, however they define being better off. The rational decision maker then compares expected costs and expected benefits of a potential decision or action (or bet at a casino). A person should only act if he or she expects the benefits to outweigh the costs.

Then what is *addiction*? Economics provides a very interesting answer to this. Although some psychologists believe problem gambling is a disease, similar to alcoholism, economists have developed alternative theories. The most prominent theory, the "theory of rational addiction," was developed by Nobel Prize–winning economist Gary Becker and his colleagues.[20] Basically, this theory suggests that addictions are just *very strong preferences*. The initial decision that leads a person to engage in gambling is a rational choice. In short, addiction is a choice, or it is at least the result of a rational choice.[21]

Consider, for example, the first time Marge puts a quarter in the slot machine. Before she gambles for the first time, as a rational person, she must recognize that there is some potential that she will really like the activity. Then the choice to gamble for the first time—even if it leads to "addiction"—may still be a rational decision. The idea of "rational addiction" is a somewhat abstract one. A more important aspect of this issue may be how addictions or the potential for addictive behavior should affect public policy. Is it the responsibility of government to prevent people from consuming goods or services that may ultimately harm them? What goods or services carry no risk of harm? A key question is, Should government act to prevent you from harming yourself?

Conclusion

We never see whether Mr. Burns' Casino ends up increasing economic development in Springfield. But assuming local government acted competently and set reasonable tax rates on the casino, Springfield likely saw some tax benefits from the casino.[22] The casino surely helped with employment in the city; since more jobs were available, workers had better options. The casino increased competition for workers, which generates upward pressure on the wage rate. Finally, the consumers who enjoy casino games benefited from having the casino in Springfield.

However, there were also likely some costs. Some other industries may have been harmed as a result of the casino opening. The casino may lead to a higher crime rate, and there are some other potential negative externalities generated by the casino. Most of the "social costs" of gambling that are not simply trans-fers (pecuniary externalities) are due to problem gamblers, perhaps like Marge.

Finally, the casino had a profound impact on Marge. Homer and her chil-dren will always remember her gambling problem, no matter how short-lived it was. Yet Homer does offer advice to Marge to help her quit gambling. When Marge suggests that she should seek professional help, Homer replies that treat-ment is too costly and instead she should just quit cold turkey. If problem gam-bling is a rational addiction, then Homer's advice may be surprisingly sound.

HOMER ECONOMICUS OR HOMER SAPIENS?

Behavioral Economics in *The Simpsons*

Jodi Beggs

BEHAVIORAL ECONOMICS is an emerging field at the intersection of psychology and traditional economics. If you've ever taken an economics course, you may recall that one of the central assumptions of nearly all traditional economic models is that individuals and companies act "rationally"—that is, in ways that maximize their long-term happiness or well-being.[1] Since the world is a complex place, this assumption technically requires that everyone has (or at least acts as though they have) unlimited information-processing capabilities, perfect self-control, complete and objective knowledge regarding the usefulness of every item available for purchase, and so on. It's not hard, however, to look around at our neighbors, our friends, and probably even ourselves to see that this assumption is unreasonable when applied literally in the real world.

Traditional economists acknowledge that people aren't perfect, but they contend that the "errors" in judgment that people make are reasonably random and just create noise in an otherwise well-functioning economic world. Behavioral economists, on the other hand, are interested in describing the ways in which people exhibit consistent irrational biases in decision making and judgment. To err is human, as the saying goes, and behavioral economists want to understand the ways in which economic actors are, well, human.[2]

It's generally more entertaining to watch humans than to watch economic robots, so it's not surprising that movies, books, and television shows generally focus on characters who are imperfect, in some ways irrational, and often downright goofy. *The Simpsons* is no exception to this model, and the world has had the privilege of watching the characters' economic missteps for the past twenty-one years. Shortly after we meet him for the first time, for example, we watch Homer Simpson take his paycheck to the dog track and bet on Santa's Little Helper (at 99:1 odds no less) because he took the dog's name as a sign.[3] It's unlikely that this was the optimal way for Homer to spend his paycheck (just ask Marge), and it's certainly not a sound betting strategy.[4] Therefore, the viewer is probably not shocked that, rather than getting the big payout he was convinced he had coming, Homer ends up with Santa's Little Helper as a pet.

In general, the fascinating part about the members of the Springfield community is that, despite being fictional characters created for entertainment purposes, their biases correspond quite well to those observed by behavioral economists in real people. Lisa even notes in the first episode of the show that Homer has the same frailties as all human beings,[5] and this theme is certainly exemplified throughout the show, perhaps even to a larger degree than the writers realized. This chapter provides an introduction to some of the basic principles of behavioral economics and shows the ways in which the characters in *The Simpsons* embody these principles. The following discussion is in no way an exhaustive introduction to the subject, as there are too many concepts in behavioral economics to be covered in one chapter. Instead, it covers a smattering of topics that are particularly relevant to the show and, it is hoped, particularly interesting to the reader. The chapter concludes with a discussion of how irrational and "human" the characters are overall.

Time-Inconsistency, Procrastination, and Commitment Devices

We need only take a quick look at the world around us in order to be reminded that self-control problems are a fact of life. Let's face it—we procrastinate, we eat too much, we don't go to the gym enough, and we don't save enough for retirement, even when doing too much or too little of these activities is at odds with our long-term happiness. Traditional economists don't have a good way to account for this behavior because it contradicts the assumption that everyone is a perfectly rational utility maximizer. Everyone is "time-consistent" in the traditional economist's world, which means that people's choices never cause them to ever look back and say, well, "D'oh!"[6]

Homer, on the other hand, is certainly not time-consistent, as his preferences for activities often seem to change from one moment to the next. Consider the time that Homer vowed to never drink another beer—and then the beer vendor came by and Homer decided to buy ten beers.[7] Or the time that

Homer vowed to not look forward to anything—and then immediately got excited about a two-for-one sale on piano benches, of course.[8] Even Homer's resolution to never eat chili again only lasted for a few seconds, or exactly until he was presented with more chili.[9]

Economists acknowledge that timing is an important factor in calculating happiness or utility—after all, it's pretty easy to see that receiving $10 today is more attractive than receiving $10 a year from now.[10] Therefore, when calculating happiness, it's important to discount future costs and benefits compared to those that occur in the present. For example, maybe getting $10 in one year makes you as happy as getting $9 today would. Traditional economists would infer that your future is discounted at 10 percent per year and would conclude that $11.11 paid out two years from now is also equivalent to $9 today, and so on.[11] In other words, these hypothetical numbers imply that you would be willing to delay gratification as long as that gratification increased by enough to counteract the 10 percent discount on it for each year you are kept waiting. This approach has the nice feature of the time-consistency just described, since the optimal choices from today's perspective will still be optimal in the future.[12] On the other hand, the model suffers a considerable weakness in that it can't explain the behavior that Homer exhibits.

Behavioral economists use the notion of time-inconsistency to explain procrastination and the overwhelming desire for immediate gratification, and they employ a concept called hyperbolic discounting to model this type of bias.[13] In hyperbolic discounting models, behavioral economists not only discount future costs and benefits as just described, they also add an additional discount factor that applies equally to all future costs and benefits (but not to current costs and benefits). Continuing the previous example, if we assume that this additional discount factor is another 10 percent, hyperbolic discounting implies that $9 today is equivalent to $11.11 one year from now, $12.35 two years from now, and so on. Alternatively, we could note that these preferences imply that you would be willing to delay a future payout by one year if the payout increased by enough to counteract a 10 percent discount (as before), but the payout would need to increase by enough to overcome two 10 percent discounts in order to make you willing to delay from today to one year in the future.

This feature in the model reflects the observation that, while people would rather get something one day from now than get it two days from now (and vice versa for costs), they *really* prefer getting things today rather than getting them tomorrow. Time-inconsistency occurs when the payout increases by enough to delay gratification from one future day to the next but doesn't increase enough to delay gratification from today until tomorrow.[14] In the example, if a payout option starting several years from now increases by 15 percent per year, you would say today that you would wait indefinitely to cash in. However, when the future rolls around and the payout is available in the present, the desire for immediate gratification takes over and you will decide that the extra 15 percent no longer makes waiting worthwhile. When applied to costs rather than benefits, this model implies that even when "doing it tomorrow" is the best choice right now, it's no longer the preferred option when tomorrow becomes today. Procrastination, therefore, occurs because individuals find it in their short-term best interests to renege on their earlier decisions and postpone action when the time to act rolls around. For example, when Homer wants to go to the mall to meet Mr. T, he tells himself over and over that he'll just go a little later, but when he finally overcomes his procrastination and decides to go, it's too late and he misses his opportunity with Mr. T.[15] Homer Simpson is lucky in that all he missed was meeting Mr. T at the mall, since counterproductive procrastination tends to pop up in many important facets of life.

The key to overcoming procrastination is recognizing that the future always eventually becomes the present. Unfortunately, not everyone is adept at this task, and Homer seems to be particularly lacking in this department. Not surprisingly, when speaking to his loan officer in "No Loan Again, Naturally," Homer claims that he was told that he wouldn't have to repay the money he borrowed until the future and then balks at his responsibility on the grounds that it's still the present rather than the future.

On the basis of this evidence, it's tempting to conclude that Homer is what behavioral economists (and likely most of the world) call naive. In the context of time-inconsistency and procrastination, one who is naive is unaware of his or her own time-inconsistency. In other words, when Homer chooses to put off activities until the future, he seems to honestly believe that when the future arrives he is going to make good on his earlier choices. "Sophisticated" individuals, on the other hand, are aware of what their preferences are going to look like in the future, and they can therefore control their procrastination with reasoning of the form "Well, I don't want to do it now, but I'm not going to want to do it tomorrow when tomorrow becomes now either, so I might as well get it over with."

Individuals who are aware of their own procrastination tendencies can sometimes just suck it up and force themselves to complete unpleasant activities in a timely manner. For example, Ned Flanders probably realizes that he is never going to want to do his taxes, so he gets the task over with as soon as possible, even going so far as to show up at the post office right when it opens on the first day of the year.[16] (Alternatively, it's possible that he actually likes doing his taxes—after all, it *is* Ned Flanders.) The rest of the town, in contrast, is shown waiting in long, frantic lines to mail their tax forms at the last minute.

Sometimes people can't just force themselves to behave rationally and not procrastinate, so they instead turn to what economists call commitment devices. Commitment devices, simply put, are schemes that serve to restrict an individual's future choices so that she is forced to act in ways consistent with her long-term self-interest. For example, Christmas clubs—savings accounts for which depositors pay to have their savings tied up until the holiday season—have historically been popular commitment devices, and the concept can be traced all the way back to ancient mythology, when Ulysses has his crew tie him to his ship's masts because he knows that he won't be able to resist the Sirens.[17]

Despite the earlier naive procrastination examples, the presence of commitment devices as a recurring theme throughout the series implies that Homer and his comrades are at least partially aware of their own weaknesses. Even in the first episode, a Christmas club is listed as an item that gets taken out of Homer's Santa Claus paycheck.[18] In "Bart's Dog Gets an F," Homer argues that the family has to commit themselves to put out the ad to find a new owner for Santa's Little Helper before the dog fails his obedience test. In "Blood Feud," Bart mails a letter that Homer wrote to Mr. Burns because he thought that Homer might change his mind otherwise. In "He Loves to Fly and He D'ohs," Homer's life coach convinces him to quit his job so that he is more committed to finding a better job. Homer even employs an ultimate commitment device when he gets his stomach stapled in "Husbands and Knives."

Reference-Dependent Utility, Narrow Bracketing, and the Endowment Effect

Economists observe that people generally exhibit risk-averse behavior in their daily lives—for example, most people would take a guaranteed payout of $50 over a 50 percent chance of winning $100.[19] (In fact, many people would likely prefer a guaranteed payout of, say, $45 rather than a 50 percent chance of $100.) Traditional economists assume that people form preferences over risky choices by comparing the expected levels of their overall wealth in all scenarios. In the initial example, traditional economists model the decision as a choice between one's current net worth plus $50 versus a 50 percent chance of current net worth plus $100.

Behavioral economists take this concept a step further and theorize that, in addition to considering resulting levels of wealth when making a decision, people also think specifically about whether an outcome represents a gain or a loss. More specifically, behavioral economists have found that people tend to evaluate outcomes in relation to some psychological reference point, and they generally feel about twice as much pain from what they perceive as a loss as they do pleasure from an equivalent gain.[20] Therefore, people are not only risk averse but also "loss averse," according to behavioral economists. This finding is important because it implies that people are sensitive to the framing of choices and outcomes as gains and losses. In particular, individuals are more sensitive to what they perceive as explicit losses as opposed to foregone gains. As a result, Homer would probably have been less upset about Marge's refusal to lie in court if he could have framed the resulting zero-dollar settlement as a foregone gain rather than thinking that Marge cost him a million dollars, even though both scenarios result in the same dollar outcome.[21]

In addition to being loss averse, Homer is susceptible to what behavioral economists call "narrow bracketing"—examining choices and outcomes in isolation rather than in a larger context. In "Lady Bouvier's Lover," for example, Homer finds out that Bart charged $350 on his credit card. On the upside, Bart gives Homer $350 in cash to make up for it. Unfortunately, or at least irrationally, Homer seems to have acclimated pretty quickly to the idea of the $350 being charged to his credit card, so when Bart hands him the cash he sees it as a gain and decides to use the cash to buy seventy transcripts of *Nightline*. A rational individual, of course, would recognize that the two transactions just cancel each other out, but instead Homer reacts as though he has been given a gift.[22] In a similar vein, Homer perceives a loss and gets upset when his "you may already have won" check can't be cashed, even though this setback didn't result in an actual loss.[23]

Furthermore, in "Simpsoncalifragilisticexpiala(D'oh)cious," Bart supposedly takes up smoking and then offers to quit in order to help the family save money. Homer gives Bart a dollar as a reward for quitting smoking (since, according to Homer, giving up smoking is one of the hardest things Bart will ever have to do), even though Bart had only taken up smoking for the purpose of having something to give up. Lisa, always the voice of reason, points out that Bart didn't actually do anything and thus doesn't deserve a reward, but Homer is unconvinced. The concept of narrow bracketing and myopia (short-sightedness) can even explain the many instances of gambling shown throughout the series.

Asymmetry in the perceptions of gains and losses (as well as the psychology of ownership[24]) results in a phenomenon known as the "endowment effect." Have you ever been given an item and later felt a strange reluctance to give it up, even though you didn't really want the item in the first place? Daniel Kahneman, Jack Knetsch, and Richard Thaler documented this phenomenon in a series of experiments involving Cornell University undergraduates and Cornell bookstore coffee mugs.[25] As a first step, they randomly chose students to receive coffee mugs. They then asked students who had mugs to report the minimum amount they would be willing to sell their mugs for, and they asked the mugless students how much they would be willing to pay for one of the mugs. Since the mugs were randomly distributed, it isn't likely that the students who got mugs just happened to like mugs more than the students who didn't get mugs. Therefore, it stands to reason that, on average, the amount that students were willing to sell their mugs for should be about the same as the amount that others were willing to pay for them. The economists' main finding, however, is that the students who had been endowed with mugs demanded about twice as much money to sell them as people who didn't own a mug were willing to pay. Traditional economists don't account for this phenomenon in their models since they assume that people have only one objective valuation of an item that is relevant in both a buying and a selling context.

The endowment effect can lead to irrational behavior, such as when Homer frantically ran down the street to catch the Goodwill truck after Marge donated some old items from the attic, including, most important of course, the family's spare Christmas tree stand.[26] It's pretty unlikely that Homer would have expended the same level of effort to obtain a spare Christmas tree stand that he didn't already own. Similarly, when Milhouse buys Bart's soul for $5 and Bart decides that he wants it back, Milhouse decides that his selling price is $50.[27] Granted, part of the price increase is likely due to the fact that Bart doesn't have a whole lot of negotiating power, but, according to behavioral economists, Milhouse generally wouldn't have sold Bart's soul for less than about $10.

In these scenarios, the irrationality exhibited appears to be counterproductive to economic and societal functioning, but loss aversion and the endowment effect that it creates can have an upside in some cases. In "And Maggie Makes Three," for example, Homer is not too keen on the idea of another child, but, fortunately, he is clearly pleased to have Maggie once she arrives.

Bounded Rationality and the Problem of Overchoice

If economic actors were able to perfectly process all of the relevant information about all of the choices available to them, it would be pretty clear that more choice is always better. After all, no one is forced to choose that two hundredth variety of toothpaste just because it's there, so its presence can't make a perfectly rational individual worse off, and it might even make him better off if he decides that the new variety is the best toothpaste for him. Unfortunately, people exhibit what behavioral economists call "bounded rationality," which is a tactful way of saying that people are stupid or, at the very least, unable to process unlimited amounts of product information in order to make perfectly optimal choices. Furthermore, evaluating the multitude of goods and services available for consumption takes effort, and therefore a plethora of choices can be more frustrating than helpful.

This notion of "overchoice" is one of the central themes of Barry Schwartz's *The Paradox of Choice*, and Schwartz even goes so far as to show that having too many choices available can cause people to refrain from making a choice at all.[28] As an example, he cites an experiment by Sheena Iyengar and Mark Lepper in which subjects at a food store were offered the option to sample and buy a particular type of jam.[29] In one condition, the subjects were offered six different flavors to sample, whereas subjects in the other condition were offered twenty-four flavors. The researchers found that, contrary to what traditional economic theory predicts, subjects who were presented with fewer options actually went on to purchase more jam. The rationale is that, as choices get harder to analyze exhaustively, the chance of making a suboptimal choice goes up, and the fear of making a suboptimal choice causes people to avoid making a choice at all.

In "It's a Mad, Mad, Mad, Mad Marge," for example, Becky was trying to kill Marge in order to steal her family, but she got derailed by the six different shovel options at the hardware store and just decided to give up on her murder plan instead. This "choosing to not choose" is usually counterproductive, but at least Marge benefited from Becky's choice paralysis in this case. On the other hand, overchoice was not so good to Milhouse when he was confronted with multiple flavors of Jell-O to choose from in the school cafeteria and ended up not only with no Jell-O (because the lunch lady told him to scram after fifteen minutes of deliberating) but also with a suspicion that the yellow Jell-O was his pet canary.[30] The overchoice problem causes Milhouse to go without dessert, though in this case the decision to abstain from choosing was made for him. The guy who got crushed under the edge of the dome in *The Simpsons Movie* because he couldn't decide whether he wanted to be inside or outside can probably relate.

Even when they want to make choices, people sometimes find it difficult to make the "right" choices due to limited cognitive resources. Baba Shiv and Alexander Fedorikhin examined this phenomenon via an experiment involving numbers, fruit salad, and chocolate cake.[31] In the experiment, one group of participants was given a two-digit number to remember, and a second group was given a seven-digit number to memorize. The participants were then offered a mid-experiment snack, but they were not clued in to the fact that the choice of snack was the real experiment. What the researchers found was that, when the subjects were given the easier task, more of them chose the fruit salad, which can be construed as the option that is more in line with their long-term best interests (or at least in line with a rational, cognitively driven choice). In contrast, participants given the more difficult task were more likely to choose the more decadent but unhealthy chocolate cake.

The theory is that, when cognitive resources are scarce or otherwise occupied, individuals' affective (that is, visceral) responses take over and they choose the most immediately gratifying option rather than the long-term "best" option. It is not surprising, then, that the vending machines at Springfield Elementary come equipped with neuro-jammers to disrupt the judgment centers in students' brains.[32] (Wouldn't it just be easier to give them numbers to memorize?) It's also not surprising that Lisa forgets her locker combination, forgets how to play her saxophone, and generally has trouble functioning properly when she is preoccupied with solving the brain teaser that seems easy for everyone else.[33]

Mental Accounting

To traditional economists, money is just money, and economically rational individuals see money as fungible and sitting in one big pile waiting to either be spent or saved. Humans, on the other hand, often think in terms of a budget with different "mental accounts"—the rent account, the food account, the toys account, and so on—and people tend to compartmentalize resources in this way in order to organize their finances and overcome self-control weaknesses. Despite the fact that these accounts are not physically separate, money and other goods can't be moved from one account to another without a good reason, and this feature can lead to biases in consumption choices. In "Old Yeller-Belly," for example, Marge initially refuses to prepare a ham because Homer asks for a celebration ham and, by her mental accounting, the only hams left are the earthquake ham and the condolence ham. (Interestingly enough, it's Homer who is the voice of reason this time and points out that they're all just hams.) It's not hard to see that it would have been suboptimal for Marge to not prepare a ham simply because the "account" for the celebration ham was empty.

In addition to organizing mental accounts by consumption category, people often have "regular income" versus "windfall income" mental accounts, and the purchases paid for from these two accounts can look quite different. Carrie Heilman, Kent Nakamoto, and Ambar Rao find, for example, that unplanned purchases made as a result of surprise in-store coupons tend to be of the treat or indulgence sort rather than of a more practical nature.[34] The Simpsons appear to be quite familiar with this bias, since much of the family's windfall spending results in what are likely less than practical purchases. When Bart and Lisa each get a $100 inheritance, for example, Bart wants to buy a hundred tacos from Taco Mat and Lisa wants to donate her money to the corporation for public broadcasting. (Luckily, Marge steps in and takes the kids to the bank to open savings accounts.)[35] In addition, Bart seems particularly susceptible to this windfall spending phenomenon, exemplified in "'Round Springfield" when he wastes an unexpected $500 on what is supposedly the ultimate Pog. This point is further driven home when Bart imagines what he would do with a surprise $1,000—apparently, he would have a party in outer space in his very own moon mansion.[36]

Homer isn't much more rational in this regard, as evidenced by the situations in which he buys gifts with his gambling winnings rather than fixing the house's termite problem[37] and asks Maggie if she can think of a better way for him to spend a hard-won $50 than on a new bowling ball.[38] Marge, on the other hand, seems to be the voice of reason and rationality on this subject—not only does she want the kids to put their inheritances in the bank, she also thinks that the family should be practical with the $2,000 award that Homer wants to spend on a massage chair because she feels that windfall money is a blessing and thus shouldn't just be spent on creature comforts.[39]

Traditional economists are quick to point out that no gift is better than cash, since cash can be used to buy whatever the recipient wants most. Behavioral economists, on the other hand, acknowledge that sometimes gifts can be superior to cash when people use mental accounts to help overcome self-control problems. By this logic, a $50 bottle of wine could be more beneficial to a wine lover than $50 cash if the recipient really likes wine but arbitrarily doesn't allow herself to spend $50 on a single bottle. Perhaps it is similar logic that persuaded Bart, when given the choice between an elephant and $10,000 cash, to prefer the elephant.[40] Even if Bart could buy an elephant with the $10,000 cash, he was probably aware that his parents wouldn't allow it and therefore found it in his best interests to force the issue and choose the elephant directly.

Transaction Utility and the Power of Free

Back in 1983, when behavioral economics was still very much a nascent field, Richard Thaler noted that "a consumer's behavior depends not only on the value of goods and services available relative to their respective prices but also on the consumer's perception of the quality of the financial terms of the deal."[41] To formally model this idea, Thaler developed the concept of "transaction utility," which is the amount of happiness one gets from feeling like he got a good deal. In his model, the total amount of happiness, or utility, that an individual gets from purchasing and consuming something is the sum of the happiness from actually using the item (referred to as acquisition utility, or just plain old utility) and the happiness that the act of purchasing in and of itself generates for the consumer (transaction utility). It is worth noting that transaction utility is positive if the customer feels like she got a bargain and is negative if the customer feels like she got ripped off.

At first glance, it's not obvious how transaction utility can lead to irrational decisions. Consider a situation, however, in which the inherent usefulness of an item isn't enough to justify the item's price, but the transaction utility is high enough to cause the consumer to purchase the item.[42] Unless the person really enjoys talking about how he got such a good deal on the item (which is admittedly a possibility), the transaction utility dissipates fairly quickly and leaves the consumer with a feeling of buyer's remorse. When Patty and Selma are clipping coupons, for example, Patty doesn't seem that enthused about grape jelly in general but notes that she loves it if it's thirty-five cents off.[43] Objectively, the thirty-five-cent discount shouldn't make Patty actually like the jelly more (even though she would be more willing to purchase it at the lower price), but this is the effect that transaction utility tends to have on people. Unfortunately, Patty would likely be initially happy with her purchase but then less than pleased with the grape jelly decision once the shine of the good deal wears off.

Adding to the "problem" of transaction utility is the fact that people do strange things when the prospect of free is dangled in front of them. Behavioral economist Dan Ariely shows evidence of this "FREE!" phenomenon in his book

Predictably Irrational when he states, "Zero is not just another price, it turns out. Zero is an emotional hot button—a source of irrational excitement."[44] Given the preceding discussion of transaction utility, this is not surprising—what can make someone feel like she got a good deal more than getting something for free? Homer seems to be particularly susceptible to the power of FREE! in "Funeral for a Fiend," when he buys a $200 Tivo (plus a two-year contract) in order to get a fifty-cent battery for free—and then not only makes it clear that he doesn't know what a Tivo is, but also almost manages to leave the Tivo at the store.

Part of the reason that the irrational attraction to the concept of free is problematic is that the appeal of the free item often precludes individuals from noticing the true (all-inclusive) cost of the item or considering more useful non-free options. For example, Homer falls for a "free beer" trap set by Bart and Milhouse because he is so focused on the idea of FREE! that he doesn't stop to consider that if something seems too good to be true, it probably is.[45] In addition, when Homer is presented with the option of a free movie, he accepts the offer without even asking what movie he will be watching.[46] This is potentially problematic for two reasons. First, the movie could be terrible and actually give Homer negative utility, especially if he is too stubborn or lazy to walk out of the theater if he doesn't like the movie. Second, the free movie causes Homer to mindlessly forego other movies and uses of his time in general that may be utility maximizing despite not being free. Finally, the destructive effect of FREE! is particularly salient when Homer skips out on disposing of waste properly in *The Simpsons Movie* because the donut shop is giving away free donuts. Given the trouble that the waste ended up causing not only for Homer but also for the whole community, opting for the free donuts was clearly not a rational choice.

Nudges, Anchoring, and Framing

Richard Thaler and Cass Sunstein wrote an entire book on the power of "nudges"—small changes in the framing of choices that can have big effects.[47] The power of nudges is certainly not lost on Apu, as evidenced when he strategically puts cans of corn out on the Simpsons' counter. When Marge mentions that the family usually keeps the cans in the cupboards, Apu points out that that's not a good strategy if she actually wants people to eat the corn. As it turns out, Apu was quite correct in his intuition, since shortly thereafter Lisa and Bart see the corn on the counter and develop a craving for it.[48]

The small change in the placement of the canned corn shouldn't, theoretically speaking, have a large effect on consumption, but in practice it very much does. In a similar vein, establishing a hypothetical reference price, or anchor, for an item shouldn't change an individual's willingness to pay for that item, but in practice it is a very powerful force. When Marge ponders purchasing a discounted Chanel suit, for example, she initially balks at the $90 price tag, but her opinion changes drastically when Lisa points out that the suit had been marked down from $2,800.[49]

In this example, the $2,800 price serves as an anchor, and as soon as Marge considers whether she would have paid $2,800, the $90 seems like a deal in comparison. It's entirely likely that the high price anchor increases the amount that Marge is willing to pay for the item despite the fact that the original price was fairly arbitrary (especially since the item didn't sell at the regular price). Economists have even found that having people write down the last two digits of their social security numbers, which results in obviously random numbers, and then having them decide whether they would pay that number of dollars for an item affects the amount that they would subsequently be willing to pay.[50]

Along those same lines, it is interesting to note that the Tom Sawyer principle[51] is alive and well within both behavioral economics and *The Simpsons*, as when Principal Skinner announces that honor students will be rewarded with a trip to an archaeological dig but detention students will be punished with a trip to an archaeological dig.[52] This principle (no near-pun intended) is just an extreme version of the concept of framing and anchoring—in this case, the anchor is whether the students are primed to think of the dig as a positive or negative activity. Even if the two groups of students did not differ in their objective preferences for the activity, it is very likely that the honor students will hold a more favorable view of it both before and after the event. Dan Ariely was able to elicit a similar response (that is, a higher willingness to pay) in his students by simply asking the question, "How much would you pay to listen to me read poetry?" rather than the question "How much would I have to pay you to get you to listen to me read poetry?"[53]

Other Biases

As stated earlier, there are far more concepts in behavioral economics than can possibly be covered adequately in a single chapter. There's the illusion-of-control bias, which makes people falsely believe that they can affect the outcomes of random events. Homer certainly exhibits the illusion of control, for instance, when he is convinced that his duck is going to win the rubber duck race (and a computer for Marge) because his duck really looks like he wants it.[54]

People also tend to exhibit what is known as a false belief in mean reversion, when they expect independent repeated outcomes to be self-correcting.[55] (This is sometimes referred to as the gambler's fallacy.) Mr. Burns, who is generally not known for his irrational behavior, illustrates this principle when suggesting that Homer, the guy who always screws up, watch his house because Homer is due for a good performance.[56]

As extensively noted in psychology, people are subject to the placebo effect. The characters in *The Simpsons* are no exception to this phenomenon, whether it's Barney getting drunk off of non-alcoholic champagne,[57] Crazy Cat Lady being lucid until Marge tells her that her drugs are just Reese's Pieces,[58] or Homer thinking that he can climb the Murderhorn because he's been eating Powersauce bars.[59] Neuroscientists have even found that subjects who are told they are consuming Coca-Cola have different and more positive brain activity than people who are simply given Coca-Cola and not told what it is.[60] This concept is neatly illustrated in *The Simpsons'* commercial for Coca-Cola when Apu relieves Mr. Burns' sadness by giving him a bottle of the soft drink, and the implication is that it's unlikely that another beverage (aside from perhaps a vodka shot or two) would have had the same effect.

Last, the failure to ignore sunk costs is a common bias observed by behavioral economists. Sunk costs are costs that have already been incurred and can't be recovered. Because of this property, sunk costs should be ignored in decision-making processes since the costs are incurred regardless of what action is chosen. People are not always good at recognizing this, as is the case when Homer goes to the go-kart track. Homer manages to break the go-kart such that his rear end is dragging on the ground, yet he refuses to stop despite being in a lot of pain. He justifies his decision by asserting that he paid for fifty laps and he's therefore determined to take them.[61] This sort of bias is also responsible for the escalation of commitment, or what is more commonly referred to as a "slippery slope." This concept is exemplified when Homer and Lisa break into the museum and Lisa is hesitant to cross the velvet ropes to touch the exhibits. Homer argues that Lisa can't just come this far and then not go farther,[62] even though ignoring the irreversible choices and making the optimal decision regarding actions from that point forward is the rational thing to do.

How "Econ" Is Homer Economicus?

Despite the numerous examples of economically irrational behavior present in the series, none of the characters are, in Richard Thaler and Cass Sunstein's term, purely "Human." Homer, for example, is clearly pretty far toward the Human end of the spectrum (as when pondering vastly overpriced extended warranties in "HOMR"), but even he has his moments of objective rational self-interest.

It's pretty common knowledge in the economic world that economists, who are essentially taught to think and behave rationally, tend to donate less to charity than non-economists of equal wealth, age, and so on. To bolster the anecdotal evidence on this topic, economist Robert Frank and psychologists Thomas Gilovich and Dennis Regan surveyed academics in various fields and found that economics professors, in addition to having lower donations on average compared to professors in other fields with similar incomes, are more likely to not give to charity at all.[63] Economists Yoram Bauman and Elaina Rose even used data on student giving at the University of Washington to support the hypothesis that not only do less-charitable individuals tend to choose economics as a major, taking economics courses leads students to become less charitable.[64] This isn't entirely surprising since traditional economic models don't explicitly account for altruism and fairness. Homer seems to have jumped on this rational economist bandwagon when he belittles charities for actually thinking that he might give them money, for example.[65]

For similar reasons, "pay what you want" systems are somewhat perplexing to traditional economists, and they are perplexing to Homer as well. When Homer is confronted with the "suggested donation" pricing policy at the museum and confirms that zero is in fact a valid price, he thinks it's hilarious that people might pay $4.50 when they don't have to, and he doesn't have particularly high hopes for the viability of the museum's pricing strategy.[66] In practice, however, many organizations, ranging from sandwich chain Panera Bread to the rock band Radiohead, have had significant success with the pay what you want model. (It probably also doesn't hurt that the $4.50 serves as an anchor for donation amounts.)

Homer, like traditional economists, even acknowledges the superiority of cash to gifts, at least once he stops and thinks. In "Boy-Scoutz 'N the Hood," for example, Homer is initially disappointed when he finds $20 under the couch, since he had been looking for a peanut. However, his inner monologue reminds him how the economy works—that $20 can buy many peanuts because money can be exchanged for goods and services—and Homer is then quite pleased with his cash discovery.

Mr. Burns, on the other hand, is portrayed as the classic "Econ"—he is a bad tipper,[67] he is clearly a penny pincher, and he seems to have no room for emotion in his decision-making processes. However, even he has his Human moments—he illustrated the false belief in mean reversion, and he has episodes of time inconsistency, as when he promises Bobo the stuffed bear that he'll never leave him behind again even though he's left Bobo behind every time before (despite likely having made similar promises in the past).[68] Sometimes, Mr. Burns' penny pinching is even on the irrational side, as when he almost drowns trying to retrieve a penny from a fountain and responds by immediately trying to get the penny again.[69]

Conclusion

Behavioral economists generally conclude that, in the real world, no one is purely Econ or purely Human. The same can be said of the characters in *The Simpsons*, and that feature certainly adds not only to the show's entertainment value but also to its lasting relevance. Given both the continued popularity of *The Simpsons* and the speed at which behavioral economic research is progressing, one can't help but ponder what biases Homer and others are going to exhibit next.

FROM RABBIT EARS
TO FLAT SCREEN

It's Getting Better All the Time

Steven Horwitz and Stewart Dompe

AT FIRST GLANCE, a 2014 episode of *The Simpsons* makes it seem as though little has changed since 1989: Mr. Burns is still the richest man in Springfield, Barney is still an incorrigible drunk, and Ned Flanders abides. America's favorite upper-lower-middle-class family has stayed upper-lower-middle class. However, first looks can be deceiving. Despite what appears to be a lack of upward mobility, their material well-being has nonetheless improved notably. Even though all of Homer's various get-rich-quick schemes over the years have failed mightily, by simply maintaining his relative place, he has nonetheless become progressively more able to provide a better life for his family, as the productive power of the marketplace has delivered newer and better goods at cheaper prices, especially when calculated in terms of the labor time it takes to purchase them. The Simpsons of 2010 are just as upper-lower-middle class as they were in 1989, but they are notably richer in absolute terms. A closer look at what they have in their house and what they are able to purchase and consume more generally, all still on Homer's modest nuclear plant technician's salary (the guys in sector 7-G haven't seen big raises over the years), will make clear the increase in their standard of living.

This should come as no surprise, as the increased well-being of the Simpson family is very representative of the experience of both the average American family and the poorest American families over the past forty years. The media are full of doom-and-gloom stories about how well-being has stagnated for American families and how kids today are worse off than their parents, but this flies in the face of both the statistical evidence and the smart phone; laptop computer; digital camera; micro-fridge; flat screen TV; Blu-ray player; and cheap, tasty, and fast food that fill the typical American household and dorm room. Without intending it, the evolution of the Simpsons' consumption patterns is an excellent illustration of the ways in which life for most Americans keeps getting better and better all the time.[1]

Markets: Is There Anything They Can't Do?

There are two parts to seeing how the standard of living of the average American family has increased in the past several decades. First, we can offer some data that document that increase, and then we can show some additional data that help explain why and how that increase has taken place. The most concise way to see the gains is to look at the data collected by the Census Bureau's periodic survey of "Extended Measures of Well-Being."[2] In this survey, they ask households whether or not they have a variety of consumer goods in their home. This survey has been done over a number of years, and the major results are summarized in Table 16.1.

These data tell at least three separate stories. The first are the gains made by poor households from 1984 to 2005. These are the households in the bottom

TABLE 16.1. Percentage of households with various consumption goods, 1984–2005

Households with:	Poor 1984	Poor 1994	Poor 2003	Poor 2005	All 1971	All 2005
Washing Machine	58.2	71.7	67.0	68.7	71.3	84.0
Clothes Dryer	35.6	50.2	58.5	61.2	44.5	81.2
Dishwasher	13.6	19.6	33.9	36.7	18.8	64.0
Refrigerator	95.8	97.9	98.2	98.5	83.3	99.3
Freezer	29.2	28.6	25.4	25.1	32.2	36.6
Stove	95.2	97.7	97.1	97.0	87.0	98.8
Microwave	12.5	60.0	88.7	91.2	1.0	96.4
Color TV	70.3	92.5	96.8	97.4	43.3	98.9
VCR	3.4	59.7	75.4	83.6	0.0	92.2
Personal Computer	2.9	7.4	36.0	42.4	0.0	67.1
Telephone	71.0	76.7	87.3	79.8	93.0	90.6
Air Conditioner	42.5	49.6	77.7	78.8	31.8	85.7
Cellular Telephone			34.7	48.3	0.0	71.3
One or More Cars	64.1	71.8	72.8 (2001)		79.5	

SOURCE: U.S. Census Bureau, 2005, and prior years.

20 percent of the income distribution for the year in question. In 1984, this was households with an income of less than $9,500 ($18,680 in 2009 dollars), and in 2005 it was an income less than $19,178 ($21,071 in 2009 dollars).[3] If we compare, for example, the poor in 1984 and 1994, we can see the significant gains of just one decade. With the exception of freezers (mostly likely due to them being built into refrigerators), the poor are more likely in 1994 to have every one of the surveyed consumption goods than in 1984. The increases in the cases of new technology are very large: microwaves are five times more likely to be found in a poor household, and a VCR almost twenty times more likely! Gains in items that middle-class families take for granted, such as a washer and a dryer, were also significant: almost 25 percent for washers and over 40 percent for dryers.

The data from 2003 and 2005 tell much the same story, with dishwashers, microwaves, and VCRs all gaining significant ground, while personal computers and air conditioners made large gains. The year 2003 marked the entrance of the cell phone into the survey, and these spread quickly among the poor. There are numerous other goods that have become common since the data from 2005 were collected, such as DVD players, digital cameras, and high-definition TVs, and future surveys will likely show the same gains for the poor in those categories as well.

If we shift from looking solely at the poor to looking at the last two columns, which compare all American households between 1971 and 2005, we can see the enormous gains of a generation. A forty-year-old in 2005 would have been six in 1971, and his parents would have likely been around the same forty years old that he is in 2005, making this difference truly a generational one. Every single category is higher in 2005 than it was in 1971, with items we now think of as "standard" household possessions becoming much more common. For example, clothes dryers went from less than half of households to over 80 percent. Dishwashers were a luxury of the rich in 1971, but were in a majority of households by 2005. Color TVs (much less high-definition ones with five hundred channels) had not penetrated half of American households in 1971, but were in just about 100 percent of them by 2005. If you think these are just frivolous consumption goods, consider the life-saving properties of air conditioning, which was relegated to less than a third of households in 1971 but possessed by almost 86 percent by 2005.[4] Finally, note all of the goods *that basically did not even exist in 1971* that were now in 66 to nearly 100 percent of households: microwaves, VCRs, personal computers, and cell phones. It is this set of trends that is most vividly illustrated by the over twenty years of *The Simpsons.*

One last way to look at these data is to compare the *average* household in 1971 with the *poorest* households in 2005. With very few exceptions (washers, freezers, and telephones, with the latter offset by the gain in cell phones), poor households today are more, and in many cases significantly more, likely to possess what we now think of as "basic" consumption goods than the average family was in 1971. In addition, almost half of poor households have all of four goods that more or less did not exist in 1971: microwaves, VCRs, personal computers, and cell phones. These data suggest very strongly that poor Americans today live considerably better than did the average American household in 1971. What they also show is that despite the media portrayal of an America in decline, the reality is that life for most Americans, at least as measured by these data, has never been better.

What makes this possible? The answer is a combination of more productive labor and more efficient production processes. Workers are, on average, richer, and firms are able to produce goods more cheaply. These two trends reinforce each other. Contrary to what you might believe, the average private sector wage has risen faster than inflation.[5] More important is the astounding reduction in the cost of producing goods that has led to lower consumer goods prices. One way to show these reinforcing trends is to compute the number of labor hours it would take to buy various goods at the average private sector wage. Economist Mark Perry has done this calculation for a set of goods similar to what we looked at earlier, and the results are show in Table 16.2.[6] When it takes a half to a quarter of the labor hours to earn the income to buy household basics that it did a generation ago, it's no surprise that households are more likely to have these goods and to afford all of the new technologies that have come into existence in the meantime.

Perry also illustrated this process another way. He calculated the labor hours necessary to purchase a stereo system sold at $379.95 in 1964 and then figured out what those labor hours would earn today and what they could purchase. It would have taken 152 hours at the average wage to buy that stereo back then. Today, 152 hours would earn you about $3,000. So instead of spending 152 hours working to buy a mediocre stereo with a turntable and small speakers, you could buy *all* of the following for under $3,000: a Panasonic home theater system, an Insignia fifty-inch plasma HDTV, an Apple 8GB iPod Touch, a Sony 3D Blu-ray disc player, a Sony 300-CD changer, a Garmin portable GPS, a Sony 14.1-megapixel digital camera, a Dell Inspiron laptop computer, and a TiVo high-definition digital video recorder. It is also noteworthy that not *one* of

TABLE 16.2. Change in work hours needed to purchase consumption goods, 1973–2009

Household Appliances	Retail Price, 1973	Hours of Work at $4.12 per hour	Retail Price, 2009	Hours of Work at $18.72 per hour	% Change, 1973 to 2009
Washing Machine	$285	69.2	$400	21.4	−69.1
Clothes Dryer	$185	44.9	$400	21.4	−52.4
Dishwasher	$310	75.2	$570	30.4	−59.5
Refrigerator	$370	89.8	$425	22.7	−74.7
Freezer	$240	58.3	$265	14.2	−75.7
Stove	$290	70.4	$650	34.7	−50.7
Color TV	$400	97.1	$300	16.0	−83.5
Coffee Pot	$37	9.0	$30	1.6	−82.2
Blender	$40	9.7	$32	1.7	−82.4
Toaster	$25	6.1	$30	1.6	−73.6
Vacuum Cleaner	$90	21.8	$100	5.3	−75.5
				Average	−70.8

SOURCE: Perry, 2009.

those items was even available at any price as an alternative to the Radio Shack stereo in 1964.

The economics of production efficiencies and a higher-skilled, better-educated workforce combine to expand the consumption possibilities of all Americans in leaps and bounds beyond what the generation before could do. So, armed with this knowledge, we return to sleepy Springfield to take a closer look and see how the Simpson family and their friends and neighbors reflect the fact that life for the upper-lower-middle class has never been better.

Television: Teacher, Mother, Secret Lover

The Simpsons has always been a TV show that made fun of television, often by putting the TV in the center of the life of Springfield and the plots of numerous episodes. Even the opening credits make this clear, ending as they do with a shot of the family watching TV. Given the importance of TV in the life of Springfield, we shouldn't be surprised to find a number of ways in which it reflects the increased living standards of the past twenty years.

For starters, the TV the family watches in the opening credits changed over the years. When *The Simpsons* first aired, it had rabbit ears and knobs on the side to change the channel, and was most definitely not "cable ready." In the early episodes, the family is clearly unhappy with their TV. When they get double their money back after failing out of Doctor Marvin Monroe's family therapy center, Homer takes his $500 and plans on buying a twenty-one-inch television ("There's No Disgrace Like Home"). Even by 1990 standards, this was a fairly modest TV, and it still ran them close to $500.

The opening credits in recent years features a different TV at the end. This one is clearly a larger, high-definition flat screen, that is certainly "cable-ready." A fairly typical thirty-two-inch LCD can be bought for under $400, and the $500 Homer got from Marvin Monroe can buy a lot of TV nowadays. He could have bought a forty-two-inch plasma for that price with some careful shopping. Plasma is a bit better than simple flesh tones, as you can see all the wrinkles on Kent Brockman's forehead! The evolution of the TV also points out that improvements in living standards are not just a matter of basic goods costing less (keep in mind that Homer would have to work far fewer hours to earn that $500 than twenty years ago), but also that we can get far-superior-quality goods for less as well. It would be one thing to have to work far fewer hours to get the same twenty-one-inch realistic flesh tones, but to both work fewer hours *and* get a forty-two-inch plasma's spectacular quality and size is the real gain.

But even this understates the real gains. The experience of TV today is hardly that of twenty or thirty years ago, given the rise of cable, satellite, and digital and on-demand programming, not to mention DVRs and TiVo. The Simpson family has shared in this bounty as well. In 2002, the Simpsons finally get satellite television ("Bart vs. Lisa vs. the Third Grade"), but before such an achievement, they had stooped much lower. Years earlier, in "Homer vs. Lisa and the 8th Commandment," Homer bribed the cable repairman with $50 to illegally install cable. He presented it to his family with MTV for the kids, VH1 for the adults, and a grand total of sixty-eight channels. This included movie channels and adult programming. The typical number of possible channels for most cable systems these days is in the hundreds. In that episode, Ned Flanders wanted to subscribe to the new Arts and Crafts channel; today there are numerous special interest channels catering to a wide variety of diverse interests, including cooking and hunting. As the diversity of channels has increased, so too has their ability to cater to specialized audiences. The ever-increasing number of television channels represents a gain in living standards, as families have more choices and that means a more precise match between their preferences and what's on TV.

This makes it all the more amusing when people still manage to complain that "there's nothing good on TV."

Now Moe Can Find Amanda Huggenkiss Anywhere

Cell phones are a triumph of progress. When *The Simpsons* first aired, they were owned solely by the rich, they looked like bricks, and with their poor reception they barely performed their intended function. Today cell phones are tiny, reception towers are numerous, and the phones possess a functionality previously reserved for personal computers, which themselves were not present in many households when *The Simpsons* first aired. More important, cell phones are a household staple, as even young teenagers have their own, and they have spread tremendously throughout even the poorest areas of the world. The ways that the cell phone has enabled us to stay in touch with other people and to get access to information at our fingertips has dramatically improved human well-being. To see this, watch an episode of a TV show even as recent as *Seinfeld* and ask how much easier it would have been to avoid the disasters they created for themselves if they only had had cell phones. Yes, the show wouldn't have been as funny, but avoiding social discoordination is one benefit of having a cell phone handy.

The Simpsons' relationship to the cell phone is quite typical. In 2003's "Brake My Wife, Please," a frantic Marge finds herself unable to reach Homer. Bart has been hospitalized after an accident, and without Homer's insurance card, he will remain chained to a radiator. As it did for Homer, the ability to get in touch in such emergencies probably drove many to adopt the new technology. Homer's purchase is also illustrative because in the first season he had to raid the kids' college fund, eighty dollars, and pawn the TV to purchase a single session of family therapy, while fourteen years later he can afford this kind of technology, thanks both to its low price and the higher value of Homer's labor. Paraphrasing the economist Joseph Schumpeter's observation that the great triumph of capitalism is not that the Queen can afford nylons, but that the average housewife can, cell phones are remarkable not because people like Mr. Burns own them, but because people like Homer Simpson can afford them.

In later episodes, we see how cell phones are now common among middle-class children. In "Lost Verizon," from 2008, Bart is cruelly mocked by the other children for lacking a cell phone. His response is to acquire a job selling used golf balls to golfers at the local country club. At a dollar a ball he works and saves until his plan is foiled by Groundskeeper Willie. What was once only available to the rich and connected is now within the grasp of a child and a part-time job. In "Father Knows Worst," a year later, a group of girls holds a cell phone decorating party, and in "Bart Gets a 'Z'" from that same year, the class spikes Mrs. Krabappel's coffee after she confiscates their cell phones. The ease with which even families of modest means can afford a technology that was a $3,000 plaything of the rich twenty years earlier nicely illustrates the ways in which life for most Americans is getting better all the time.

They Have Internet on Computers Now

The decreasing cost of computers has revolutionized society. Computing power that once occupied a large room can now sit comfortably upon your lap or in the palm of your hand. For a number of seasons, the family did not even own a computer, which was not all that unusual. Eventually the personal computer made its way into the Simpsons' lives. Several episodes indicate both the ways in which it became within their reach and how it enhanced their well-being.

In "The Computer Wore Menace Shoes," from 2000, a sleazy salesman convinces Homer that he needs a $5,000 computer to check his email. Homer is obviously buying too much machine for his needs, but what is interesting to note is that even with inflation, a cutting-edge PC today (over ten years later) retails at around $3,999. As a percentage of income, particularly measured as labor hours, we are spending much less and we are getting a much better machine. The top-of-the-line computer Homer bought for $5,000 years ago would barely stack up, if at all, to entry-level machines today. The same forces of competition and efficiency would now allow Homer to do probably more than he could on the $5,000 machine for as little as $299 for a very small netbook. And if it was really just email and basic Internet, why buy a computer at all? A smartphone, which can often be had for free if one pays for the data plan, will do the trick. The cell phones that the residents of Springfield hold in their hands do much of what Homer's $5,000 machine did eight seasons ago.

Computers improve our standard of living by allowing us an unprecedented access to information. Having access to Wikipedia on the iPhone has ended the most heated of trivia debates and saved friendships if not lives. In "Bart vs. Australia," from 1995, Bart collect calls Australia to ask if their water drains clockwise or counterclockwise, stiffing a local boy with a massive phone bill. This of course starts an international incident. With a computer, not only could Bart have Googled the Coriolis effect, he could have found a YouTube video illustrating it.

Computers also play a central role in the episode "Marge Gamer," from 2007. Even though this episode takes place several seasons after "The Computer Wore Menace Shoes," the initial premise is almost the same: Marge lacks an email address. Instead of buying a new computer, Lisa teaches Marge about the Internet using the family's laptop. The rest of the episode focuses on Marge's burgeoning Internet addiction and her virtual interactions with Bart in an on-line game. *The Simpsons* have come a long way since Homer had to take out an-other mortgage to afford a computer. Several things are worth noting. The first is that the family has multiple computers: a desktop and a laptop. Second, the desktop is in Bart's room and, given his distaste for academics, it is essentially a toy. Third, since both computers are capable of running an online game, they both have some power and cannot be bottom-of-the-barrel machines. Last, their Internet connection is capable of simultaneously supporting two people playing video games, which suggests some form of high-speed Internet. Like many American households, the Simpsons went from no computing power to an expensive, simple machine with a basic Internet connection to multiple ma-chines with considerable computing power, connected by high-speed Internet and possibly a household wireless network. And all of this on the basic salary of a sector 7-G employee.

Why Would Anyone Think Otherwise?

Given what the Simpson family teaches us about the increasing well-being of the typical American family over the past twenty years, why would so many people think things have gotten worse? There are a variety of statistics and ar-guments that people use to make the claim that American families are no better off than they used to be, but all of them are full of problems that are worth exploring as a way to think more critically about what the statistics do and do not show.

One of the most frequently cited statistics along these lines is "median household income." Median household income is the household income level at which half of households earn more and half of households earn less. Thus it is often used as a measure of how the "middle class" is doing. In 1990, median household income was $47,637 as measured in 2009 dollars. In 2009, median household income was $49,777.[7] Looked at this way, it appears as though twenty years has produced only about a $2,100 increase in the income of a middle-class family. However, there at least two problems with using this statistic to measure how the "typical" family is doing that need to be noted.

First, we have to remember what it means to compare medians over time. Because the number of households changes from year to year, we are not com-paring exactly the same households when we compare medians through time.

This is important because as the number of households grows from year to year, it is possible that even as the median stays stagnant, each and every household in the original group of households could be richer. Think about test scores as an example. Suppose we have a class of five students who score 40, 50, 60, 70, and 80. The median score is 60. Now suppose two new students enter the class before the next exam. Now suppose they both score 40, but every other student's score goes up by ten, so we have: 40, 40, 50, 60, 70, 80, 90. Notice that the median score is still 60 (half did better, half did worse), but *every student scored better on the second exam than on the first*. The same is true of households: because the pool of households grows each year, and "new" households are usually new entrants to the labor market (either young people or immigrants), those new households are usually relatively poor, so they enter below the median. The implication is that even if the median is fairly stagnant, a large number of households could still be notably better off than they were in prior years. So our evidence about the increasing material well-being of the typical American household is not at odds with the fact that median household income in 2009 dollars has remained pretty flat over the same period.

A second problem with the median household income data is that they do not account for the fact that the average American household is smaller than it used to be. This trend is more noticeable over a longer period than twenty years, but even over the twenty years of *The Simpsons*, the average U.S. household has shrunk from about 2.6 members to 2.5.[8] With fewer members, on average, a household's income will enable the individuals in that household to live better. An income of $49,000 will go farther with only three people than with four. When we add together the fact that the falling costs of goods makes for a better life at a given income, the fact that a stagnant median is compatible with most individual households doing better, and the fact that households are shrinking, we can see that the data on median household income is not a reliable indicator of how the typical family has done over the past twenty years.

Raising the point about the declining cost of goods enables us to make one more observation about the use of median household income as an indicator of standard of living. Ultimately, what we care about is not the money income that people earn, but what that income enables them to do in terms of feeding, clothing, and housing themselves. In some sense, the really fundamental indicator is consumption, and the data presented in the earlier sections make clear how the falling real costs of most goods and services have broadened what the average (and the typical poor) family can consume. One final statistic to make this point: over the course of the twentieth century, the percentage of the average family's income that was devoted to food, clothing, and shelter fell from 75 percent to around 35 percent.[9] Although that trend has slowed, it has not stopped. Each year, the average American family has more discretionary income to spend on non-necessities, which helps to explain the changes we observe in the Simpson family.

Another hotly debated issue that is raised by critics is the question of income mobility. Mobility refers to the degree to which households can move up the income ladder over time. So we might wish to know what percentage of households in the lowest 20 percent of the income distribution are able to move up at least one quintile (that is, one group of 20 percent) in a certain number of years (say, five or ten or fifteen). The easier it is for people to move up, the more income mobility we have. Mobility is another way to measure the degree to which the typical household has become better or worse off over time.

We do not have the space to enter into all of the controversies around these data, but a few points are worth making. First, by some accounts, there remains a significant degree of such mobility in the United States in recent years. U.S. Treasury data indicate that of the poor households in 1996, 57 percent had moved up by 2005. Of middle-class families in 1996, 75 percent were still in the middle class (33 percent) or had moved up (42 percent) by 2005.[10] The study also concluded, "The degree of mobility among income groups is unchanged from the prior decade (1987 through 1996)." Finally, those data also reveal that the real median income of all taxpayers included in the entire sample grew by 24 percent over that period, which is consistent with our test score example from above. The median incomes of the lower-income groups also increased more than the median incomes of the higher-income groups. So even though the rich did get richer, the poor and middle class got richer faster!

As positive as the data on quintile mobility might be, they also understate the real gains to households. The reason is that as we grow richer overall, the size of each quintile expands, which means it takes progressively more income to rise from one quintile to another. It is more likely that households can be moving up the income ladder in terms of their income without jumping a quintile now than it was when the quintiles were more narrow in years past. For example, in 1990, the average incomes in the second-lowest and middle-income quintiles were $18,030 and $29,781. In 2009, the averages were $29,257 and $49,534. (All of these are not adjusted for inflation, as we are interested in comparing the nominally valued quintiles in each case.) The distance from typical lower-middle to middle class was about $11,700 in 1990 but over $20,000 in 2009. In 2009, the range of the lower-middle and middle-class quintiles was $20,712 to $39,000 and $39,000 to $62,725, which compares to the 1990 values of $12,500 to $23,662 and $23,662 to $36,200. Being lower-middle class went from an $11,162 range in 1990 to an $18,288 range in 2009, while being middle class had a $12,538 range in 1990 and a $23,725 range in 2009. The lower-middle-class range expanded by 64 percent, while the middle-class range grew by 89 percent.

This is more evidence that even if families did not move up income quintiles as easily, it does not mean they weren't getting richer or that they lacked upward mobility. The fact that mobility stayed roughly constant over the two periods in the Treasury data is some evidence that families were doing better and that mobility is understated, as we know the quintiles expanded over that period. So even as the mobility data show a significant degree of upward mobility, the reality for most families is that they are more upwardly mobile than those data indicate.

Critics might also note that there is one aspect of the Simpson family that is less typical than was the case in years past: they are a single-earner family. Yes, Marge had a number of part-time jobs over the years, but they have largely survived on Homer's income alone. Some observers have argued that the rise in dual-earner households has happened out of necessity, as families were not able to afford to live middle-class lives on one income. The evidence, however, suggests otherwise. First, the increased labor force participation of married women has been on an upward trend for a hundred years, with no major jump in the last generation, other than for the mothers of very young children. Second, the economic evidence is that the main reason women have joined the labor force is because, with their higher levels of education and the greater demand for labor deriving from increasing wealth, they are able to command notably higher wages than in years past. Along with the improvements in household technology and smaller family sizes that have reduced the need for labor time in the household, these higher wages have drawn women into the workforce out of desire, not necessity. Finally, the evidence suggests that the higher the husband's income, the *more* likely his wife is to have a full-time job. So it is not that struggling middle-class men need working wives to keep up with the Joneses. Rather the Joneses are able to consume more because the payoff to both spouses working is higher and the need for one to be home is lower.[11]

There is much more that could be said about these issues, and we encourage readers to follow up on some of our endnotes to read more about the ways in which life for most American families has improved notably over the past two decades.

Conclusion

A careful watching of the twenty-year evolution of *The Simpsons* would reveal more examples than we have provided here. Despite the fun they've had with Dr. Nick, Dr. Hibbert, and Marvin Monroe, the family has been able to afford medical treatment (think of all the damage Homer has done to Bart and to himself over the years) that prior generations would not have had access to, in some cases at any price. Although the Simpsons have driven the same car for twenty years, a 2010 episode, "Stealing First Base," included a portable GPS unit in that car, something else that is now commonplace in American households that was not commercially available when the show first aired. Having the same car is an interesting example, because cars have actually not dropped all that much in price calculated by labor time. However, cars have steadily increased in quality and amenities over the decades, and the fact that their pink car continues to run after twenty years reflects a major advance over cars of the 1960s or 1970s. (Plus, the one time Homer tried to design his own car, that didn't work out so well ["Oh Brother, Where Art Thou?"]).

The central joke of *The Simpsons* has always been their status as a "typical American family." That typicality is effectively illustrated by the ways in which the gradual increase in their absolute standard of living parallels that of the average overbite-lacking, five-fingered American family of the real world. From the very television they parody, to cell phones, computers, iPods, medical care, and all the rest, the evolution of the daily lives of Homer, Marge, Bart, Lisa, and all of Springfield is the story of a gradual and cumulative increase in material well-being. The process is slow, and the world is still a familiar one from day to day, but with the distance of twenty years, we can see that the surface similarities mask a world that keeps getting better all the time.

THE CONTRIBUTORS

Jodi Beggs is best described as a freelance economist. She has taught economics at both the undergraduate and graduate levels, is an editor for an online learning company, and writes about economics on her web site "Economists Do It with Models" and for various other publications. Jodi has a Master's degree in economics from Harvard University, and she will finish her Ph.D. dissertation as soon as people stop allowing her to count watching cartoons as work. Like Homer Simpson, Jodi thinks that *The Economist* is the real type of "adult" magazine, and this project has given her a compelling urge to purchase a saxophone.

Peter J. Boettke is the BB&T Professor for the Study of Capitalism at the Mercatus Center at George Mason University and also University Professor of economics at GMU. Professor Boettke is the author of several books on the history of, collapse of, and transition from socialism in the former Soviet Union as well as books and articles on the history of economic thought and methodology. With David Prychitko and the late Paul Heyne, he is coauthor of the widely used textbook *The Economic Way of Thinking*, now in its thirteenth edition. In addition to GMU, Boettke has held faculty positions at the London School of Economics, the Hoover Institution at Stanford University, and New York University.

Per Bylund is a research professor in the Department of Management and Entrepreneurship in Baylor University's Hankamer School of Business and the John F. Baugh Center for Entrepreneurship and Free Enterprise. He is also an associate fellow of the Ratio Institute in Sweden and a research fellow at the McQuinn Center for Entrepreneurial Leadership at the University of Missouri.

Art Carden is an assistant professor of economics and business at Samford University and a regular contributor to Mises.org and Forbes.com. His research interests include economic development; the economic history of the South; and the economic, political, and social impact of big box retailers such as Walmart.

Anthony M. Carilli is a professor of economics and director of the Center for Study of Political Economy at Hampden-Sydney College in Virginia. He earned M.A. and Ph.D. degrees from Northeastern University. Dr. Carilli's research interests are varied; he has published papers on rural firefighting, NASCAR, social capital, Austrian business cycle theory, monetary regimes, and so on. Outside of academics, Dr. Carilli serves as a volunteer firefighter and baseball umpire. He umpired professionally for four years in the independent Northern League, where he worked the championship series in his final season. He also has worked many Virginia State high school playoff games.

John Considine is an economist. You might remember him from articles such as "The Simpsons: Public Choice in the Tradition of Swift and Orwell" and "Yes Minister: Invaluable Material for Teaching the Public Choice for Bureaucracy" or from teaching economics to students at University College Cork, Ireland.

Stewart Dompe is an adjunct professor at Johnson & Wales University. When not watching *The Simpsons* he researches Austrian economics and political economy. He enjoys the occasional Duff Beer and Krusty Burger. He dreams of one day releasing the hounds.

Robert J. Gitter is a professor of economics at Ohio Wesleyan University. He holds M.A. and Ph.D. degrees in economics from the University of Wisconsin-Madison and a B.A. degree in economics from the University of Michigan. In the past several years his primary research focus has been on Mexican migration issues, and he has published an article along with his son, Seth, and another coauthor. He has published on a wide range of issues in labor economics in *The American Economic Review*, *The Monthly Labor Review*, and *Economics Letters* as well as in German and Mexican journals. He was awarded Ohio Wesleyan's Herbert Welch Meritorious Teaching Award. The university provost made the award at graduation, citing, among other reasons, Gitter's ability to relate to the students through the use of *The Simpsons*. Like Homer, Gitter has three children and a very loving and understanding wife.

Seth R. Gitter is an associate professor of economics at Towson University. He holds a Ph.D. degree from the Agricultural and Applied Economics Department at the University of Wisconsin-Madison and a B.A. degree in economics from Grinnell College. His main area of research focuses on human capital accumulation in Latin America. He has received research grants from the Inter-American Development Bank and the British Government (DFID) to study the effects of conditional cash transfers on early childhood development. His work has been published in *World Development*, *World Bank Economic Review*, and *The Journal of Development Studies*. He has enjoyed watching *The Simpsons* with his father and coauthor, Robert Gitter, since he was Bart's age. With his wife, Marie, he has a daughter, Sylvia, who is Maggie's age.

Joshua Hall is an associate professor of economics at West Virginia University. He earned his bachelor and master degrees in economics from Ohio University and his

Ph.D. degree from West Virginia University in 2007. Prior to returning to his alma mater, he was the Elbert H. Neese, Jr. Professor of Economics at Beloit College. Formerly an economist for the Joint Economic Committee of the U.S. Congress, he is a coauthor of the widely cited *Economic Freedom of the World* annual reports. In addition, he is author of over fifty articles in journals such as *Contemporary Economic Policy, Journal of Economic Behavior and Organization, Journal of Economic Education, Journal of Labor Research, Southern Economic Journal, Public Finance Review,* and *Journal of Public Administration Research and Theory.*

Lauren Heller is an assistant professor of economics at Berry College in Rome, Georgia. A Ph.D. graduate from the University of North Carolina at Chapel Hill, she earned her B.A. degree in economics from Capital University. Her research interests focus primarily on issues pertaining to international health and applied econometrics.

Christopher M. Holbrook has an M.A. degree in political science from the University of South Dakota, and is pursuing a Ph.D. degree in political science at the University of Missouri.

Steven Horwitz is Charles A. Dana Professor of Economics at St. Lawrence University in Canton, New York, and an Affiliated Senior Scholar at the Mercatus Center in Arlington, Virginia. He is the author of two books, *Microfoundations and Macroeconomics: An Austrian Perspective* (2000) and *Monetary Evolution, Free Banking, and Economic Order* (1992), and he has written extensively on Austrian economics, Hayekian political economy, monetary theory and history, and the economics and social theory of gender and the family. His work has been published in professional journals such as *History of Political Economy, Southern Economic Journal,* and *The Cambridge Journal of Economics.* He has also done public policy research for the Mercatus Center, Heartland Institute, Citizens for a Sound Economy, and the Cato Institute, with his most recent work being on the role of Walmart and other big box stores in the aftermath of Hurricane Katrina. He is currently working on a book on classical liberalism and the family.

Shannon M. Kelly is an economics major at the College of Charleston. Originally from Canada (like Homer Simpson), she was raised in Watertown, New York. Besides dual citizenship, she shares much in common with Homer Simpson, as she is also a lover of beer and donuts. However, she has greater ambition than Homer and would like to attend graduate school to further her studies in economics.

Peter G. Klein is an associate professor of applied social sciences and associate professor of public affairs at the University of Missouri, adjunct professor at the Norwegian School of Economics and Business Administration, and director of the McQuinn Center for Entrepreneurial Leadership. His research focuses on the economics of organization, entrepreneurship, and corporate strategy, with applications to diversification, innovation, food and agriculture, economic growth, and vertical coordination. He taught previously at the Olin School of Business; the University of California, Berkeley; the University of Georgia; and the Copenhagen Business School. During the 2000–2001 academic year, Klein was a senior economist with the Council of Economic Advisers.

David T. Mitchell is an assistant professor of economics at the University of Central Arkansas. He took his Ph.D. degree in economics from George Mason University and his undergraduate degree from Clemson University. His notable publication outlets include the *Southern Journal of Economics*, the *Cato Journal*, and Forbes.com. His favorite classes to teach are microeconomics, public economics, and experimental economics. He is currently researching post-Katrina rebuilding on the Gulf Coast.

Gregory M. Randolph is an associate professor of economics in the School of Business, Southern New Hampshire University. He received his B.A. degree from Grove City College and his M.A. and Ph.D. degrees in economics from West Virginia University.

Douglas Rogers was an H. B. Earhart Dissertation Fellow in the department of Economics, George Mason University. Tragically, he passed away in a car accident in 2011. He was awarded his Ph.D. degree in economics posthumously in 2011, when he was awarded the Israel M. Kirzner Award for Outstanding Dissertation in Austrian Economics for "Organizing Crime: Towards a Theory of the Criminal Firm." He graduated summa cum laude with a B.A. degree in economics in 2007 from West Virginia University.

Justin M. Ross is an assistant professor of public finance at Indiana University in the Bloomington School of Public and Environmental Affairs. He earned his Ph.D. degree in economics from West Virginia University, and his research interests lie in state and local public finance, especially property-tax-related issues. His interest in the benefit-view of property taxation also leads him to study zoning and other institutional features of local government.

Diana W. Thomas is an assistant professor of economics at Utah State University. Her research is in the areas of public choice, where she mostly explores entrepreneurship in the political sphere, and development economics. Diana teaches international economics and microeconomic principles. In an earlier life, Diana was a portfolio manager for a German investment management company. Working in finance, she learned rather quickly that "If something's hard to do, then it's not worth doing." So she chose a life of the mind, and "Who would have guessed reading and writing would pay off?!"

Mark Thornton is a senior fellow at the Ludwig von Mises Institute. He serves as the book review editor of the *Quarterly Journal of Austrian Economics*. He served as the editor of the *Austrian Economics Newsletter* and as a member of the editorial board of the *Journal of Libertarian Studies*. He has served as a member of the graduate faculties of Auburn University and Columbus State University. He has also taught economics at Auburn University at Montgomery and Trinity University in Texas. Mark served as assistant superintendent of banking and economic adviser to Governor Fob James of Alabama (1997–1999), and he was awarded the University Research Award at Columbus State University in 2002. His publications include *The Economics of Prohibition* (1991), *Tariffs, Blockades, and Inflation: The Economics of the Civil War* (2004), *The Quotable Mises* (2005), *The Bastiat Collection* (2007), and *An Essay on Economic Theory* (2010). He is a graduate of St. Bonaventure University and received his Ph.D. degree in economics from Auburn University.

Douglas M. Walker is a professor of economics at the College of Charleston. His research on gambling has been published in journals such as *Journal of Health Economics*, *Public Choice*, *Contemporary Economic Policy*, and *Public Finance Review*. His book *The Economics of Casino Gambling* was published in 2007. His lifelong dream, which he achieved in June 2010, was completing the requirements to join the Beer Club at the Charleston Mellow Mushroom.

Andrew T. Young is an associate professor of economics at the College of Business and Economics, West Virginia University. His research is in macroeconomics, including the study of business cycles, economic growth, and monetary policy. His work is published in such journals as the *Review of Economics and Statistics*, the *Journal of Money, Credit, and Banking*, the *Southern Economic Journal*, and the *Review of Austrian Economics*.

Preface

1. Hall, 2005.

2. Hall and Gillis, 2010.

3. For an excellent overview of the evolution of the phrase *homo economicus,* see Persky (1995). McCloskey (1993) points out that while it has come to mean "economic man," *homo economicus* is more appropriately translated as "economic human."

Chapter 1

1. Fortunately for us, many of Bastiat's essays on economics have been collected into three volumes: *Economic Harmonies* (Bastiat 1995a), *Economic Sophisms* (Bastiat 1995b), and *Selected Essays on Political Economy* (Bastiat 1995c).

2. Bastiat, 1995c.

3. Imagine the episode: there would be a parade, Bart and Milhouse would be the toast of the town, Lisa would be angry, Marge ecstatic, and Homer confused.

4. And possibly allows Fudd Beer to gain a stronghold in Springfield.

5. Bastiat, 1995c, p. 1.

6. The budget constraint need not be limited to money or income. It can include proclivities, predilections, talents, and the like: Lisa is smart, Bart mischievous, Marge caring, and Homer—well he's just Homer.

7. That is even the title for a successful introductory economics text, *The Economic Way of Thinking* (Heyne, Boettke, and Prychitko 2010).

8. Mankiw, 2009.

9. Gwartny, Stroup, Sobel, and Macpherson, 2008.

10. Frank and Bernanke, 2009.

11 For an interesting discussion of opportunity cost, see Munger (2006).

12. See Buchanan (1969) for the most comprehensive discussion of this topic.

13. See Buchanan (1969) for a wonderful discussion of subjective valuation.

14. The apprentice chef prepares the fugu because the head chef is having a brief tryst with Mrs. Krabappel in his car.

15. His "successes" include a fifteen-mile-per-hour speed limit on Main Street, a speed bump, and a dip sign, in addition to the stop sign at D Street and Twelfth.

16. *The Wealth of Nations* (Smith [1776] 1937, p. 3) begins, "The greatest improvement in the productive powers of labour, and the greater part of the skill, dexterity, and judgment with which it is any where directed, or applied, seem to have been the effects of the division of labour."

17. Adam Smith ([1776] 1937, p. 4) describes the specialization in the pin factory: each worker has his own task, so pin making "is divided into a number of branches, of which the greater part are likewise peculiar trades. One man draws out the wire, another straights it, a third cuts it, a fourth points it, a fifth grinds it at the top for receiving the head; to make the head requires two or three distinct operations; to put it on, is a peculiar business, to whiten the pins is another; it is even a trade by itself to put them into the paper; and the important business of making a pin is, in this manner, divided into about eighteen distinct operations. . . ."

18. Smith, [1776] 1937, p. 11.

19. Changes in tastes and preferences can also change plans. In the opening scene of "The Sweetest Apu," Apu questions his wife Manjula's judgment in bringing the octuplets to work as they run roughshod all over the Kwik-E-Mart. He asks that she take the children home because men buying adult magazines are too embarrassed to bring them to the counter.

20. This does not suggest that an individual won't sometimes experience *ex post* regret; after the trade, he may discover he was mistaken in his evaluation of the items being traded. In "Bart Sells His Soul," convinced that there is no such thing as a soul (a soul has zero value), Bart exchanges his soul with Milhouse for $5. After the exchange some strange things begin to happen to Bart, and he decides that his soul was worth more than $5 (he experiences *ex post* regret) and sets out to retrieve it.

21. Since money is another good, saying "at different prices" is the same as saying "for other goods."

22. The labor theory of value holds that the value of anything is given by the labor embodied in it. So something that takes more labor to produce would therefore be more valuable than something that uses less labor in its production. By the labor theory of value, Homer's spice rack would be more valuable than one built in half the time by a more skilled artisan. The labor theory of value is intuitively powerful, so much so that even Adam Smith believed it.

Chapter 2

1. Heyne, Boettke, and Prychitko, 2010, 6.

2. For more, see Boettke and Dirmeyer (2008) and Blaug (2008).

3. Private property rights are a precondition to economic exchange and growth, and thus it is vital to understand how property rights emerge and how they function

in order to understand economics in general. See Coase, "The Problem of Social Cost" (1960); Alchian, "Some Economics of Property Rights" (1965); and Demsetz, "Toward a Theory of Property Rights" (1967) for three seminal works on the emergence and function of property rights in a market economy. The critical issue with property rights is that they help establish the rules of access to the use of scarce resources, assign accountability for that use, and provide the foundation for the trade of those access rights to higher-valued users of the resource.

4. Specialization is essential for individuals to get the most out of trade. Consider the case of the pin factory in Adam Smith's *An Inquiry into the Nature and Causes of the Wealth of Nations* ([1776] 1937), described in Chapter 1. Specialization increased the average output per worker from twenty pins at most to four thousand eight hundred pins per day!

5. To see why this is the case, some basic algebra is necessary. Going from Table 2.1, Dr. Hibbert's productive capabilities can be expressed by the equation $H = 10 - 2S$, where H represents hallways cleaned and S represents surgeries performed. Once again, if he chooses to only clean hallways, he can clean ten but that leaves no time for performing surgeries. He can also choose to perform five surgeries but this leaves no time for cleaning hallways. If he were to split his time evenly between activities he could perform two-and-a-half surgeries and five hallway cleanings. This corresponds to the table, in which his opportunity cost of performing one surgery is two hallways cleaned.

6. It is worth noting that the exact terms of the exchange need not be three hallways for one surgery. There are many different price ratios that are mutually beneficial; that is, in which both parties benefit. Any price ratio in which both parties benefit from the trade is possible.

7. In one of the most important and highly cited papers in economics, Hayek (1945) explains the role that prices play in a market economy. He shows how prices solve the central problem in economics, what is commonly referred to as "the knowledge problem." Prices aggregate the dispersed knowledge, held by individual consumers, regarding the market value of scarce resource. Prices not only let us know what things are worth, they also ensure that resources flow to their highest-valued use.

Chapter 3

1. This chapter is inspired by and based on discussions I led during summer writing camps at Rhodes College.

2. More on the Austrian School can be found in Boettke (2008).

3. For a critique of this argument, see Whitman (2006).

4. Landsburg, 1995.

5. Acemoglu and Angrist, 2001.

6. DeLeire, 2000a. DeLeire (2000b) gives a nice summary of this literature.

7. Block (2008) offers an entertaining defense of the person who shouts "fire!" in a crowded theater; his defense inspires the discussion in this text.

8. Bastiat, 1995; Hazlitt, [1946] 2009.

Chapter 4

1. For those whose interest is piqued by what follows, an excellent and detailed discussion of the nature of money is provided by Ludwig von Mises (1981), in particular, chapters 1–6.

2. Federal Reserve, 2010. There are other definitions of the money supply in the U.S. economy. For example, a more narrow measure is M1, which is cash plus checking account deposits. (In other words, M1 equals M2 minus savings account deposits.) M3, on the other hand, is a broader definition of the money supply (that is, it includes assets other than cash and bank accounts). If you want to know how much the money supply is in the U.S. economy, according to various measures, the FRED database at the St. Louis Federal Reserve branch is an excellent source: http://research.stlouisfed.org/fred2/categories/24.

3. In the past few years, several U.S. localities have attempted to issue their own currencies to encourage people to buy locally. However, while they are designed to only be acceptable locally, the problem with them is that *they are only acceptable locally!* See, for example, Gangemi (2007). (There is more on this further on in the chapter. An effective money will arise from an asset that is, among other things, *widely used in payment for goods and services.*)

4. For more on the relationship between money and double-entry bookkeeping and profits historically, see Weatherford (1997, chapters 4–5) and Ferguson (2008, chapter 1).

5. For a wealth of examples of commodities that served as monies in the American colonies, see Brock (1975).

6. Inflation is a phenomenon that has plagued many economies, disrupting the store of value function of money and breaking down the ability of people to exchange goods and services. This is especially true during *hyper*inflations (for example, the German experience following World War I), when the purchasing power of money can fall by over 300 percent in a single month! Nobel Laureate Milton Friedman (1994) provides a wonderful overview of several inflationary episodes and explains why, invariably, the culprits are governments that indulge in the creation of excessive amounts of new money.

7. Hagenbaugh, 2006.

8. Weatherford, 1997, pp. 21–22.

9. For example, see Radford (1945) and Lankenau (2001).

10. Rothbard, 2008, chapter 4.

11. Moving from a gold standard to a fiat currency is desirable from the point of view of governments largely because it provides them with an implicit (and less visible) means of taxing its citizens. See Murray Rothbard (2008, chapter 3) for a presentation of this argument.

12. Alternatively, George Selgin (2008) provides a fascinating story from late 1700s to early 1800s Britain. During this time (which is the beginning of the Industrial Revolution), the government failed to provide enough small-denomination coinage. In response, private manufacturers started to offer competing issues of coins that gained wide acceptance. Despite being "tokens" in the sense that their exchange value was greater than their metallic value, these constituted Britain's small denomination circulation until 1821, when they were outlawed by the government.

Chapter 5

1. Carroll, 2007.

2. For more information on entrepreneurship, see Kirzner (1973), Schumpeter ([1934] 1993), and Baumol (1990).

3. For more information on opportunity costs, see Buchanan (1969).

4. For more information on economic profits, see Knight (1921) and Rothbard (2009).

5. For more information about competition, see Hayek (1978) and Kirzner (1997).

6. McAfee, Mialon, and Williams (2004) provide a nice discussion of what an entry barrier is. For information on the impact of entry barriers on entrepreneurship and economic progress, see Sobel, Clark, and Lee (2007).

7. An individual firm may be able to continue to earn economic profits by constantly providing differentiated goods or services from its competitors. For more information about how firms compete in the market process, see Hayek (1945; 1978).

8. For a discussion of some economist's views on postal services, see Geddes (2004).

9. See the episode "Bart Gets Hit by a Car."

10. For an interesting application of business licensure, see Levitz (2010). The article discusses a legal battle between Benedictine monks and the state funeral board in Louisiana regarding the right to sell caskets.

11. In fact, the effect of licensure on the wages of physicians was a portion of Nobel Laureate Milton Friedman's doctoral dissertation, eventually published as Friedman and Kuznets (1945). In the book they find that physicians' salaries were one-third higher than those of dentists in large part because the barriers to entry were greater (at the time) for physicians than for dentists. For more discussion of this episode, see Friedman and Friedman (1998, p. 71).

12. For a discussion of the diamond industry of the twentieth century, see Epstein (1982).

13. Economists generally refer to a firm in an industry in which there are high entry barriers and no close substitutes for the good or service provided as a monopoly. For more information on monopolies, see Harberger (1954) and Bork (1978).

14. In addition to the suggested readings and standard classroom economics textbooks, see Henderson (2007) to read more about each topic.

Chapter 6

1. Compare Klein (2008), Casson (1982), and Knight (1942).

2. Parker, 2004.

3. Hamilton, 2000.

4. Acs and Audretsch, 1990.

5. Foss, Foss, and Klein, 2007.

6. Baumol, 1990.

7. Witt, 1999.

8. See, for example, Mises ([1949] 1998) and Salerno (2008).

9. Knight, 1921; Foss, Foss, and Klein, 2007; and Yu, 2002.

10. Cantillon, [1775] 1931; Knight, 1921; Foss and Klein, 2005; and Mises [1949] 1998.

11. Kirzner, 1973; 1979; and 1992.

12. Foss and Klein, 2010.

13. Schumpeter, [1934] 1993.

14. Schultz, 1975 and 1980.

15. Casson, 2000.

16. Witt, 1998 and 1999.

17. Casson, 1982.

18. Mises, [1949] 1998.

19. Baumol, 1990.

20. Mises, [1949] 1998, p. 249.

21. Lachmann, 1956, p. 16.

Chapter 7

1. Smith, [1776] 1937, book I, chapter 2, p. 14.

2. Smith [1776] 1937, book IV, chapter 2, p. 423.

3. Hirshleifer, 2005, p. 506.

4. For a full description of economic efficiency, see Heyne, Boettke, and Prychitko (2010).

5. The assumptions underlying perfect competition are described in every microeconomics textbook. They usually include at least conditions 1–3 described here, but sometimes there are additional criteria and some authors limit themselves to conditions 1 and 2. See, for example, Mankiw (2009).

6. Burns realizes it is a monopoly in "Who Shot Mr. Burns? (Part One)" when he notes that he already owns the electric company, the water works, and a hotel on Baltic Avenue.

7. For more on how technological advance can reduce the need for policy intervention, see Klein and Foldvary (2003), especially chapters 9, 10, and 11.

8. For a more detailed discussion of the tragedy of the commons, see Hardin (1968).

9. You can find a more detailed description of the California water basin problem as well as other examples of local self-governance solutions to commons problems in Ostrom (1990).

10. According to the restaurant owner, Bart's shirking now means his children will go to a state university.

11. This episode also had one of the most insightful commentaries on parents' motivations and higher education.

12. Yellen (1984) discusses efficiency wages in more detail.

13. Notice that this theory assumes no repeat interaction because consumers would presumably not purchase a brand of beer for a second time if they had had a bad experience with it previously.

14. Klein discusses this in "The Demand and Supply of Assurance" (2002).

15. Conversely, when in Spittle County one orders Fudd Beer, which is widely available even though it makes hillbillies blind, according to Moe ("Midnight Towboy").

16. In the episode "Marge in Chains," we find out that the seal on the wall of Mayor Joe Quimby's office reads "Corruptus in Extremis" (extremely corrupt).

Chapter 8

1. Those familiar with economics may recognize this sentence as a play on a famous passage from Adam Smith's *An Inquiry into the Nature and Causes of the Wealth of Nations* ([1776] 1937, p. 423): "It is not from the benevolence of the butcher, the brewer, or the baker that we expect our dinner, but from their regard to their own self-interest." Smith was a Scottish moral philosopher and is considered the father of economics.

2. A shorter essay written for policymakers that tries to address these questions can be found in Ross (2009).

3. In economics, a "rent" is the portion of a payment to a factor of production that is beyond what is required to keep that factor employed in its current use. In the case of a monopoly rent, the producer is restricting total output so that the last unit of production sells at a higher price, causing a larger transfer from consumers to the producer to occur. The origins of this concept can be traced back to a famous economist, David Ricardo, who provided a similar definition in his book *On the Principles of Political Economy and Taxation* (1821).

4. The implications of this point for policy, namely that special-interest groups and politicians are unlikely to differentiate between externalities, is elaborated on in Holcombe and Sobel (2001).

5. According to Levy and Peart (2001), "The Dismal Science" was a pejorative term for economics coined by Thomas Carlyle in his 1849 essay, "An Occasional Discourse on the Negro Question." At the time, economists such as John Stuart Mill used institutions to explain wealth differences across nations, whereas members of the eugenics movement such as Carlyle and Sir Thomas Malthus offered that race was the primary explanation.

6. In standard economic theory, it is not necessary that the $2 go to any such group. What is important is that resources are allocated efficiently, while the issue of who gets the $2 per Duff becomes a distribution-and-equity issue.

7. Social welfare analysis is a type of cost-benefit analysis that economists conceptualize or estimate for society at large. It takes the total social benefits and subtracts the social costs of the resources, resulting in "net social welfare" or "social net benefit." For example, the social net benefit of this chapter will be the value of it to the reader, less the production costs such as materials, labor, and the best forgone alternative use of the time spent by the reader enjoying this chapter.

8. In this particular case, parents do not bear the full cost of their children because of public policy, not because of natural market forces. Thus, even though the analysis of the consequences are the same, the underlying cause is not a internal market failure but a result of the political process that finances public education through taxation.

9. Pigouvian taxation receives its name from the influential economist and author of "The Welfare of Economics" (1932), A. C. Pigou. Pigou's welfare analysis is the basis for normative economic analysis in a wide range of fields, but the use of taxation makes it particularly evident in public finance (Sobel 2005).

10. The "Cap and Trade" bill that failed in the 2010 Congress is an example of this attempt to create property rights. Other policy examples can be found in Ross (2009).

11. See Armen Alchian's essay on property rights in the *Concise Encyclopedia of Economics, 2nd ed.* (2008) for a richer discussion.

12. This idea was first considered in Coase (1960). Ronald Coase won the Nobel Prize for Economics in 1991.

13. This approach is commonly used in welfare analysis, and is known as "compensating variation."

14. Oliver Williamson, a former student of Ronald Coase, was the 2009 Nobel Prize winner in economics for his work in understanding the role of transaction costs in economic organization. See Williamson (2010) for an overview of his life's work.

15. Economists use the term *transaction costs* very loosely. For instance, if it were simply impossible to communicate with other parties in your group, economists would refer to this situation as having "infinite transaction costs," even though that may sound a bit perplexing to those outside the science.

16. For an introduction to how politics matters in the judicial system, see Lopez (2010).

17. This problem is sometimes referred to as "The Tragedy of the Anticommons." See Heller (1998) for an explanation, as well as the coining of the phrase.

18. For a deeper description of the similarities and differences of these two schools, see Mitchell (2001).

19 Stigler, 1971.

Chapter 9

1. Why the negative stereotyping? Obviously those who decided to use the word *failure* had not seen the episode "Homer to the Max." This episode illustrates the well-known phenomenon that stereotyping can have powerful feedback effects. Max Power is a far more dynamic character than Homer Simpson. That said, Frank Grimes is amazed at, and irritated by, Homer's success ("Homer's Enemy").

2. Market failure occurs when the costs or benefits to the individual are different from those facing society. A standard example is when the costs of smoking are borne by nonsmokers.

3. Government failure, like market failure, occurs when the costs or benefits to the individual are different from those facing society. The difference between government failure and market failure is that the former arises from decisions made in a government setting while the latter occurs in a market setting. In addition, many deem it a government failure that public officials would make decisions based on their private interest rather than in the public interest.

4. Individual failure occurs when individuals have irrational biases in their decision making. For example, when Homer is rushing to submit his tax returns he still stops to purchase an ice cream ("The Trouble with Trillions"). These issues are dealt with in more detail in Chapter 15, on behavioral economics.

5. The beginning of the public choice school is usually linked to the publication of Buchanan and Tullock (1962).

6. Shughart, 2008, p. 428.

7. Gordon Tullock says, "higher-level British bureaucrats will tell you that they simply carry out the instructions of their 'masters.' Although this may be true, to some extent the relationship between the senior bureaucrats and the political heads of their departments is rather like the caricatures in the British television situation comedy *Yes Minister*" (Tullock, Seldon, and Brady 2002, pp. 53–54). An account of the public choice aspects of this comic relationship is provided in Considine (2006).

8. The politician needs to keep the median voter happy. Or put another way, the median voter determines the outcome.

9. If for whatever reason the individual does vote, he or she is unlikely to be well-informed because of the costs of acquiring information on the candidates or issues.

10. Olson (1965) explains this phenomenon.

11. Might this explain the narrow acceptance or rejection of ballots on publicly funded stadia presented in Rosentraub (1997)?

12. There are also references to the other Capra and Stewart classic *It's a Wonderful Life* in "Fear of Flying," "Two Cars in Every Garage and Three Eyes in Every Fish," "When Flanders Failed," "Miracle on Evergreen Terrace," and "Sampson and Delilah."

13. A common theme in the government failure literature is when costs are strategically underestimated and benefits strategically overestimated. In this case the lobbyist's cartoon rendition of the benefits of logging is strategically overestimated.

14. The mutual political support for policies is labelled logrolling by public choice scholars. The pigs eating dollar bills from barrels is a reference to pork barrel politics or the bringing home of the bacon. It is a situation in which a political representative succeeds in getting preferential treatment of his or her constituency.

15. The government inspection official that Burns tries to bribe in "Two Cars in Every Garage and Three Eyes in Every Fish" is one exception. Other exceptions are Rex Barron and Ray Patterson. The IRS officials also seem to be public spirited even if not so bright.

16. References to "real-life" democrats and republicans suggest these too have their faults. President Clinton admitted that he was a bad president in "Saddlesore Galactica," while his Republican alternative George Bush was far from the ideal neighbor in "Two Bad Neighbors."

17. The issue of prohibition is dealt with in more depth in Chapter 13.

18. Shughart, 2008, p. 430.

19. In Federalist Paper No. 51, James Madison (1788) pointed out that "If men were angels, no government would be necessary. If angels were to govern men, neither external nor internal controls on government would be necessary."

20. No, Bono is not Colin's father.

21. Snake also sees the opportunity provided by the town meeting to burgle the attendees' empty houses.

22. Logan (2005) explains how Lanley used the social psychology of group membership and influence to achieve his aim. Homer also tells Marge she should have written a song like Lyle Lanley did. The importance of imagery in politics can be seen by how the Republicans used a photo of Michael Dukakis in a military tank against him in the 1988 presidential campaign. They also used the example of Willie Horton to claim Dukakis was soft on crime in a manner similar to the way the Springfield Republicans claimed Quimby was soft on crime for releasing Sideshow Bob ("Sideshow Bob Roberts").

23. Although children don't vote, they do represent a clearly defined interest group that others identify with. It is no coincidence that Quimby and Sideshow Bob campaign in both the Elementary School and the Retirement Castle.

24. Gordon Tullock says, "its [tax avoidance] mere existence puts a certain amount of restraint on the government. Whether the restraint is good or bad depends on what government does" (Tullock, Seldon, and Brady 2002, p. 70).

Chapter 10

1. One of the fathers of economics, Alfred Marshall (1890, p. 94), said, "Economics has as its purpose firstly to acquire knowledge for its own sake, and secondly to throw light on practical issues." Hence, studying immigration continues in this tradition.

2. Wait a second, do people use terms such as *value of migration* in making their decisions? Probably not, unless they are economists. But these are just our words to describe their thought processes. For classic articles on migration, see Todaro (1969) and Sjaastad (1962).

3. See Pritchett (2006) and Clemens (2010).

4. Chiquiar and Hanson, 2005.

5. Government Accounting Office, 2006.

6. Reyes and Mameesh, 2002.

7. If you don't think future benefits need to be discounted, then how do you feel about a lottery in which you win a million dollars paid out a rate of a dollar a year for one million years?

8. Borjas, 1987.

9. S.H.I.T.? How did this one get by the Fox censors?

10. Another example of getting on a path to citizenship occurred in "Coming to Homerica," when Homer attempted to marry off Marge's sister Selma to Thorbjørn, a recent migrant from Ogdenville. Such a marriage would not have been legal, as marriage to Selma would be considered cruel and unusual punishment. In addition, their marriage would not have been seen as credible given that Selma Bouvier-Terwilliger-Hutz-McClure-Stu-Simpson had previously been married to Sideshow Bob, Lionel Hutz, Troy McClure, Disco Stu, and Abe Simpson.

11. Except for selling "Out of Business" signs.

12. Mr. Burns took advantage of immigrant labor in the episode "The Last Temptation of Homer"; he replaced one of Homer's colleagues, Charlie, with Zutroy, an immigrant of unknown origin. Mr. Burns paid the relatively small wage of one shiny penny a day. For Mr. Burns, having cheap labor is a benefit, since he is hiring. For Charlie, however, there is a cost in that he no longer has his job. Similarly, when Mr. Burns produced his biopic masterpiece film, he hired Stephen Spielbergo, the Mexican director, whose wage was substantially less than that of Stephen Spielberg, the American director.

13. The idea that the native-born population would resent immigrants working for lower wages is not new. After the Irish potato famine in 1845, many people emigrated from Ireland to the United States and England. The native-born population of the host nations thought that the Irish immigrants might undercut their wages. To keep their customers and other employees happy, firms would advertise for help with a note stating that no Irish need apply. It appears in the Simpsons, too, as a sign that says "Help Wanted: No Irish Need Apply" at Moe's bar in "Homer vs. the Eighteenth Amendment." For the view that claims about labor market discrimination against the Irish are overstated, see Jensen (2002).

14. Chiquiar and Hanson (2005) found in 2000 that more than half of Mexican migrants to the United States did not complete ninth grade, compared to only one in twenty native-born U.S. citizens.

15. You might be wondering if Homer is in the more educated group. He did in fact attend Springfield University in "Homer Goes to College."

16. Burtless, 2009.

17. For a review of a number of studies, see Levine (2010).

18. Sometimes migrants possess skills that Americans don't. We admit some migrants to the United States under the H1B visa program because they possess special skills. Perhaps H1B visas were used to hire the Ogdenvillians to build a wall to keep Ogdenvillians out because no Americans had the skills.

19. Or not, if you checked your Gmail and googled five things while trying to read this chapter.

20. "The City of New York vs. Homer Simpson."

21. Wadsworth, 2010; and Butcher and Piehl, 1998.

22. Sometimes undocumented immigrants contribute taxes without receiving benefits. If someone is using a social security number that is not theirs, he or she will be paying into the system yet receiving no benefits. Since the persons doing this are not in the country legally, it is difficult to survey them and find out how frequently this occurs.

23. Some students under the age of twenty-one also purchase fake papers to have a Duff Beer.

24. Congressional Budget Office, 2007.

25. Borjas, 1995.

26. Congressional Budget Office, 2007.

27. This assumes someone actually listens to economists.

28. Borjas, 2001.

Chapter 11

1. The title of this chapter is a play on the title of Ehrenreich (2002).

2. I'm waiting for the episode in which Homeland Security comes to find out what Homer is doing with all that uranium. I hope there's a Mos Eisley Cantina scene at Moe's in the same episode.

3. Even Homer's super-boss Hank Scorpio ("You Only Move Twice") was greedy and self-interested. He gave the United Nations seventy-two hours to deliver the gold or else he would use a doomsday device.

4. As Scorpio did with Homer in "You Only Move Twice."

5. Economists call this "on the margin," meaning one more or less (workers) at the relevant range. If football teams had fifty million players each, then Peyton Manning might not be so valuable. Since each team is only allowed eleven players at a time, Peyton Manning is very valuable. Replacing him with a different quarterback (a change of one player, or a marginal change) would be a huge difference. Replacing Homer with a different safety inspector might not be such a big difference, so Homer makes much less than Peyton.

6. In some episodes Homer only has a high school diploma, but in this one he goes to college and fails, so his friends hack into the school's computer to change his grade. In the episode "The Front," we find that Homer was one credit short of actually graduating from high school.

7. On the basis of all the jobs he's had, it would seem at first glance that Homer has lots of possible options.

8. Even though Scotland has many golf courses and he has to live in a shack on school property in the United States.

9. This isn't normally the case. See, for example, Harrigan (1999).

10. U.S. Department of Commerce, Bureau of Economic Analysis, 2010.

11. As evidence of how his co-workers perceive him, Lionel Hutz tells Gil not to drag Marge down with him in "Last Exit to Springfield."

12. After all, he gets to shine his head in the "Shine-O Ball-O."

13. We see in "I Married Marge" that this is Homer's last job before working at the power plant.

14. "Hello Gutter, Hello Fadder."

15. This is sometimes called the two-tiered labor market.

16. See Chapter 3 in this volume for more on unintended consequences.

17. See more on entrepreneurship in Chapter 6 of this volume. Economist Andrew Oswald suggests a very different reason for Homer's entrepreneurship. Homer doesn't like his job but can't easily move because he owns his house. If selling his house were easier, Homer might move and take a different job. Landsburg (1997) includes a nice discussion of Oswald's work on the relationship between home ownership and job loss.

18. This is the reason Burns lets Homer watch his house when he goes to the Mayo Clinic in "Mansion Family."

19. U.S. Department of Labor, Bureau of Labor Statistics, 2010a.

20. Many people have made this point, but Bryan Caplan (2007) is the strongest proponent of college as signaling.

21. Most people aren't as honest as Homer; some people are tempted to embellish their resumes. In "I Married Marge," Homer doesn't know how to lie his way through an interview with Smithers. Rather than saying his worst quality is that he works too hard, he mentions that he is a slow learner.

22. Detail-oriented, by the way, is just code for "I can take your drudgery and eat it like chocolate ice cream."

23. For more on this research, see Heckman, Humphries, and Mader (2010).

24. Homer Simpson Syndrome is when the brain is cushioned with an exceptionally thick layer of fluid. As a result, he can't be knocked out by normal punches or a surgical two-by-four ("The Homer They Fall").

Chapter 12

1. For an interesting study of the relationship between health outcomes and time preference by a prominent health economist in the field, see Fuchs (1982).

2. Some recent empirical work examines the incentives facing smokers, especially as it pertains to their ability to quit. To see an example of new ways that economists are studying these incentives, see Gine, Karlan, and Zinman (2010).

3. For further reading, see Grossman (1972).

4. For a detailed discussion of the economic incentives facing doctors, auto mechanics, and other providers of "credence" goods, see Dulleck and Kerschbamer (2006).

5. For an example of the ways in which medical malpractice risk has influenced the specialties of obstetrics and gynecology, see Reyes (2010).

6. For evidence supporting a movement away from employer-linked provision and toward a model of individual health care exchange, see Dafny, Ho, and Varela (2010).

7. For a good introductory discussion of the economics of the employer provision of health care, see Folland, Goodman, and Stano (2009).

8. The amount that individuals actually pay for their own health services is known as an "out of pocket" payment. The share of health expenditures that are paid out of pocket has decreased over time, as shown in Figure 12.2.

9. Nobel Prize–winning economists Milton Friedman and Simon Kuznets examined the barriers to entry for physicians and other specialized fields as early as 1945. To obtain further details pertaining to this work, see Friedman and Kuznets (1954).

10. Currently, a black market for kidneys and other organs exists in the United States and elsewhere, because it is illegal to sell organs in most countries. For an interesting study of the market for organs, including an argument supporting incentives for organ exchange, see Becker and Elías (2007).

Chapter 13

1. The author would like to thank Briggs Armstrong, Jedidiah Becker, and Willard Sitz for their contributions to this chapter.

2. Writing in *The Daily Telegraph*, Walton (2007) named the episode one of the ten best *Simpsons* episodes ever. Robert Canning (2009) of IGN Entertainment called it his favorite episode of the series.

3. Yandle, 1983.

4. The generic term for people who transport products illegally is *smuggler*. The term *bootlegger* is often applied to those who smuggle alcohol over land, while *rum runner* is the term for someone who smuggles alcohol over water.

5. See, for example, DeSombre (1995), Yandle (1999), and Brandt and Svendsen (2009).

6. Many states had local option laws that allowed city or county governments to go "dry."

7. For an example of the role of prejudice against minorities in the adoption of prohibition, see Thornton (1991a, pp. 66–68).

8. For more details concerning the history and adoption of prohibitions in the United States, see Thornton (1996) and Thornton (1997).

9. The economics and politics of the adoption and repeal of Prohibition are analyzed in Thornton and Weise (2001).

10. For a review of the major consequences of Prohibition, see Thornton (1991b).

11. For more information on the term *prohibition*, see Thornton (1994; 2003).

12. During Prohibition it was legal to make your own beer, wine, and distilled spirits for personal consumption as was well as for medicinal and sacramental proposes.

13. For more on the way that most cost-benefit studies related to alcohol use ignore the benefits of alcohol consumption, see Stringham and Pulan (2006).

14. For more on the crime and corruption that result from prohibitions, see Thornton (1991a).

15. National Commission on Law Observance and Enforcement, 1931, p. 90.

16. Robert Stack played Agent Elliot Ness in the television series *The Untouchables* (1959–1963). Stack received an Emmy award for best actor in 1960. Rex Banner's image and voice is based on Stack. The narrator's voice in this episode is based on the voice of Walter Winchell, the narrator of *The Untouchables*.

17. At first I thought to describe Homer's network of pipes (similar to that in the introduction to the *Super Mario Brothers* television show) as a labyrinth. However, I was reminded that Homer (the ancient Greek philosopher, not the nuclear power plant employee) wrote about Daedalus, the mythical craftsman who built amazing devices and machines including the Labyrinth on Crete used to imprison the half-man, half-bull creature, Minotaur. A Rube Goldberg machine is probably a better description of Homer's creation.

18. For more information on the potency of illegal drugs and alcohol, see chapter 4 of Thornton (1991a).

19. For more information on the issue of repealing prohibition, see Thornton (1998).

Chapter 14

1. Kelly acknowledges financial support for this project from the Initiative for Public Choice and Market Process at the College of Charleston.

2. It is unclear why the citizens of Springfield allow Mr. Burns to build a casino, given his long history of bad behavior. In a 1997 survey of 804 TV-viewing adults,

the following question was asked: "From a list of prime time's most notorious evil-doers, who do you think is most likely to go to hell?" Montgomery Burns "won," getting 18 percent of women's' votes and 22 percent of men's. In second place was Dr. Michael Mancini, of *Melrose Place*, and coming in third was Cigarette Man, from *The X-Files* (Kaufman 1997, p. 34).

3. This is a summary of Franklin's (1994) testimony.

4. See the American Gaming Association's *State of the States, 2010* for a variety of state-level data on the casino industry.

5. If we actually knew in which state Springfield is located, we could offer a more precise analysis of the likely economic impacts of Mr. Burns' Casino, as casino legislation is a state and local decision and most casino policies are state-specific.

6. Walker and Jackson, 2011. It should be noted that empirical study results are often very sensitive to the model specification. The results for a particular state could be different from the overall results found in this study.

7. American Gaming Association, 2010.

8. Homer's other life-long dreams include being a contestant on *The Gong Show*, eating the world's biggest sub at the State Fair, and working at a bowling alley.

9. Cotti, 2008.

10. By "consumer surplus," economists mean the different between consumers' willingness to pay and the market price for a good or service. "Producers' surplus" can be thought of as profit, or the difference between the market price and production cost.

11. Schumpeter, [1934] 1993, 66.

12. This may especially be a problem with the lottery, which is one—if not the only—way to get very rich overnight.

13. The crime rate is often used as a measure of the risk of being victimized by crime. So the crime rate is typically measured as the number of crimes divided by the population at risk.

14. The best empirical study on this issue is by Reece (2010). Walker (2010) provides a comprehensive review of the casino-crime literature.

15. Diagnostic criteria for problem gambling can be found in the *DSM-IV* (American Psychiatric Association, 1994).

16. In more technical terms, social costs are technological, but not pecuniary, externalities. For a detailed discussion of this distinction, see Justin Ross's chapter on externalities, in this book.

17. Walker, 2007.

18. Petry, Stinson, and Grant (2005) found that around 73 percent of problem gamblers have other serious behavioral problems.

19. Our discussion here is extremely general and simplistic. There is an enormous amount of debate over the definition of "social costs" and the appropriate measurement techniques. For a detailed discussion of the social costs of gambling, see Walker (2007, chapters 6–8).

20. Becker and Murphy's "Theory of Rational Addiction" (1988) is a key paper on this issue.

21. Some psychologists also hold this view. Schaler (2002) argues that addictions are *behaviors*, and all behaviors are actions and therefore cannot be diseases.

22. This admittedly is a questionable assumption, given what we know about other decisions Springfield policymakers have made: being scammed into building a monorail, building a freeway over a residential neighborhood, implementing the stealth bomber Bear Patrol along with the smallest tax increase in history, and so on.

Chapter 15

1. Economists developed the concept of utility as a quantifiable measure of happiness, so it follows that rational behavior involves maximizing one's long-term utility.

2. In *Nudge: Improving Decisions About Health, Wealth and Happiness*, Richard Thaler and Cass Sunstein (2008) explicitly define this distinction as being "Human" versus being "Econ."

3. "Simpsons Roasting on an Open Fire."

4. In addition to lacking hedging or diversification, this betting strategy suffers from what Richard Griffith (1949) described as the favorite-longshot bias. The favorite-longshot bias states that, in horse (and presumably dog) racing, favorites are consistently underpriced and longshots are consistently overpriced. The theory is that this bias arises due to people who irrationally bet on the longshot in order to quickly make up for previous losses, because it's the end of the day, and so on.

5. "Simpsons Roasting on an Open Fire."

6. Specifically, time-consistent preferences don't induce regret, since, if an individual is time consistent, her preferences regarding an action don't change depending on how far before or after the potential action she is evaluating the action.

7. "A Star Is Burns."

8. "Co-Dependent's Day."

9. "I'm with Cupid."

10. This is both because people generally like things sooner rather than later and because money not spent earns interest over time.

11. This is because $10 per minute at a 10 percent discount equals $9, and $11.11 minus two successive 10 percent discounts also equals $9.

12. In other words, if it was worth it for you to wait two years to get $11.11 rather than $9 today or $10 in one year, you're not going to turn around next year and choose the $10 over waiting one more year for $11.11.

13. *Hyperbolic*, in this context, refers to the shape of the graph of the discounting function. The model for rational, time-consistent discounting of future costs and benefits is called exponential discounting.

14. This concept holds regardless of whether the time periods are days, months, years, centuries, or so on.

15. "Deep Space Homer."

16. "The Trouble with Trillions."

17. For this reason, commitment devices are sometimes referred to as Ulysses pacts or Ulysses contracts.

18. "Simpsons Roasting on an Open Fire."

19. Note that, on average, both of these options would yield $50.

20. For example, this would imply that it hurts as much to lose $1 as it feels good to win $2.

21. "Bart Gets Hit by a Car."

22. Appropriately enough, we will examine how windfalls are often spent on frivolous items in a later section.

23. "Mr. Lisa Goes to Washington."

24. For more on the psychology of ownership, see Morewedge, Shu, Gilbert, and Wilson (2009).

25. Kahneman, Knetsch, and Thaler, 1990.

26. "Little Big Mom."

27. "Bart Sells His Soul."

28. Schwartz, 2005.

29 Iyengar and Lepper, 2000.

30. "To Surveil with Love."

31. Shiv and Fedorikhin, 1999.

32. "The Heartbroke Kid."

33. "Lisa, the Simpson."

34. Heilman, Nakamoto, and Rao, 2002.

35. "Bart the Fink."

36. "The Regina Monologues."

37. "Lisa the Greek."

38. "The Telltale Head."

39. "Brother, Can You Spare Two Dimes?"

40. "Bart Gets an Elephant."

41. Thaler, 1983, p. 229.

42. Anyone who's ever watched a commercial for Christmas Tree Shops should be familiar with this concept.

43. "Treehouse of Horror XVI."

44. Ariely, 2008, p. 55. See also Shampanier, Mazar, and Ariely 2007.

45. "There's Something About Marrying."

46. "Home Away from Homer."

47. Thaler and Sunstein, 2008.

48. "Homer and Apu."

49. "Scenes from the Class Struggle in Springfield."

50. Ariely, Loewenstein, and Prelec, 2003.

51. The "Tom Sawyer principle" refers to the anecdote in Mark Twain's novel in which Tom gets Ben Rogers to pay him for the right to paint the fence by pretending that the chore is a fun and rewarding activity.

52. "Lisa the Skeptic."

53. Ariely, Loewenstein, and Prelec, 2006.

54. "Bart Has Two Mommies."

55. Anyone who's ever watched a baseball player at the plate and thought something of the form "He's due for a big hit" is already familiar with this concept.

56. "The Mansion Family."

57. "Deep Space Homer."

58. "Homer and Ned's Hail Mary Pass."

59. "King of the Hill."

60. McClure and others, 2004.

61. "My Fair Laddy."

62. "Lost Our Lisa."

63. Frank, Gilovich, and Regan, 1993.

64. Bauman and Rose, 2011.

65. "Any Given Sundance."

66. "Lisa's Substitute."

67. "A Hunka Hunka Burns in Love."

68. "Rosebud."

69. "He Loves to Fly and He D'ohs."

Chapter 16

1. For an overview of the way in which "it's getting better all the time" and has been for the past hundred years, see Moore and Simon (2000).

2. U.S. Census Bureau, 2005.

3. U.S. Census Bureau, 2010. It is worth noting the increase in the maximum income that defined the lowest 20 percent of income earners.

4. Air conditioning is perhaps the number one reason that heat-related deaths have fallen in the developed world. Data from the United States indicate that heat-related deaths in twenty-eight major cities fell by 75 percent from the 1960s to the 1990s. See Davis, Knappenberger, P., Michaels, P., and Novicoff (2003), who list air conditioning as a primary reason why, particularly given that average urban temperatures have risen over that period.

5. The average private sector weekly earnings in 1990 was $349.75 and in 2009 it was $617.11. If we adjust $349.75 for changes in the consumer price index, it was worth $574.00 in 2009 dollars. So the real value of the average private sector wage rose about 7.5 percent over that period. See U.S. Department of Labor, Bureau of Labor Statistics (2010b) and author's calculations.

6. Perry, 2009. More data of this sort can be found in Cox and Alm (1999).

7. U.S. Census Bureau, 2010.

8. U.S. Census Bureau, 2003. In particular, see "Table HS-12: Households by Type and Size: 1900 to 2002."

9. U.S. Department of Labor, Bureau of Labor Statistics, 2006, pp. 3–6; and Visual Economics, 2010.

10. U.S. Department of the Treasury, 2007.

11. The interested reader should consult a standard text on labor markets or the economics of gender to see the particular data. A good place to start would be Jacobsen (2007).

REFERENCES

Acemoglu, D., and Angrist, J. (2001). Consequences of employment protection? The case of the Americans with Disabilities Act. *Journal of Political Economy* 109:915–957.

Acs, Z., and Audretsch, D. (1990). *Innovation and small firms.* Cambridge MA: MIT Press.

Alchian, A. (1965). Some economics of property rights. *Il Politico* 30:816–829.

Alchian, A. (2008). Property rights. In D. Henderson (ed.), *The concise encyclopedia of economics, 2nd ed.* http://www.econlib.org/library/Enc/PropertyRights.html. Accessed August 23, 2010.

American Gaming Association. (2010). *State of the states, 2010: The AGA survey of casino entertainment.* Washington, DC: AGA.

American Psychiatric Association. (1994). *Diagnostic and statistical manual*, 4th ed. Washington, DC: APA.

Ariely, D. (2008). *Predictably irrational: The hidden forces that shape our decisions.* New York: HarperCollins.

Ariely, D., Loewenstein, G., and Prelec, D. (2003). Coherent arbitrariness: Stable demand curves without stable preferences. *Quarterly Journal of Economics* 118:73–105.

Ariely, D., Loewenstein, G., and Prelec, D. (2006). Tom Sawyer and the construction of value. *Journal of Economic Behavior & Organization* 60:1–10.

Bastiat, F., trans. G. B. de Huszar, ed. W. Hayden Boyers. (1995a). *Economic harmonies.* Irvington-on-Hudson, NY: The Foundation for Economic Education.

Bastiat, F., trans. A. Goddard. (1995b). *Economic sophisms.* Irvington-on-Hudson, NY: The Foundation for Economic Education.

Bastiat, F., trans. S. Cain. (1995c). *Selected essays on political economy.* Irvington-on-Hudson, NY: The Foundation for Economic Education.

Bauman, Y., and Rose, E. (2011). Selection or indoctrination: Why do economics students donate less than the rest?" *Journal of Economic Behavior and Organization* 79:318–327.

Baumol, W. (1990). Entrepreneurship: Productive, unproductive and destructive. *Journal of Political Economy* 98:893–921.

Becker, G., and Elías, J. (2007). Introducing incentives in the market for live and cadaveric organ donations. *Journal of Economic Perspectives* 21:3–24.

Becker, G., and Murphy, K. (1988). A theory of rational addiction. *Journal of Political Economy* 96:675–700.

Blaug, M. (2008). Invisible hand. In S. Durlauf and L. Blume (eds.), *New Palgrave dictionary of economics*, pp. 564–566. London: Palgrave Macmillan.

Block, W. (2008). *Defending the undefendable.* Auburn, AL: Ludwig von Mises Institute

Boettke, P. (2008). Austrian school of economics. In D. Henderson (ed.), *The concise encyclopedia of economics*, pp. 23–27. Indianapolis: Liberty Fund.

Boettke, P., and Dirmeyer, J. (2008). Spontaneous order. In S. Durlauf and L. Blume (eds.), *New Palgrave dictionary of economics*. London: Palgrave Macmillan.

Borjas, G. (1987). Self-selection and the earnings of immigrants. *American Economic Review* 77:531–553.

Borjas, G. (1995). "The economic benefits from immigration." *Journal of Economic Perspectives* 9:3–22.

Borjas, G. (2001). *Heaven's door: Immigration policy and the American economy.* Prince—ton, NJ: Princeton University Press.

Bork, R. (1978). *The antitrust paradox.* New York: Basic Books.

Brandt, U., and Svendsen, G. (2009). Trawling for subsidies: The alignment of incentives between fishermen and marine biologists. *Journal of European Public Policy* 16:1012–1029.

Brock, L. (1975). *The currency of the American colonies, 1700–1764.* New York: Arno Press.

Buchanan, J. (1969). *Cost and choice: An inquiry in economic theory.* Chicago: University of Chicago Press.

Buchanan, J., and Tullock, G. (1962). *The calculus of consent.* Ann Arbor: University of Michigan Press.

Burtless, G. (2009). Impact of immigration on the distribution of well-being. Center for Retirement Research Working Paper 2009-34.

Butcher, K., and Piehl, A. (1998). Cross-city evidence on the relationship between immigration and crime. *Journal of Policy Analysis and Management* 17:457–493.

Canning, R. (2009). The Simpsons flashback: Homer vs. the eighteenth amendment review. June 1, 2010. http://tv.ign.com/articles/101/1012765p1.html.

Cantillon, R. ([1755] 1931). *Essai sur la nature du commerce en général.* London: Macmillan.

Caplan, B. (2007). Page one of my next book. Econlog weblog. http://econlog.econlib.org/archives/2007/03/page_one_of_my.html. Accessed November 27, 2010.

Carroll, L. (2007). Simpsons trivia, from swearing Lisa to 'Burns-Sexual' Smithers.

MTV. http://www.mtv.com/news/articles/1565538/20070725/story.jhtml. Accessed November 27, 2010.

Casson, M. (1982). *The entrepreneur: An economic theory.* New York: Rowman & Littlefield.

Casson, M. (2000). An entrepreneurial theory of the firm. In N. Foss (ed.), *Competence, governance and entrepreneurship: advances in economic strategy research.* New York: Oxford University Press.

Chiquiar, D., and Hanson, G. (2005.). International migration, self-selection, and the distribution of wages: Evidence from Mexico and the United States. *Journal of Political Economy* 113:239–281.

Clemens, M. (2010). A labor mobility agenda for development. Center for Global Development Working Paper 201.

Coase, R. (1960). The problem of social cost. *Journal of Law and Economics* 3:1–44.

Congressional Budget Office. (2007). *The impact of unauthorized immigrants on the budgets of state and local governments.* Washington, DC: Government Printing Office.

Considine, J. (2006). Yes Minister: Invaluable material for teaching the public choice of bureaucracy. *Economic Affairs* 26:55–61.

Cotti, C. (2008). The effect of casinos on local labor markets: A county level analysis. *Journal of Gambling Business and Economics* 2:17–41.

Cox, W. M., and Alm, R. (1999). *Myths of rich and poor: why we're better off than we think.* New York: Basic Books.

Dafny, L., Ho K., and Varela, M. (2010). Let them have choice: Gains from shifting away from employer-sponsored health insurance and toward an individual exchange. National Bureau of Economic Research Working Paper 15687.

Davis, R., Knappenberger, P., Michaels, P., and Novicoff, W. (2003). Changing heat-related mortality in the United States. *Environmental Health Perspectives* 111:1712–1718.

DeLeire, T. (2000a) The wage and employment effects of the Americans with Disabilities Act. *Journal of Human Resources* 35:693–715.

DeLeire, T. (2000b). The unintended consequences of the Americans with Disabilities Act. *Regulation* 23:21–24.

Demsetz, H. (1967). Toward a theory of property rights. *American Economic Review* 57:347–359.

DeSombre, E. (1995). Baptists and bootleggers for the environment: The origins of United States unilateral sanctions. *Journal of Environment & Development* 1:53–75.

Dulleck, U., and Kerschbamer, R. (2006). On doctors, mechanics, and computer specialists: The economics of credence goods. *Journal of Economic Literature* 44:5–42.

Ehrenreich, B. (2002). *Nickel and dimed: On (not) getting by in America.* New York: Henry Holt.

Epstein, E. (1982). Have you ever tried to sell a diamond? *The Atlantic* 249:23–34.

Federal Reserve. (2010). *Federal reserve statistical release H.6, money stock measures.* http://www.federalreserve.gov/releases/h6/current/h6.htm. Accessed August 10, 2010.

Ferguson, N. (2008). *The ascent of money.* New York: Penguin.

Folland, S., Goodman, A., and Stano, M. (2009). *The economics of health and health care,* 6th ed. Upper Saddle River, NJ: Prentice Hall.

Foss, K., Foss, N., and Klein, P. (2007). Original and derived judgment: An entrepreneurial theory of economic organization. *Org Stud* 28:1–20.

Foss, N., and Klein, P. (2005). Entrepreneurship and the economic theory of the firm: Any gains from trade? In R. Agarwal, S. Alvarez, and O. Sorenson (eds.), *Handbook of entrepreneurship: Disciplinary perspectives.* Norwell, MA: Kluwer.

Foss, N., and Klein, P. (2010). Entrepreneurial alertness and opportunity discovery: Origins, attributes, critique. In H. Landström and F. Lohrke (eds.), *The historical foundations of entrepreneurship research.* Aldershot, UK: Edward.

Frank, R., and Bernanke, B. (2009). *Principles of economics,* 4th ed. New York: McGraw-Hill/Irwin.

Frank, R., Gilovich, T., Regan, D. (1993). Does studying economics inhibit cooperation? *Journal of Economic Perspectives* 7:159–171.

Franklin, W. (1994). Testimony and prepared statement. In U.S. House of Representatives, Committee on Small Business. *The national impact of casino gambling proliferation.* 103rd Cong., 2nd sess., Sept. 21, 1994.

Friedman, M. (1994). Money mischief: Episodes in monetary history. Orlando: Mariner Books.

Friedman, M., and Friedman, R. (1998). *Two lucky people: Memoirs.* Chicago: University of Chicago Press.

Friedman, M., and Kuznets, S. (1945). *Income from independent professional practice.* New York: National Bureau of Economic Research.

Fuchs, V. (1982). Time preference and health: An exploratory study. National Bureau of Economic Research Working Paper 0539.

Gangemi, J. (2007). Buy local—with town currency. *Bloomberg Businessweek.* http://www.businessweek.com/smallbiz/content/jul2007/sb20070717_097103.htm. Accessed August 11, 2010.

Geddes, R. (2004). Do vital economists reach a conclusion on postal reform? *Econ Journal Watch* 1:61–81.

Giné, X., Karlan, D., and Zinman, J. (2010). Put your money where your butt is: A commitment contract for smoking cessation. *American Economic Journal: Applied Economics* 2:213–235.

Government Accounting Office. (2006). Illegal immigration: Border-crossing deaths have doubled since 1995. U.S. Government Accountability Office Report GAO-06-770.

Griffith, R. (1949). Odds adjustment by American horse race bettors. *American Journal of Psychiatry* 62:290–294.

Grossman, M. (1972). *The demand for health: A theoretical and empirical investigation.* New York: Columbia University Press.

Gwartney, J. D., Stroup, R. L., Sobel, R. S., and Macpherson, D. (2008). *Economics: private and public choice,* 12th ed. Mason, OH: South-Western College Publishing.

Hagenbaugh, B. (July 6, 2006). A penny saved could become a penny spurned. *USA Today*.

Hall, J. (2005). Homer economicus: Using *The Simpsons* to teach economics. *Journal of Private Enterprise* 20:165–176.

Hall, J., and Gillis, M. (2010). Using *The Simpsons* to improve economic instruction through policy analysis. *American Economic Review* 55:84–92.

Hamilton, B. (2000). Does entrepreneurship pay? An empirical analysis of the returns to self-employment. *Journal of Political Economy* 108:604–631.

Harberger, A. (1954). Monopoly and resource allocation. *American Economic Review* 44:77–87.

Hardin, G. (1968). The tragedy of the commons. *Science* 162:1243–1248.

Harrigan, J. (1999). Estimation of cross-country differences in industry production functions. *Journal of International Economics* 47:267–293.

Hayek, F. (1945). The use of knowledge in society. *American Economic Review* 35:519–530.

Hayek, F. (1978). Competition as a discovery procedure. In F. Hayek, *New studies in philosophy, politics, economics and the history of ideas*, pp. 179–190. London: Routledge and Kegan Paul.

Hazlitt, H. ([1946] 2009). *Economics in one lesson*. Auburn, AL: Ludwig von Mises Institute.

Heckman, J., Humphries, J., and Mader, N. (2010). The GED. National Bureau of Economic Research Working Paper 16064.

Heilman, C., Nakamoto, K., and Rao, A. (2002). Pleasant surprises: Consumer response to unexpected in-store coupons. *Journal of Marketing Research* 39:242–252.

Heller, M. (1998). The tragedy of the anticommons: Property in the transition from Marx to markets. *Harvard Law Review* 111:621–688.

Henderson, D. (2007). *The concise encyclopedia of economics*, 2nd ed. Indianapolis: Liberty Fund. http://www.econlib.org/library/CEE.html.

Heyne, P., Boettke, P., and Prychitko, D. (2010). *The economic way of thinking*, 12th ed. Upper Saddle River, NJ: Pearson Education.

Hirshleifer, J. (2005). *Price theory and applications*, 7th ed. Cambridge: Cambridge University Press.

Holcombe, R., and Sobel, R. (2001). Public policy toward pecuniary externalities. *Public Finance Review* 29:304–325.

Iyengar, S., and Lepper, M. (2000). When choice is demotivating: Can one desire too much of a good thing?" *Journal of Personality and Social Psychology* 79:995–1006.

Jacobsen, J. (2007). *The economics of gender*, 3rd ed. New York: Blackwell.

Jensen, R. (2002). 'No Irish need apply:' A myth of victimization. *Journal of Social History* 36:405–429.

Kahneman, D., Knetsch, J., and Thaler, R. (1990). Experimental tests of the endowment effect and the Coase theorem. *Journal of Political Economy* 98:1328–1348.

Kaufman, J. (March 29, 1997). Tuning in to God: A *TV Guide* poll reveals just how deeply today's viewers are yearning for more prime-time piety. *TV Guide*.

Kirzner, I. (1973). *Competition and entrepreneurship*. Chicago: University of Chicago Press.

Kirzner, I. (1979). *Perception, opportunity, and profit: Studies in the theory of entrepreneurship*. Chicago: University of Chicago Press.

Kirzner, I. (1992). *The meaning of the market process*. London: Routledge.

Kirzner, I. (1997). *How markets work*. London: Institute of Economic Affairs.

Klein, D. (2002). The demand and supply of assurance. In T. Cowen and E. Crampton (eds.), *Market failure or success*. Oakland, CA: Independent Institute.

Klein, D., and Foldvary, F. (2003). *The half-life of policy rationales: How new technology affects old policy issues*. New York: New York University Press.

Klein, P. (2008). Opportunity discovery, entrepreneurial action, and economic organization. *Strategic Entrepreneurship Journal* 2:175–190.

Knight, F. (1921). *Risk, uncertainty and profit*. Boston: Houghton-Mifflin.

Knight, F. (1942). Profit and entrepreneurial functions. *Journal of Economic History* 2:126–132.

Lachmann, L. (1956). *Capital and its structure*. London: Bell and Sons.

Landsburg, S. (1995). *The armchair economist*. New York: Free Press.

Landsburg, S. (1997). Buy a house, lose your job. *Slate*. http://www.slate.com/id/2044/. Accessed November 27, 2010.

Lankenau, S. (2001). Smoke 'em if you got 'em: Cigarette black markets in U.S. prisons and jails. *Prison Journal* 81:142–161.

Levine, L. (2010). *Immigration: The effects on low-skilled and high-skilled native-born workers*. Washington, DC: Congressional Research Service.

Levitz, J. (August 25, 2010). Coffins made with brotherly love have undertakers throwing dirt. *Wall Street Journal*.

Levy, D., and Peart, S. (2001). The secret history of the dismal science: Part I, economics, religion, and race in the 19th century. http://www.econlib.org/library/Columns/LevyPeartdismal.html. Accessed August 11, 2010.

Logan, C. (2005). Lyle Lanley, you're my hero. In A. Brown (ed.), *The psychology of the Simpsons*. Dallas: Benbella Books.

Lopez, E. (ed.). (2010). *The pursuit of justice: the law and economics of legal institutions*. New York: Palgrave Macmillan.

Madison, J. (1788). The federalist no. 51: The structure of the government must furnish the proper checks and balances between the different departments. *Independent Journal*.

Mankiw, G. N. (2009). *Principles of economics*, 5th ed. Mason, OH: South-Western Cengage Learning.

Marshall, A. (1890). *Principles of economics*. London: Macmillan.

McAfee, R., Mialon, H., and Williams, M. (2004). What is a barrier to entry? *American Economic Review* 94:461–465.

McCloskey, D. (1993). Some consequences of a conjective economics. In M. Ferber and J. Nelson (eds.), *Beyond economic man: Feminist theory and economics*. Chicago: University of Chicago Press.

McClure, S., Li, J., Tomlin, D., Cypert, T., Montague, L., and Montague, R. (2004). Neural correlates of behavioral preference for culturally familiar drinks. *Neuron* 44:279–387.

Mises, L. von. ([1949] 1998) *Human action*. Auburn, AL: Ludwig von Mises Institute.

Mises, L. von. (1981). *The theory of money and credit*. Indianapolis: Liberty Fund.

Mitchell, W. (2001). The old and new public choice: Chicago versus Virginia. In W. Shughart and L. Razzolini (eds.), *The Elgar companion to public choice*. Cheltenham, UK: Edward Elgar.

Moore, S., and Simon, J. (2000). It's getting better all the time: 100 greatest trends of the last 100 years. Washington, DC: Cato Institute.

Morewedge, C., Shu, L., Gilbert, D., and Wilson, T. (2009). Bad riddance or good rubbish? Ownership and not loss aversion causes the endowment effect. *Journal of Experimental Social Psychology* 45:947–951.

Munger, M. (2006). A fable of the OC. http://www.econlib.org/library/Columns/y2006/Mungeropportunitycost.html. Accessed September 14, 2010.

National Center for Health Statistics. (2010). *Health, United States, 2009: With special feature on medical technology*. Hyattsville, MD: National Center for Health Statistics.

National Commission on Law Observance and Enforcement. (1931). *Enforcement of the prohibition laws of the United States*. Washington, DC: Government Printing Office.

Olson, M. (1965). The logic of collective action. Cambridge, MA: Harvard University Press.

Ostrom, E. (1990). *Governing the commons: The evolution of institutions for collective action*. Cambridge, MA: Cambridge University Press.

Parker, S. (2004). *The economics of self-employment and entrepreneurship*. Cambridge, MA: Cambridge University Press.

Payscale.com. (2010). *Best undergrad college degrees by salary*. http://www.payscale.com/best-colleges/degrees.asp. Accessed April 21, 2010.

Perry, M. (2009). The rich are getting richer and the poor are getting richer: The good old days are now. http://mjperry.blogspot.com/2009/11/rich-are-getting-richer-and-poor-are.html. Accessed November 26, 2010.

Persky, J. (1995). Retrospectives: The ethology of *homo economicus*. *Journal of Economic Perspectives* 9:221–231.

Petry, N., Stinson, F., Grant, B. (2005). Comorbidity of DSM-IV pathological gambling and other psychiatric disorders: Results from the National Epidemiological Surveys on Alcohol and Related Conditions. *Journal of Clinical Psychology* 66:564–574.

Pritchett, L. (2006). Let their people come: Breaking the gridlock on global labor mobility. Washington, DC: Center for Global Development.

Radford, R. A. (1945). The economic organisation of a P.O.W. camp. *Economica* 12:189–201.

Reece, W. (2010). Casinos, hotels, and crime. *Contemporary Economic Policy* 28:145–161.

Reyes, B., and Mameesh, L. (2002). Why does immigrant trip duration vary across U.S. destinations? *Social Science Quarterly* 83:580–593.

Reyes, J. (2010). The effect of malpractice liability on the specialty of obstetrics and gynecology. National Bureau of Economic Research Working Paper 15841.

Ricardo, D. (1821). On the principles of political economy and taxation, 3rd ed. http://www.econlib.org/library/Ricardo/ricP.htmlRoss. Accessed August 23, 2010.

Rosentraub, M. (1997). *Major league losers: The real cost of sports and who is paying for it*. New York: Basic Books.

Ross, J. (2009). What should policy makers know when economists say "market" failure? *Georgetown Public Policy Review* 14:27–32.

Rothbard, M. N. (2008). What has government done to our money? Auburn, AL: Ludwig von Mises Institute.

Rothbard, M. (2009). *Man, economy, and state: A treatise on economics, scholar's edition*. Auburn, AL: Ludwig von Mises Institute.

Salerno, J. (2008). The entrepreneur: Real and imagined. *Quarterly Journal of Austrian Economics* 11:188–207.

Schaler, J. (2002). *Addiction is a choice*. Chicago: Open Court.

Schultz, T. (1975). The value of the ability to deal with disequilibria. *Journal of Economic Literature* 13:827–846.

Schultz, T. (1980). Investment in entrepreneurial ability. *Scandinavian Journal of Economics* 82:437–448.

Schumpeter, J. ([1934] 1993). *The theory of economic development*. New Brunswick, NJ: Transaction.

Schwartz, B. (2005). The paradox of choice: Why more is less. New York: Harper-Perennial.

Selgin, G. (2008). *Good money: Birmingham button makers, the royal mint, and the beginnings of modern coinage, 1775–1821*. Ann Arbor, MI: The Independent Institute.

Shampanier, K., Mazar, N., Ariely, D. (2007). Zero as a special price: The true value of free products. *Marketing Science* 26:742–757.

Shiv, B., and Fedorikhin, A. (1999). Heart and mind in conflict: The interplay of affect and cognition in consumer decision making. *Journal of Consumer Research* 26:278–292.

Shughart, W. (2008). Public choice. In D. Henderson (ed.), *The concise encyclopedia of economics*. Indianapolis: Liberty Fund.

Sjaastad, L. (1962). The costs and returns of human migration. *Journal of Political Economy* 70:80–93.

Smith, A. ([1776] 1937). *An inquiry into the nature and causes of the wealth of nations*. New York: Modern Library.

Sobel, R. (2005). Welfare economics and public finance. In J. Backhaus and R. Wagner (eds.), *Handbook of public finance*. New York: Springer.

Sobel, R., Clark, J., Lee, D. (2007). Freedom, barriers to entry, entrepreneurship, and economic progress. *Review of Austrian Economics* 20:221–236.

Stigler, G. (1971). The theory of economic regulation. *Bell Journal of Economics and Management Science* 3:3–18.

Stringham, E., and Pulan, I. (2006). Evaluating economic justifications for alcohol restrictions. *American Journal of Economic Sociology* 65:971–990.

Thaler, R. (1983). Transaction utility theory. In R. Bagozzi and A. Tybout (eds.), *Advances in consumer research*, vol. 10, pp. 229–232. Ann Arbor, MI: Association for Consumer Research.

Thaler, R., and Sunstein, C. (2008). *Nudge: Improving decisions about health, wealth, and happiness*. New Haven, CT: Yale University Press.

Thornton, M. (1991a). *The economics of prohibition*. Salt Lake City: University of Utah Press.

Thornton, M. (1991b). *Alcohol prohibition was a failure*. Policy Analysis No. 157. Washington, DC: Cato Institute.

Thornton, M. (1994). The economics of prohibition. In P. Boettke (ed.), *The handbook of Austrian economics*, pp. 358–361. Cheltenham, UK: Edward Elgar.

Thornton, M. (1996). The fall and rise of puritanical policy in America. *Journal of Libertarian Studies* 12:143–160.

Thornton, M. (1997). Prohibition: The ultimate sin tax. In W. Shughart (ed.), *Taxing choice: The predatory politics of fiscal discrimination*, pp. 171–198. New Brunswick, NJ: Transaction.

Thornton, M. (1998). Perfect drug legalization. In J. Fish (ed.), *How to legalize drugs: Public health, social science, and civil liberties perspectives*, pp. 638–660. Lanham, MD: Jason Aronson.

Thornton, M. (2003). Prohibition. In C. Rowley and F. Schneider (eds.), *Encyclopedia of public choice*, pp. 437–439. New York: Springer.

Thornton, M., and Weise, C. (2001). The great depression tax revolts revisited. *Journal of Libertarian Studies* 15:95–105.

Todaro, M. (1969). A model of labor migration and urban unemployment in less developed countries. *American Economic Review* 69:486–499.

Tullock, G., Seldon, A., and Brady, G. (2002). *Government failure: A primer in public choice*. Washington, DC: Cato Institute.

U.S. Census Bureau. (2003). *Statistical abstract of the United States: 2003 edition*. Washington, DC: Government Printing Office.

U.S. Census Bureau. (2005). *Extended measures of well-being: Living conditions in the United States, 2005*. http://www.census.gov/population/www/socdemo/extended-05.html. Accessed November 26, 2010.

U.S. Census Bureau. (2010). *Income*. http://www.census.gov/hhes/www/income/data/historical/household/index.html. Accessed November 26, 2010.

U.S. Department of Commerce, Bureau of Economic Analysis. (2010). *State per capita and state personal income news release archive*. http://www.bea.gov/newsreleases/relsarchivespi.htm. Accessed November 27, 2010.

U.S. Department of Homeland Security. (2010). *Yearbook of immigration statistics*. Washington, DC: Department of Homeland Security.

U.S. Department of Labor, Bureau of Labor Statistics. (2006). *100 years of consumer spending: Data for the nation, New York City, and Boston.* http://www.bls.gov/opub/uscs. Accessed November 26, 2010.

U.S. Department of Labor, Bureau of Labor Statistics. (2010a). *Usual weekly earnings of wage and salary workers: Third quarter 2010.* http://www.bls.gov/news.release/pdf/wkyeng.pdf Accessed: September 1, 2010.

U.S. Department of Labor, Bureau of Labor Statistics. (2010b). *Establishment data: Historical hours and earnings.* ftp://ftp.bls.gov/pub/suppl/empsit.ceseeb2.txt. Accessed November 26, 2010.

U.S. Department of the Treasury. (2007). *Income mobility in the United States from 1996 to 2005.* http://www.ustreas.gov/offices/tax-policy/library/incomemobility study03-08revise.pdf. Accessed November 26, 2010.

Visual Economics. (2010). *How the average U.S. consumer spends their paycheck.* http://www.visualeconomics.com/how-the-average-us-consumer-spends-their -paycheck/. Accessed November 26, 2010.

Wadsworth, T. (2010). Is immigration responsible for the crime drop? An assessment of the influence of immigration on changes in violent crime between 1990 and 2000. *Social Science Quarterly* 91:531–553.

Walker, D. (2007). *The economics of casino gambling.* New York: Springer.

Walker, D. (2010). Casinos and crime in the USA. In B. Benson and P. Zimmerman (eds.), *Handbook on the economics of crime.* Northampton, MA: Edward Elgar.

Walker, D., and Jackson, J. (2011). The effect of legalized gambling on state government revenue. *Contemporary Economic Policy* 29: 101–114.

Walton, J. (July 7, 2007). The 10 best Simpsons TV episodes (in chronological order). *Daily Telegraph.*

Weatherford, J. (1997). *The history of money.* New York: Crown.

Whitman, G. (2006). Against the new paternalism: Internalities and the economics of self-control. Cato Policy Analysis No. 563.

Williamson, O. (2010). Transaction cost economics: The natural progression. *American Economic Review* 100:673–690.

Witt, U. (1998). Imagination and leadership: The neglected dimension of an evolutionary theory of the firm. *Journal of Economic Behavior & Organization* 35:161–177.

Witt, U. (1999). Do entrepreneurs need firms? A contribution to a missing chapter in Austrian economics. *Review of Austrian Economics* 11:99–109.

Yandle, B. (1983). Bootleggers and baptists: The education of a regulatory economist. *Regulation* 7:12–16.

Yandle, B. (1999). After Kyoto: A global scramble for advantage. *Independent Review* 4:19–40.

Yellen, J. (1984). Efficiency wage models of unemployment. *American Economic Review* 74:200–205.

Yu, T. (2002). The Knightian firm: Uncertainty, entrepreneurial judgement and coordination. *Journal des Economistes et des Etudes Humaines.* 12:459–473.

Note: page numbers followed by *f* and *t* refer to figure and tables, respectively. Those followed by n refer to notes, with note number.

leadership and coordination, as characteristic
of entrepreneurs, 68
lemons problem, 79
Lepper, Mark, 168
Levy, D., 203n5
licenses and permits, as entry barrier, 58–59
Limbaugh, Rush, 140
liquidity: properties contributing to, 45–47; as
property of money, 45
Lisa (character): Bart and, 24, 46; and
bounded rationality, 169; and casino
gambling, 152; and compensating
differentials, 121; and environmental
concerns, 94; and externalities, 88; and
health care, asymmetric information in,
130; Homer and, 9, 11, 30, 32, 35, 88, 101–
2, 148, 162, 166–67; and irrational biases,
170, 172, 173, 174; and markets, 23; and
opportunity costs, 21, 53; and political
corruption, 96–97, 99, 100; and standard
of living, 185
Logan, C., 206n22
logic of collective action, 96
loss aversion, 166, 167
losses: and departure of market competitors,
56–57; as incentive in market economy,
55; pain of vs. lack of gain, 166
Lovejoy, Reverend (character), 12, 47, 152, 156

Macpherson, D., 6
MADD. See Mothers Against Drunk Driving
Madison, James, 205n19
Maggie Simpson (character), 6–7, 31, 82, 93,
116, 121, 167, 170
Malthus, Sir Thomas, 203n5
Manjula Nahasapeemapetilon (character),
109–10, 198n92
Mankiw, G. N., 6
Manning, Peyton, 117–18, 208n5
Marge Simpson (character): Becky's attempted
murder of, 68; Burns' political career and,
75; on Canyonero SUV, 89; and
comparative advantage, 11; and
economizing, 10; as entrepreneur, 57, 58,
67; and gambling, 153, 157–58, 158–59,
160; and health care, 129, 132, 183;
Homer and, 9, 18, 67, 162, 166, 167; and

Homer's weight gain, 30, 34; immigrants
and, 111; and irrational biases, 169–70,
172, 173, 174; jobs held by, 58, 116, 188;
and markets, 22, 26, 57; money and, 46,
49; and opportunity costs, 7–8, 21, 53, 54,
170; as parent, 18, 141; pregnancy of, 121;
and Prohibition, 148, 149; and public
goods, 76, 101; and quality of life
improvements, 184–85
marginal benefits (MB): and efficiency, 9;
future, discounting of, 163–64; as
incentives, 32; vs. marginal cost, in choice,
22, 27–28, 29, 32–34; social (SMB), vs.
private, 86f, 87
marginal costs (MC): and efficiency, 9; future,
discounting of, 163–64; as incentives, 32;
vs. marginal benefit, in choice, 22, 27–28,
32–34
marginal value, law of diminishing, 13
margins, choice as made at, 29, 34, 37
market: as basic concept, 6, 14; and
comparative advantage, discovery of, 11;
definition of, 14; in equilibrium,
definition of, 71; and resources, best use
of, 26–27; rules, importance of, 22–27;
and social cooperation, 22; and supply,
adjustment of, 15–18, 16f, 17f; and wealth
production, 24
market, efficient: conditions necessary for, 70–
71; definition of, 70. See also efficiency
market economy: exchange externalities in,
82–83, 85–86, 85f (See also externalities);
"invisible hand" guiding, 20–21, 84–85;
profits as incentive in, 27–28, 33, 55, 81;
role of price in, 16–18, 16f, 17f, 25–26,
199n7; in The Simpsons, as best among
bad choices, 98; unintended consequences
of interfering with, 35–37
market failure: asymmetric information as,
78–79; externalities and, 204n2;
government-based solutions to, 77, 79;
government failure as greater than, 95,
100; monopolies as, 72–76; nongovernment solutions to, 77–78, 79–80;
public goods as, 76–78; in The Simpsons,
94; theory vs. real world and, 80; types
of, 72

wages: cost of employee benefits and, 123; efficiency, 78; and employers' competition for labor, 119–20, 124–25; impact of immigration on, 110–12, 111*f*, 114, 207nn12–13; increase in, as attraction to immigrants, 107–8; increase in *vs.* inflation, 180, 214n5; profitability of employees and, 117, 118*f*; for technical *vs.* non-technical fields, 118–19, 119*f. See also* price of labor

War on Drugs: and increased potency of marijuana, 148–49; U.S. as leader of, 142; violence and crime generated by, 145

WCTU. *See* Women's Christian Temperance Union

wealth: as basic concept, 6, 18; definition of, 18, 24

The Wealth of Nations (Smith), 198n16

wealth production: specialization and, 24–25, 25*t*, 199n4; through markets, 24; unintended consequences of regulation and, 35–36

"The Welfare of Economics" (Pigou), 204n9

"What Is Seen and What Is Not Seen" (Bastiat), 36

widely valued asset, as property of money, 45–46, 50, 51

Wiggum, Clancy (character), 12, 42, 97–98, 136, 146–47, 149

Williamson, Oliver, 204n14

windfall *vs.* regular income, and irrational bias, 170

Wittman, Donald, 92

women in workforce, motives of, 188

Women's Christian Temperance Union (WCTU), 142

Woods, Tiger, 140

work environment, unpleasant, compensating differentials for, 121, 122, 126

World War I: and gold standard, 48; hyper-inflation in Germany following, 44, 200n6

World War II, and gold standard, 48

Yandle, Bruce, 141

zealots, as social class, 139–40